Research Reports ESPRIT

Project 2315 · TWB · Volume 1

Edited in cooperation with the European Commission

M. Kugler K. Ahmad
G. Thurmair (Eds.)

Translator's Workbench

Tools and Terminology for Translation and Text Processing

Springer

Volume Editors

Marianne Kugler
Philips Kommunikations-Industrie AG
Thurn-und-Taxisstr. 10, D-90327 Nürnberg, Germany

Khurshid Ahmad
AI Group, Department of Mathematical and Computing Sciences
University of Surrey, Guildford, Surrey GU2 5XH, UK

Gregor Thurmair
Sietec Systemtechnik
Carl-Wery-Str. 22, D-81739 München, Germany

ESPRIT Project 2315, TWB (Translator's Workbench), belongs to the Peripheral Systems, Business Systems and House Automation sector of the ESPRIT Programme (European Specific Programme for Research and Development in Information Technologies) supported by the European Commission.

The main results of the TWB project were two prototype versions of the Translator's Workbench: a high-end or workstation version integrating all tools mentioned under FrameMaker (and thus Unix), and a low-end or PC version integrating a subset of tools under MS Windows. In addition, there are stand-alone versions of, among others, a machine-assisted terminology elicitation system, of standard and advanced proof-reading tools, and of document converters to and from the TWB editor.

CR Subject Classification (1991): J.5, I.2.7, I.7.1-2

ISBN-13: 978-3-540-57645-7 e-ISBN-13: 978-3-642-78784-3
DOI: 10.1007/978-3-642-78784-3

CIP data applied for

Publication No. EUR 16144 EN of the
European Commission,
Dissemination of Scientific and Technical Knowledge Unit,
Directorate-General Information Telecommunications, Information Market
and Exploitation of Research,
Luxembourg.

SPIN: 10132150 45/3140-543210 – Printed on acid-free paper

Preface

The Translator's Workbench Project was a European Community sponsored research and development project which dealt with issues in multi-lingual communication and documentation.

This book presents an integrated toolset as a solution to problems in translation and documentation. Professional translators and teachers of translation were involved in the process of software development, starting with a detailed study of the user requirements and ending with several evaluation-and-improvement cycles of the resulting toolset.

English, German, Greek, and Spanish are addressed in the contributions, however, some of the techniques are inherently language-independent and can thus be extended to cover other languages as well.

Translation can be viewed broadly as the execution of three cognitive processes, and this book has been structured along these lines:

- First, the translation pre-process, understanding the target language text at a lexico-semantic level on the one hand, and making sense of the source language document on the other hand. The tools for the pre-translation process include access to electronic networks, conversion of documents from one format to another, creation of terminology data banks and access to existing data banks, and terminology dictionaries.
- Second, the translation process, rendering sentences in the source language into equivalent target sentences. The translation process refers to the potential of conventional machine translation systems, like METAL, and of the statistically oriented translation memory.
- Third, the translation post-processes, making the target language readable at the lexical, syntactical and semantic level. The translation post-processes include the discussion of computer-based solutions to proof-reading, spelling checkers, and grammar checkers in English, German, Greek, and Spanish.

The Translator's Workbench comprises tools for making these three cognitive processes easier to execute for the translator and gives the state of the art in which translation and text processing tools are available or feasible.

The Translator's Workbench Project with its interdisciplinary approach was a demonstration of the techniques and tools necessary for machine-assisted translation and documentation.

Marianne Kugler, Khurshid Ahmad, Gregor Thurmair

December 1994

List of Authors

Ahmad, Khurshid, University of Surrey
Albl, Michaela, University of Heidelberg
Davies, Andrea, University of Surrey
Delgado, Jaime, UPC Barcelona
Dudda, Friedrich, TA Triumph Adler AG
Fulford, Heather, University of Surrey
Hellwig, Peter, University of Heidelberg
Heyer, Gerhard, TA Triumph Adler AG
Höge, Monika, Mercedes Benz AG
Hohmann, Andrea, Mercedes Benz AG
Holmes-Higgin, Paul, University of Surrey
Hoof, Toon van, Fraunhofer Gesellschaft IAT
Karamanlakis, Stratis, L-Cube Athens
Keck, Bernhard, Fraunhofer Gesellschaft IAT
Kese, Ralf, TA Triumph Adler AG
Kleist-Retzow, Beate von, TA Triumph Adler AG
Kohn, Kurt, University of Heidelberg
Kugler, Marianne, TA Triumph Adler AG
Le Hong, Khai, Mercedes Benz AG
Mayer, Renate, Fraunhofer Gesellschaft IAT
Menzel, Cornelia, Fraunhofer Gesellschaft IAT
Meya Montserrat, Siemens Nixdorf CDS Barcelona
Rogers, Margaret, University of Surrey
Stallwitz, Gabriele, TA Triumph Adler AG
Thurmair, Gregor, Siemens Nixdorf Munich
Waldhör, Klemens, TA Triumph Adler AG
Winkelmann, Günter, TA Triumph Adler AG
Zavras, Alexios, L-Cube

Table of Contents

I. Introduction

Multilingual Documentation and Communication

1. Introduction

Gerhard Heyer

Text processing has always been one of the main productivity tools. As the market is expected to approach saturation, however, two main consequences need to be taken into consideration. On the one hand, we can expect a shift of interest towards value-adding text processing tools that give the user an operational advantage with respect to, e.g. translation support, multi-media integration, text retrieval, and groupware. On the other hand, any such extensions will gain widest acceptance if they can be used as complements to or from within the most widespread text processing systems.

The project has tried to take both considerations into account by developing TWB as a set of modular tools that can equally be integrated into FrameMaker under UNIX, Word or other text processing packages for Windows (capable to communicate via DDE).

Three scenarios are expected as real life applications:

(1) Writing a text or memo in a language that is not one's native language. In a Europe that is more and more growing together, increasingly texts will have to be exchanged that are written in English, French, or German. For many colleagues in international organisations or corporations, this is reality already today. Requirements for this kind of application are in particular language checking tools for non-native writers of a language, preferably based on a comparative grammar.

(2) Translating a text from source language into target language. In this scenario, it is mainly professional translators who are concerned, but also authors in all areas of text production occasionally have to translate already existing documents into other languages. In a professional environment, translation frequently is part of a technical documentation process. Hence, requirements for this kind of application comprise powerful editors, text converters, document management, terminology administration, and translation support tools, including fully automatic translation.

(3) Reviewing a text and its translation. Once a text has been translated, either the translator himself or the person for whom he has translated the text might wish to review the translation with respect to the source text. In many cases, this will just pertain to some key terms or paragraphs. The main requirement for this kind of application, therefore, is parallel scrolling, or alignment.

TRANSLATOR'S WORKBENCH (TWB) as a pre-competitive demonstrator project covers all three scenarios, and is intended to deliver up to date and competitive results that adhere to international standards, and which can serve as a basis for future developments in the area of advanced text processing and machine aided translation.

2. Key Players

Monika Höge, Andrea Hohmann, Khai Le-Hong

In a multilingual business environment the translator generally acts as a mediator between document creators on the one hand and document users on the other. However, due to the recent growth of multilingual communication and documentation, very often both document creators and document users are confronted with the problem of producing and understanding foreign language texts. The need to support all three groups - document creators, translators, document users - with adequate tools is obvious, the marketplace ever increasing.

One can distinguish between two major potential user groups of language tools, i.e. professional users and occasional users. Professional users include in-house translators, translators in translation agencies, freelance translators, and interpreters. There is an even wider range of occasional users, i.e. commercial correspondents, managers, executives, technical writers, secretaries, typists, research staff, and publishing shops. Different users have different requirements, have to perform different tasks and consequently need different tools. Figure 1 gives an outline of the different user groups and the language-related tasks they have to perform.

	professional users				occasional users					
user group / task	in-house translators	translation agencies	freelance translators	interpreters	secretaries typists	commercial correspondents	technical writers	research staff	managers executives	publishing shops
typing texts (diff. languages)	X	X	X		X	X	X	X	X	X
understanding source texts	X	X	X	X		X	X	X	X	X
writing target/ FL texts	X	X	X			X	X	X	X	X
translating (intellectual)	X	X	X	X	X	X				X
checking texts	X	X	X		X	X	X	X		X
looking-up LGP terms	X	X	X	X	X	X	X	X	X	X
looking-up LSP terms	X	X	X	X	X	X	X	X	X	X
knowledge extraction	X	X	X	X		X	X	X	X	
terminology elaboration	X	X	X	X			X	X		

Fig. 1: User groups and language-related tasks

user group / tools	professional users				occasional users					
	in-house translators	translation agencies	freelance translators	interpreters	secretaries typists	commercial correspondents	technical writers	research staff	managers executives	publishing shops
editor	X	X	X	X	X	X	X	X	X	X
language checker	X	X	X		X	X	X	X	X	X
on-line LSP dictionaries	X	X	X	X	X	X	X	X	X	X
termbanks	X	X	X	X	X	X	X	X	X	X
translation tools	X	X	X		X	X		X	X	X
machine translation	X	X	X		X	X		X	X	
text comparison	X	X	X			X	X			
converters	X	X	X	X	X	X	X	X	X	X
terminology elaboration tool	X	X	X	X			X	X		X

Fig. 2: User groups and language tools

Taking into account the outline given in figure1, one may now easily define the tools which would be useful for the different user groups as shown in Fig. 2.

3. The Cognitive Basis of Translation

Kurt Kohn, Michaela Albl

According to a widely held belief, translating consists essentially in a process of linguistic substitution. Surprisingly, this simplifying view according to which a translator's main task is to find equivalent words and expressions seems to be quite common even among language professionals. While such a naive "common sense" understanding of translation is not necessarily in conflict with professional translational practice, it certainly does not provide an adequate conceptual orientation for the development of translation support tools.

Translational competence has a cognitive dimension. Translators need to be able to understand a source text and, on this basis, to produce a target text appropriately adapted to the inevitable changes within the communicative situation. Under the common assumption of a "container" model of meaning and translation, the tasks involved in the translational comprehension and production of texts tend to be underestimated. According to the central metaphor of this model, the source text "contains" meaning, which is then recovered by cracking the textual code, and transferred to its custom-built new home, the target text, for further communicative use.

But texts do not "contain" meaning; rather, they provide the kind of linguistic "road-signs" which support and guide readers in their attempt to create a meaningful interpretation. It is through the activation of integrated denotational, propositional and illocutionary strategies that texts perform their basic cognitive function: They trigger off and control complex processes of mental modelling leading up to a cognitive representation of the states and events a text is said to be about.

Text-based mental modelling presupposes various kinds of linguistic and non-linguistic knowledge, both in the declarative and procedural mode. World knowledge and specialized subject knowledge are exploited to feed the "content" dimension of mental modelling. Linguistic knowledge is used for the production and/or identification of the textual clues - i.e., words, phrases, syntactic structures - needed for the activation, selection and restructuring of particular pieces of factual knowledge in the course of mental modelling. The successful cognitive creation of textual meaning, in comprehension as well as in production, always requires a complex strategic exploitation, through integrated 'bottom up' and 'top down' cycles, of the linguistic and factual knowledge implicitly required by the text.

In the course of learning one (or several) natural language(s), speakers acquire and refine the highly specialized strategies underlying unilingual text comprehension and production. As they are deeply ingrained and largely subconscious, they are quite naturally activated when texts are processed for comprehension and production under translation conditions. Translating, however, imposes specific constraints under which the exclusive reliance on strategies geared towards the problems and demands of ordinary unilingual text processing is likely to cause serious processing conflicts (Kohn 1990a).

Two types of conflict are of particular importance, as evidenced by well-known and frequent deficits even in professional translations. The first one arises from the continuing presence of the source text during translation. While in ordinary unilingual text comprehension the textual meaning clues are transient road signs, processed only as far as necessary for securing a satisfactory match with the available 'top down' information, translating requires their presence throughout the entire process. The words and structures of the source text do not fade away with successful comprehension; in fact, they are kept alive and are needed for continual checks. This means that in the course of the production of the target text, translators have to create appropriate expressions while, at the same time, being forced to focus their attention on the source text. Thus, "old" textual clues relevant for the comprehension task are getting in the way of "new" ones necessary for production. This interference conflict between source and target text accounts for "translationese", which is one of the most persistent translation problems.

The second type of conflict derives from the translator's lack of communicative autonomy. Translators normally are more or less limited in the semantic control they are allowed to exercise. Unlike the ordinary unilingual producer of texts, they are not semantically autonomous. The meaning for which the translator has to find the appropriate linguistic expression is essentially determined by the source text. Translating conditions are, thus, in conflict with the meaning creating function of text production, and seriously inhibit the translators' intuitive retrieval of their linguistic knowledge; again, translationese is likely to be the unwelcome result.

Underlying this model of translating as a text-based cognitive activity is the claim that the strategies and procedural conditions of translational text processing are basically the same for translating general and special texts. This does not mean, however, that there are no differences between the two. On the contrary, depending on the kinds of factual and linguistic knowledge involved, and of the conventions controlling the adequacy of textual expressions, texts of different types create specific demands on translational processing.

In the case of special texts, more often than not, the common problems resulting from translation-specific processing constraints are magnified by the difficulties translators have with successfully keep abreast of the explosive knowledge development in specialized subject areas, and of the corresponding changes in terminological, phraseological and stylistic standards and conventions. Technical translators are not only faced with the "ordinary" problems of translation; they also have to fight a constant battle on the knowledge front.

The solutions provided by TWB account for a whole variety of needs arising in the context of multilingual documentation and translation: target text checking with respect to spelling mistakes, grammatical errors and stylistic inadequacies; the aquisition, representation and translational deployment of terminological knowledge; the encyclopaedic and transfer-specific elaboration of terms; a dynamically evolving translation memory. In the face of a fast moving multilingual information market, TWB is thus geared to support translators to achieve better and more reliable translation results and to increase their overall translational productivity.

4. User Participation in Software Development

Khurshid Ahmad, Andrea Davies, Heather Fulford, Paul Holmes-Higgin, Margaret Rogers, Monika Höge

In the last 40 years, translation has established itself as a "distinct and autonomous profession", requiring "specialised knowledge and long and intensive academic preparation" (Newmark 1991:45). Even in the United Kingdom, for example, where industry and commerce often rely on the status of English as a lingua franca, the profession is now consolidating its position.

Challenges	Consequences/Needs
- there is a growing awareness of product quality, involving extensive translation quality assurance; the target text has to meet the pragmatic, stylistic and terminological demands of user/reader/consumer.	-> terminology elaboration tools
- owing to the harmonization of the Single European Market in 1993 and the resulting problem of product liability, the accuracy and clarity of translations is gaining in importance.	-> term banks -> language checkers
- the use of recent technology means that translation is often the final step in the life cycle of a product; translations have to be delivered camera-ready and just-in-time.	-> advanced text processing systems -> desktop-publishing tools -> interchangeable text modules for documentation -> access to text databases -> text comparison tools
- in order to guarantee the information flow in a field of growing specialisation and complex technical expertise the contact between translators and experts has to be much closer and communication made easier.	-> communicating with clients (experts) via computer networks
- in order to guarantee the cost-effectiveness of translations, the organization of translation work must ensure that the goals of quality and quantity are reached.	-> user friendly, quick and easy-to-handle translation tools -> machine aided translation -> machine translation
- the technical environment is growing increasingly complex; different systems are used in different organizations and even in different parts of the same organization.	-> advanced converting facilities

Fig. 3: Challenges of the future and consequences for the translator

The Institute of Linguists has 6,000 members of whom nearly 40% belong to the Translating Division and the Interpreting Division (1991). The more recently-established Institute of Translating and Interpreting has nearly 1500 members (1991). Both organisations offer examinations in translation. In the TWB project, the professional status and expertise of translators has been explicitly acknowledged by their close involvement in all stages of software development through the integration of an IT user organisation, i.e. Mercedes-Benz AG.

Mercedes-Benz translators have been involved throughout the software design and development life-cycle, initially in a user requirements study, and subsequently in software evaluation during the project. The project consortium recognized the importance of eliciting the translators' needs before developing tools to support them in their daily work. For this reason, at the beginning of the TWB project a user requirements study was conducted by Mercedes-Benz AG and the University of Surrey. The purpose of this study was to elicit, through a questionnaire-based survey, observation study, and in-depth interviews, the current working practice of professional translators, and to ascertain how they might benefit from some of the recent advances in information technology. This study is perhaps one of the first systematic attempts to investigate the translation world from these two perspectives. The study methodology itself was innovative, drawing on and synthesizing techniques employed in psychology, software engineering, and knowledge acquisition for expert system development.

Software development and its implementation precipitates change in the user organisation which leads to an inevitable change in the original user requirements. This had to be incorporated in our work as we view software development as an evolving process, where history is as important as future development; and to this end, translators were consulted throughout the project and have taken part in software testing and evaluation (see in detail Chap. 20).

The integration of the end users into the project development work has necessitated careful change management, with a recognition of the need to introduce new technology without disturbing unduly the established working practice of translators. The user requirements study substantiated the theoretical literature on translation (see for example Newmark 1988 and 1991) by confirming that translation is a complex cognitive task involving a number of seemingly disparate high-level skills. These skills could perhaps be grouped under the broad heading of multilingual knowledge communication skills, and involve essentially an ability to transfer the meaning and intention of a message from one language to another in a manner and style appropriate to the document type. The skills fall into the following categories: linguistic (e.g. language knowledge, ability to write coherently and cohesively), general communication (e.g. sensitivity to and understanding of the styles of various documents, knowing where to locate relevant domain information, knowing how to conduct library searches), and practical abilities (e.g. word processing, typing, use of a fax machine, familiarity with electronic mail, as well as miscellaneous administrative tasks.)

4.1 User Requirements Study

In this section, translators' needs are considered within the framework of the typical professional environment in which technical translation is carried out, before the approach adopted for the user requirements study and some of its principal findings are presented. Finally, the relevance of these results to TWB software development is discussed.

4.1.1 Translation as Part of the Product Development Lifecycle

The complexity of the overall process of document translation becomes apparent when the following three factors are considered: suppliers and developers from a number of countries are often involved in the manufacturer and marketing of an individual product; companies involved in the product development lifecycle typically utilise different equipment; the use of terminology varies from company to company. Furthermore, technological advances mean that product development lifecycles are becoming shorter. In addition, similar multilingual product documentation often has to be produced in a short space of time for closely related products, such as different types of car. At the same time, quality is an increasingly important consideration. With the advent of EC product liability restrictions in 1993, the requirement for accuracy in documentation - including, of course, translations - will become even more crucial.

When working within such a multilingual office framework, where both speed and accuracy are of equal importance in the product development lifecycle, the translator requires support at two principal levels: terminology needs to be agreed and its usage standardised; tools are needed to assist in document production and transmission. The translation of documentation needs to be seen as an integral part of the development of a product, and an organisation should never lose sight of the fact that a product's documentation may significantly influence the reception and acceptance of the product itself by its intended users.

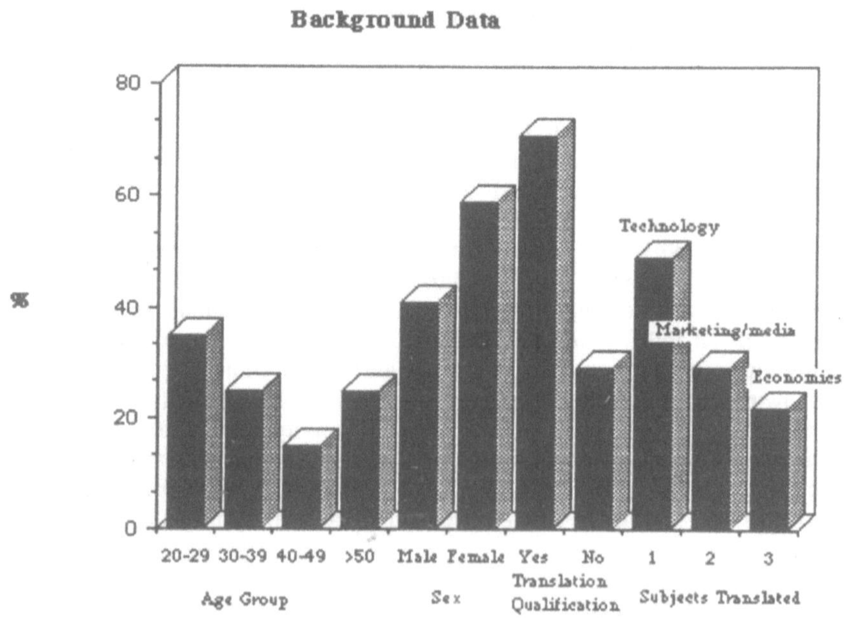

Fig. 4: Translator profile according to: age, sex, translation qualification, and principal subjects translated

Figure 3 illustrates some of the major challenges facing the translation industry of the future, and indicates the technological facilities to which translators should have access if these challenges(identified by the Language Services Department at Mercedes-Benz AG) are to be adequately faced.

4.1.2 Requirements Study: Method

The user requirements study comprised three phases: a Europe-wide questionnaire survey to which over 200 professional translators responded; an observation of six translators at work in the Mercedes-Benz AG translation department in Stuttgart; and in-depth interviews with 10 translators at Mercedes-Benz AG and freelance translators in Britain.

Questionnaire Survey

The questionnaire survey was based on a "task" model of translation, i.e. the translation of documents was viewed as a combination of tasks namely: the task of receiving the documents to be translated (input); the task of translating the document (processing) and the task of delivering the document (output). The task model provided clues to what it is the translator generally does and what particular needs the individual translator has, permitting the formation of a user profile. The task model and the user profile formed the basis of our study and enabled us to establish a clear picture of the translator and his or her working environment.

Observation Study

The observation study was conducted by the University of Surrey in the Mercedes-Benz AG translation department. Six translators were observed at work (without disrupting their normal work routine, although some did stop work to discuss various aspects of translation practice). Our primary aim was to gain an overall impression of the translation process and, in so doing, to identify some of the problems translators encounter in their daily work.

An additional aim of the observation study was to watch translators in various phases of their work, i.e. the pre-translation edit, translation phase and post-translation edit phase, to gain insight into the procedure adopted by translators in their work and the phases in which various tools, such as terminology aids, are used.

In-depth interviews

In-depth interviews were conducted with some translators in the UK and in the translation department at Mercedes-Benz. The objective of this part of our study was to gain more detailed information about translation practice and translators' requirements by allowing translators to discuss their work and the needs they have. This phase of our study was particularly useful for discussing issues which were not really suitable for presentation in the questionnaire, such as the layout of the user interface.

Some of the techniques of knowledge engineering were employed for the interviews with translators. Two forms of interviews were conducted: focussed and structured interviews. Focussed interviews provided the translators with the opportunity to discuss their work and their requirements freely; structured interviews enabled the interviewer to pose specific questions to the translators about current working practice and requirements.

The principal topics covered in interviews included translators' working methods, terminology requirements, the use of computer checking tools, and the layout of the user interface. In the discussions on the layout of the user interface, a series of storyboards was used to enable translators to visualise screen layout options, and so on.

4.1.3 User Requirements Study: Principal Findings

Each part of the study is described below.

Questionnaire Survey

People: Figure 4 indicates that the typical translator in our survey is young, female, has a university qualification, and translates technical texts.

"Inputs" and "Outputs": the major input media are non-digital, whereas the principal output media are digital. This indicates that translators make use of digital technology (i.e. computers), but may be constrained by their client's use of non-digital input media.

Processing Requirements: We investigated processing requirements for (i) terminology, (ii) word processing, (iii) spelling checking, (iv) grammar checking, and (v) style checking. The spectrum of user needs for processing tools ranged from simple look-up lexical items to more complex semantic processing. Our respondents were only aware of computer-based facilities for items (i), (ii) and (iii) above. For text processing, word processors are used by a substantial proportion of translators. The use of dictating machines was found to be rare in our sample. Most translators in our sample (over 40%) checked spelling off-line, approximately 30% manually on screen, and just over 25% using spell check programs. Less than 1% of the translators in our sample had any direct experience with term banks or with machine translation or machine-aided translation.

The terminology aids most commonly used by the translators in the survey sample were paper-based dictionaries, glossaries and word lists, although doubts were expressed about their accuracy and currency. Translators in our sample organised their terminology bilingually and alphabetically in a card index, including less information than they expect from other sources. Only very few translators organised their terminology systematically (e.g. according to a library classification), but many stated that this could be useful. Grouped in order of priority, requirements for terminological information were found to be:

foreign language equivalent, synonym, variant, abbreviation;
definition, contextual example, usage information;
date, source and terminologist's name;
grammatical information

Our survey indicated that terminological information is required throughout the translation process: during pre-translation editing to clarify the source language terms; in the translation process itself to identify and use target language terms; and during the post-translation edit phase for checking the accuracy of target language terms.

Observation Study

The chronology of translation tasks was shown to be: read source language text; mark unfamiliar terminology; consult reference works; translate text; edit translation. In addition, reference works continued to be consulted throughout the translation process to clarify further terminological problems. Hence, our study indicates that the translation process cannot be discretely divided into the three phases (pre-translation edit, translation phase and post-translation edit) commonly assumed in translation theory and in the teaching of translation.

The principal difficulty identified by translators throughout their work was the inadequacy of currently available reference material in terms of currency, degree of domain specialisation, range of linguistic detail.

Interview Study

The major points arising from the interviews are as follows:

Working methods:

Terminology clarification often takes place throughout the translation process; Translations are mostly checked on a print out rather than on screen; Word processors are the preferred tools for translation work, rather than typewriters or dictating machines.

Terminology:

More information is required than just the foreign language equivalent of a term (e.g. grammatical information); Contextual examples are often more useful than definitions as they provide both decoding and encoding information.

Checking Tools:

Positive attitude shown to computer spell checkers; if translators had spell checkers, they would use them. Translators have no experience of using grammar and style checkers and therefore found it hard to visualise how these tools will work.

User Interfaces:

A WIMP environment is favoured by translators; the interface should be as simple as possible.

4.1.4 Summary of Principal Findings and their Impact on Software Development

It was established that in view of recent advances in information technology, computational aids would be welcome in the translation environment. These aids should support the translator throughout the translation process, and include tools to assist in terminology elicitation, term bank development, terminology retrieval, multilingual text processing, the provision of machine-produced raw translations, the identification of previous translations, and spelling checking.

Based on the results of the user requirements study, the Translator's Workbench is providing the following:

- multilingual text processing facilities;
- term bank, and a term bank development environment (MATE);
- spelling, grammar, and style checkers;
- translation memory;
- remote access to an existing machine translation system (METAL) and to the term bank EURODICAUTOM;
- converters compatible with ODA (Office Document Architecture).

The results of the study were presented to the software developers in the project consortium, and in general, the reaction was positive, results being taken up and integrated into the tools being developed for TWB.

4.2 Software Testing and Evaluation - Integrating the User into the Software Development Process

This section considers some of the problems involved in software testing and evaluation during development in the particular context of TWB and presents the solutions which were agreed on.

Integration Considerations

In trying to integrate the end user into the software development process, we had to address the issue of communication difficulties between software developers and users. Owing to their general lack of computing expertise, it is difficult for the users to formulate and articulate their specific requirements in a way that the software developers can comprehend and act upon. Likewise, the software developers typically find it difficult to grasp the real issues involved in the day-to-day tasks of a translation environment. In order to bridge the gap between these two groups, a team was formed from members of the consortium (The User Requirements and Interface Group - URI). This group, made up of users, developers, and linguists, has been responsible for considering the points raised by users in the software testing and evaluation, and for communicating these points to the software developers.

Organisational Considerations

Software acceptance tests are usually conducted upon completion of the implementation phase, but in TWB, software testing took place with active user participation throughout the software development lifecycle. Adopting this approach to testing improved the chances of detecting major deficiencies in the software and of determining any significant discrepancies in the users' expectations of the software and the software performance or functionality. The TWB software development and evaluation work has therefore been a dynamic process. The approach has, however, put great demands on the software developers because they have been compelled to deliver testable software at a very early stage in the project. This was particularly difficult within the scope of TWB, since it is a pre-competitive research and development project. Nevertheless, three scenario tests have been successfully carried out on separate prototype versions of the TWB software; and furthermore, long-term tests have been conducted, in which a member of the testing team has inspected the functionality and performance of the software over a longer period of time.

The general testing procedure developed by the URI group follows a nine-step approach in which developers and users participate equally. This approach is illustrated in Figure 5 below.

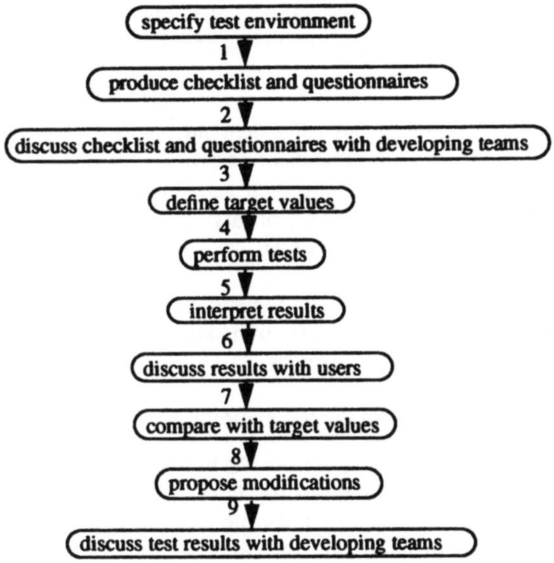

Fig. 5: The nine-step approach to TWB software testing

If the above testing procedure is followed, the software can be improved at any point in the development cycle, and in turn, the improvements can be monitored by the testing team. This has the advantage that the user is motivated by the fact that the problems identified during testing are generally solved before the next phase of tests is conducted.

Methodological Considerations

Eliciting user requirements at the beginning of the software development process is only the first stage of user participation. The later, and arguably more complex, stage of software testing and evaluation involves the assessment of how far translators' actual requirements have been met. A particular difficulty here is that users' requirements often change once the tools which have been designed to meet specified needs are in operation. Hence, the testing and evaluation of final software quality involves more than a simple check against pre-defined requirements. The notion of quality from the user's point of view must be defined and methods elaborated for the metrication of this quality by means of acceptance tests. (For details see Chap. 20)

5. TWB in the Documentation Context

Gregor Thurmair

5.1 The Context of Translation Tools

In the last few years, the job of a technical translator has changed considerably because translation has become a more important part of the technical world. It is not an "isolated activity" any more but should be considered as part of a chain of the production of technical documentation.

There are many examples of the growing demand for technical documentation; for some products it covers hundreds of thousands of pages. This is due to the fact that the products themselves become more complex, and their functionality has to be described more carefully and in more detail. There are cases of large projects where the documentation alone involves a turnover of several million ECU.

These projects require professional planning and managing; and they often involve translation work packages as well. In this way, translation becomes integrated into the product and (multilingual) documentation business.

This fact puts three constraints on the translation job:

- documentation must be multilingual, owing to the growing internationalisation of markets; this trend will be reinforced in the next few years in Europe. For large international companies, documentation must be available in at least three languages in parallel. This creates a growing demand for translation.
- documentation must be available "just in time"; its production often determines the time of delivery of a product (as products cannot be launched at foreign markets if the documentation is not available). This holds even more for translation, and it shortens the amount of time to be spent by translators for their jobs. As a result, translation is looked at more closely by product planning people, and possibilities of translation support are being considered.
- documentation is produced using special documentation or publishing systems, like Word, Interleaf, FrameMaker, and others. As the whole documentation environment will be tuned towards those systems, translators are expected to accept documents written with those documentation systems, and to deliver translations formatted in the same way. This has strong implications for the translation environment, as it must be computer based; and translators cannot be experts in all the systems their customers use (some of which even require special hardware to run on).

These facts mean that from the point of view of the translators, they find themselves in a dilemma: They have to translate more documents in more languages in shorter time, in a more constrained environment. They must be specialists in their technical areas, possibly in several languages, and in addition, they must be familiar with the most common documentation and publishing systems.

This situation requires technical support to be given to translators. This support should comprise all areas of the translation process; tools to be developed should contain:

- support for document import and export, i.e. converters
- support for translation preparation, e.g. lexicon lookup tools
- support for translation, e.g. translation memory tools, or even machine pretranslation
- support for postediting, proofreading, and reviewing
- support for archiving, document management, and version comparison
- support for accounting and billing.

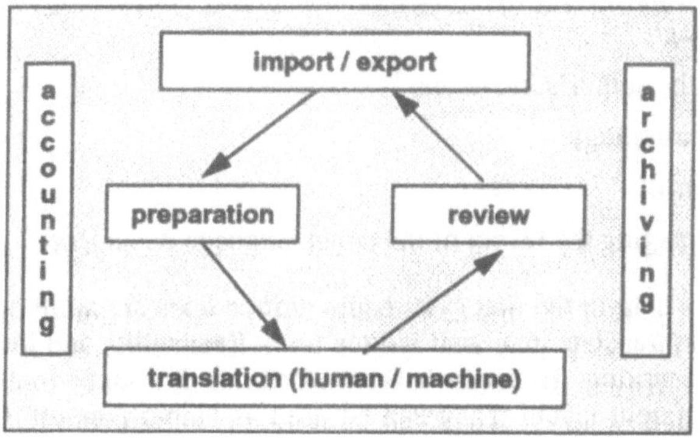

Fig. 6: Translation tools in context

Some of these tools would be useful not just for translators but also for other users. Problems of terminology apply also to (monolingual) documentation experts: consistency of terminology is certainly an issue here, as well as proofreading, checking documentation guidelines, dictionary lookup, and others such as converters for text and graphics, or archiving functions. Many of the functions to be developed can be shared by translators and documentation workers. This point has also been substantiated at workshops on documentation and translation where Translator's Workbench was presented.

There is another group of users which can profit from the developments mentioned above, and which is also confronted with the problem of multilingual document handling: offices today become more and more multilingual, owing to the fact that industry is becoming increasingly involved in international communication and business.

As a result, much business communication has to be written in non-native languages, and it is often not translated by a skilled translator. These "occasional" translators again must have the support of software tools, and those tools are similar to the ones for professional translators; among them are

- dictionary lookup facilities, with definitions of terms
- pretranslation of highly repetitive text blocks, trained for office texts
- text correction and proofreading tools for the target language

This fact influences the development of marketable translation products, as the office market is much larger than the one for professional translators. Therefore, industry has started projects for "multilingual offices" which tackle problems of language use in the office environment. These projects could serve as a basis to develop tools particularly designed for translators and technical authors such as accounting, delta version management, etc.

Some of the tools needed have been studied in more detail in Translator's Workbench (TWB).

5.2 Text Control

Investigations have shown that the most time consuming activities in the translation process are the following:

- clarification of the author's intentions
- collection of terminology
- the translation itself
- retyping and arranging the layout of the target language document

Language checkers help in the first case: badly written texts are more difficult, and therefore more costly, to translate than well written ones. Readability and intelligibility can be improved by good writing. Translator's Workbench has developed tools which allow for text control on different levels. They can be used as "input control" for the translation process, and also as "output control", to detect errors in the target language.

Language checking can be conducted on different levels:

On the **orthographic** level, TWB investigated a number of approaches to improve the poor quality of existing spellers:

- a lexicon-based speller for Greek has been developed, based on conventional techniques of lexicon lookup and similarity measuring. The challenge here was the language: Greek is a highly inflectional language with many irregularities and word stem changes, therefore the lexicon lookup needs to be organised in a sophisticated way.
- in order to create spellers with more linguistic intelligence, a Spanish spelling module has been developed which operates on the syllabic structures of Spanish. It turns out that this approach is more accurate than existing spellers, both in terms of diagnostics and of correction proposals.
- most spellers are not context-sensitive, i.e. they do not recognise errors which lead to "legal" words such as agreement errors, fixed phrases etc. In TWB, an extended speller has been developed for German, which not only recognises more difficult cases of phraseology (e.g. German capitalisation problems) but also incorporates intelligence to recognise some basic agreement errors (e.g. within noun phrases, noun - verb congruency). This shows that spelling correction requires more linguistic intelligence than a mere lexicon lookup.

The result of these efforts was a Greek speller released as a product for DOS, and improved quality for spellers with more linguistic intelligence. Two issures remain, however: the spellers must be partially redesigned from a software engineering point of view to compete with the existing ones, and they must be extended in terms of language coverage.

This is a problem for most of the TWB tools: As they involve more and more linguistic intelligence, porting them to other languages requires considerable efforts, not just in terms of lexicon replacements but also in terms of studying the syllabic structures of European languages in more detail, or even developing grammars. It may turn out that an approach which works for one language does not work for another one. This is a drawback from a product marketing point of view as several parallel approaches must be developed and maintained.

In the case of **grammar checking**, it turns out that most existing grammar checkers are not reliable, and therefore are very restricted in their usage. This is due to the fact that most of them do not use a real grammar but are based on some more or less sophisticated pattern matching techniques. However, the fact that they sell shows that there is a need for those tools.

TWB again followed several approaches in grammar checking:

- We developed a small noun phrase grammar based on augmented transition networks (ATN) for German in order to detect agreement errors. An analysis of the errors made by foreign langguage students indicated that these noun phrase agreement errors are among the most frequent grammatical errors in German texts (please see the section on Grammar and Style Checkers for more detailed information). This grammar is planned to run on a DOS machine, aş part of the extended speller mentioned above. The problem of partial parsing is of course to find the segments where to start parsing (noun phrases can have embedded clauses, prepositional attachments etc.)
- A second approach has been followed for Spanish grammar checking: Here we used an existing grammar (the METAL analysis) and enriched it by special rules and procedures to cover ungrammatical input. During parsing, it can be detected if one of those special rules has fired, and if so, the appropriate diagnostic measure can be taken.

  This approach adds a "peripheral" grammar to the core grammar which tries to identify the cases of ungrammaticality (agreement errors, wrong verb argument usage, etc.). Its success depends on two facts, however: First, the grammar writer must have foreseen the most frequent types of errors in order to allow for the grammar to react on it; and second, the coverage of the core grammar must be good enough in order not to judge a parse failure as ungrammatical sentence.
- A third approach was developed for German again: Based on a dependency grammar, we tried to implement an approach called "unification failure". The basic idea is that the grammar itself should decide what an ungrammatical input may be and where an error could be detected (namely where two constituents cannot be unified into a bigger one).

  This approach is backed by the study carried out for German mentioned above, which shows that nearly all kinds of errors one could think of really can be found in a text corpus; therefore it may be difficult to predict those errors in a "peripheral" grammar approach.

  The basic algorithms for the "unification failure" approach have been developed and implemented; some theoretical problems still have to be solved; see the chapter on syntax checking below.

As a result, it turned out that grammar checking needs much more linguistic intelligence if it is to be helpful and reliable. It requires fully developed lexicon and syntax components and some "heavy" machinery (in terms of computing power). The TWB tools are the better the more developed the underlying grammars are. This again hampers their portability to other languages as it means considerable investment.

A last area of language checking was **style checking**, or more specifically verification of controlled grammars. This is more closely related to the documentation business as it tries to implement guidelines for good technical writing, conventions for style and layout, also implying language criteria.

Such a verification of controlled grammars has been developed for German, based on the METAL grammar. It implements diagnostics for guidelines such as

- Don't write sentences longer than 20 words
- Don't use too complex sentences
- Don't use three and more part compounds

It analyses texts sentence by sentence and gives diagnostic information for each of them if necessary.

This approach seems to be feasible if the grammar coverage is large enough. It is experimented with by several documentation departments; it has to be extended to other languages.

5.3 Translation Preparation Tools

While the Language Checking Tools are important for the documentation process as such (and can be used by both authors and translators), there must be tools available particularly for translators. Some of those tools have been developed within TWB, some need to be developed.

The second main area of the translation process cited above is terminology search and preparation. TWB tries to help here by offering a set of tools, centered around a **Term Bank**.

The term bank is used in two ways: It is a medium to store and edit terminology, and it is a medium to retrieve terminology during the translation process. As a basic software device, an Oracle relational database was chosen; this was integrated both into the MATE terminology toolkit and into the term retrieval component. The structure of a terminological entry has been defined in a "multilayer" approach, and several thousand example entries (for the area of automotive engineering) have been implemented.

During the translation process, **access** to these data must be provided from the translator's wordprocessor. The TWB tools offer several possibilities here:

- The easiest way is to use the **Cut and Paste** facility offered by the UNIX/Motif window manager. Users simply highlight a text portion, paste it into the search window of the term bank, retrieve the result, and paste it back into the text. Although this approach works in general, it has problems in case of formatting characters, blanc spaces, and so on. Also, it is not the fastest way to do it.
- On DOS, it is possible to ask for lexicon information (the area being commerce, finance, and law) from the WinWord editor, by using a **hotkey** and activating internal links. In this way, translators can look up and paste terms into their document.
- This has been achieved on UNIX by implementing a special interface into the FrameMaker desktop publishing system. This interface has also proved to be suitable for other linguistic applications.

The success of using a term bank depends on the terminology which is stored in it; this is not a software issue but an issue of providing terminology in different areas: If it is too expensive to fill a term bank, or if users do not find what they search for, it will not be used.

Therefore it is essential to provide tools for **terminology maintenance**. TWB has developed software for terminology maintenance and corpus work: The MATE system comprises corpus analysis tools (production of wordlists, indices, or keywords in contexts), term inspection tools, term bank maintenance and editing, printing facilities, and so on. This allows for empirical and corpus based terminology work. Providing good terminology is central for the term bank software.

Another possibility for checking terminology is to look up external term banks, like EURODICAUTOM, TEAM, or others. This is possible with the TWB **remote access** software. Users can access the EURODICAUTOM database and search for terms they need to know. While this is technically feasible, it is time-consuming and expensive (in terms of line costs); it would be simpler to download several modules of external term banks like EURODICAUTOM into the local term bank (which raises the question of copyright problems)

In addition to the "official" terminology, released by a terminologist, and stored in a term bank, it transpired that a more private device could be helpful where translators store their particular information of any kind, ranging from private hints to phone numbers of experts.

Therefore, we developed the **Card Box** in TWB which is meant to support this kind of information base, and to allow for online access. It is implemented in the manner of a hypercard stack which can be looked up back and forth.

All the tools presented above need to be improved to be fully operational: The term bank functionalities must be better integrated, the editor - term bank connection must be stabilised, the different term formats must be made exchangeable by creating terminology interchange formats and software support. This will be an issue in the MULTILEX Esprit project. The MATE functions must be made compatible, a common user interface with just the same look and feel must be designed.

Other functions are missing in TWB, e.g. the possibility of looking up the words of a text in a term bank and extracting relevant information, for instance to produce glossaries, lists of "illegal" terms, synonym links, inconsistency checks, etc.

5.4 Translation Tools

In the third main area, the translation proper, TWB also provides some tools to increase productivity.

The TWB **Translation Memory** is a tool which looks up patterns in a database of previously translated text, and replaces the input patterns by its correspondence in the target language. The system consists of a training part which asks the user for correspondences; these relations are interpreted in a statistical model. At runtime, this model is processed to detect the target language patterns for a given input string.

Although it has only limited linguistic knowledge, this approach is promising in the area of phraseological and terminological correspondences, i.e. where local decisions can be made; and it should be trained for many small-scale text types rather than for one universal text-type.

It will help the translators to translate fixed expressions of high frequency, and expressions which have been translated before.

If texts are well written and repetitive enough, they can be completely translated by machine. Machine (pre-)translation of technical text will have a large market share in the future, given the constraints of the documentation process outlined above.

In order to experiment with this approach, TWB implemented the possibility of **remote access to a MT system**, in this case METAL.

Users send their text, specify the text format, and the lexicon modules to be used for translation, and send their text via an ODIF / X400 connection to a translation server. It is translated there and the raw translation is sent back.

The success of such an approach depends on the lexicon maintenance, the quality of a translation, and the ease of postprocessing.

Overall, the translation process can be organised in a very flexible way with the TWB tools:

- Users can translate "by hand" and look up terminology using the TWB lexicon lookup tools
- Users can pretranslate frequently used patterns using the Translation Memory, and translate only the rest manually
- Users can send the text to a translation server and postedit the raw translation being sent back.

Again, improvements can be imagined in this area: A common user interface, a better training facility for the memory, an access functionality beyond X400, additional tools like sophisticated search-and-replace functions would support the translators even more. But the general direction can be recognised: To react to the translator's needs in a flexible way, with a set of supporting tools.

5.5 Post-Translation Tools

The last main area, retyping and reformatting, has been tackled in TWB by writing **converters** between different editing and publishing systems.

To do this, we have chosen ODA/ODIF as our main interchange platform: It is a well known standard, it is supported by main software suppliers, it is well defined not only in syntax but also in its semantics, and it cooperates nicely with the X400 protocols in its ODIF interchange part.

Converters from and into ODIF have been written and are being marketed:

- Word to ODIF and back
- FrameMaker to ODIF and back
- WordPerfect to ODIF and back
- MDIF (the METAL Document Interchange Format) to ODIF and back

Other converters from and into ODIF are available, or are under development (like DCA, HIT, and others).

This eases the problem of reformatting, as translators can use their own wordprocessors and still deliver a correctly layouted document at the end. Experience shows that good converters increase the overall productivity of a translator by more than 20%

As a result, the TWB tools show the direction into which future documentation and translation processes will go, even if some of them are not yet productive and immediately usable. They reflect the fact that documentation, multilingual office, and translation have their interdependencies, and that they all need tools which interact with each other in a flexible way, guided by a "liberal" architecture (the TWB manager). Every workstation will be able to configure the sets of TWB tools according to its needs, but all tools will interact nicely.

From this point of view, TWB shows the strategic direction into which future development should go; and it demonstrates in a prototypical way what some of the components needed could look like.

6. Market Trends for Text Processing Tools

Gerhard Heyer

Information systems buying in the 1990s is generally expected to polarize, on the one hand, into growing and profitable so-called operational applications, and stagnating, so-called personal productivity and administrative applications, on the other hand. Personal productivity and administrative applications are primarily intended to reduce administrative costs, while by operational applications are meant applications that add new and better services, improve operational flexibility, or reduce operational costs. The growth in operational applications is expected to dictate the structure of computing in the 1990s, where, in particular, the operational activities will be organization-specific.

In addition to horizontal software applications, therefore, software development will also have to focus on functional solutions, i.e. general solutions to problems that are common to a number of vertical applications without becoming a product for the mass market.

Considering the main standard software packages for the PC (data base systems, integrated software packages, word processing, DTP, spreadsheets, and graphics), text processing as the key productivity tool is and will remain in the near future the single most important horizontal software application.

However, in accordance with the general tendency towards more operational applications, saturation for the word processing market is forseable, and expected to have effects from 1994 onwards.

In 1991 the main trends for text processing software are:

- integration with other packages (e.g. spreadsheet, graphics, database)
- graphical user interface (e.g. WINDOWS based),
- CD-ROM integration (e.g. for dictionaries, distribution of long texts).
- addition of extended functionality (e.g. groupware, text retrieval, translation support, proofreading, DTP)

In addition to CD-ROM, read-write magneto-optical disks for archiving purposes, scanner plus OCR software for inputting text, and flash ROM cards are also considered possible hardware extensions related to text processing. The markets for optical disks is expected to grow fast until 1994 with highest growth rate for read-write disks.

Linguistic tools to enhance text processing packages on the PC today comprise standard packages like:

- spelling checkers,
- proofreading tools,
- thesauri and synonym dictionaries (monolingual dictionaries),
- translation dictionaries,
- translation support tools,
- fully automatic translation,
- remote access facilities to large automatic machine translation systems.

Definitions:

Spellcheckers check each word against a list, or dictionary, regardless of context, and highlight only spellings which do not exist with respect to this list.

Proofreading tools make use of linguistic knowledge in terms of more complex dictionaries (like Duden for German) or grammar rules, in order to identify orthographical errors the correction of which requires knowledge of the context (e.g. correct use of article, capitalization, lack of agreement between subject and verb).

In the market forecasts below, spellcheckers and proofreading tools are collectively referred to as text editing tools.

Thesauri, synonym dictionaries, and term data bases list for each word its definition(s) and possible alternatives.

Translation dictionaries list for each word or phrase its translation(s) in one or more other languages. All electronic dictionaries can be called stand-alone or integrated into the text processing system.

Translation support tools are editors and systems for interactively composing or correcting translations.

Fully automatic translation systems are software systems that take some text as source text and non-interactively translate it into the target text.

Remote access facilities to large automatic machine translation systems is software for obtaining fully automatic translations via network services (e.g. via X400).

Conclusions for TWB

Careful evaluation of available products shows that most companies aim at particular tools only, and that there is presently no single company offering tools for all aspects of electronic writing. Thus, TWB is the first unified product for all aspects of advanced text processing.

In most cases, available products are based on inadequate linguistic data. In order to increase user acceptance, and thus to promote commercial success, TWB should continue to aim at the highest linguistic quality of tools needed.

With the exception of Microsoft's grammar checker for Word 2.0 for Windows 3.1, none of the tools are not (yet) available for standard text processing under Windows. Most products are available for English only. Again, TWB is one of the first products that offers a full range of integrated and advanced text processing tools under Windows also for languages other than English.

In summary, we can expect a growing market for extensions to standard text processing packages coping with the language problem in an increasingly international business, and TWB appears well equipped to meet that challenge.

II. Translation Pre-Processes

The 'Input' Resources

7. Document access - Networks and Converters

Jaime Delgado, Montserrat Meya

7.1 The Use of Standards for Access from TWB to External Resources

Introduction

One of the aims of the TWB project is to be open to the outside world. For this reason, some tools that interconnect TWB with external resources have been developed.

These tools include access to external term banks and access to machine translation systems, using X.400 as communication mean, and ODA/ODIF as document interchange format.

X.400 message handling systems can be used for many applications, apart from normal InterPersonal messaging [CCITT 1988] [ISO 10021]. The Office Document Architecture (ODA) and Interchange Format (ODIF) standard [ISO 8613] provides a powerful means to help the transfer of documents independently of their original format. One of our user applications combines the use of both standards, in order to provide remote access to Machine Translation Systems (MT-Systems). In this way, documents inside X.400 messages are ODIF streams.

Furthermore, the ODA standard allows TWB users to incorporate into their environment documents generated from different word processors. Converters have been developed between several word processor formats, including the one used in TWB (FrameMaker), and ODA, and between the METAL format (MDIF) and ODA. The second level ODA Document Application Profile [Delgado/Perramon 1990] has been implemented (Q112/FOD-26 [CEN/CENELEC ENV 41510] [ISO DISP 11181]). Therefore, raster and geometric graphics, as well as characters, can be converted.

An important advantage of the developments made for remote access to MT-Systems is that we can use the implemented software outside TWB: any X.400 system with ODA capabilities could be able to interchange documents with MT-Systems, and, on the other hand, ODA converters could be used to incorporate different word processor files into different word processing systems.

X.400 Electronic Mail

"X.400" is the common way to refer to the international recommendations (from the CCITT) [CCITT 1988] and standards [ISO 10021] that define the "electronic mail" application. More formally, the ISO standard is referred as "MOTIS".

The X.400 recommendations specify the format of the "InterPersonal" messages to be interchanged by electronic means. Furthermore, communication protocols based on Open Systems Interconnection (OSI) [ISO 7498] are defined.

The basic elements of an X.400 system are the User Agent (in charge of interacting with the user) and the Message Transfer Agent (in charge of interchanging the messages).

Use of the content of X.400 messages

The content of an interpersonal X.400 message, as defined in X.400/MOTIS, can be divided in two parts:

- Heading: it contains several fields to give attributes to the message. Examples of such attributes are originator, different kinds of recipients, subject, priority, message relationships, sensitivity, users to reply to, and so on.
- Body: it contains the information the user actually wants to convey. One message may contain several bodyparts with text or other content type, like ODA.

We have used this message structure to relate X.400 messages and MT-Systems. For example, in order to relate X.400 messages and MT-System commands, we use the "heading" part of the X.400 message.

Some information is common to MT-System and X.400 messages, so we can extract such information for MT-Systems from the X.400 message. Heading fields belonging to this category are:

- Sender (Originator) of the text to be translated;
- Receiver of the text to be translated (the MT-System);
- Delivery time (Date + Time);
- Document or message identifier;
- Priority;
- Reply To: Intended recipient of the translated document;

However, MT-Systems usually need more information that has to bc coded in the heading of the X.400 message. Examples are:

- Operation (Translate, Pre-Analyze, ...);
- Language pair;
- Thematic area of the document;

The solution we have taken for sending this information from our system to the MT-System, via X.400, is to use the "Subject" field defined in the X.400 message heading. Hence, operation, language pair, and thematic area are coded, straight-forwardly, in the subject attribute of the message. However, if the MT-System needs more information, another solution should be adopted.

ODA: Open Document Architecture

The Office Document Architecture (ODA) standard (which is to be renamed to "Open Document Architecture"), together with the Office Document Interchange Format (ODIF) standard [ISO 8613], provides the means to avoid knowing, or worrying about, the word processor that a recipient of a message or document we want to send uses. If we develop converters between word processor formats and ODA, we can skip this problem. All we have to do is to convert to ODA from our word processor, when sending a document; and from ODA to the word processor format, when receiving a document.

ODA document structure

The ODA standard describes a document as a set of constituents, each of which is a set of attributes specifying its characteristics or its relationships with other constituents.

In ODA, a clear distinction is made between the logical structure of a document (e.g. the organization of the document in chapters, sections, paragraphs, appendices, and so on) and its layout structure (its disposition in the presentation medium: pages, areas within pages, and so on).

Logical and layout structures may be generic or specific. Generic structures describe characteristics common to several constituents, so that they can be used to guide the process of creating the specific structures, which hold the actual content of the document.

The content information of the document is included in constituents called content portions, that are related to "Content Architectures". Currently, the ODA standard defines three content architectures: character, raster graphics, and geometric graphics.

Other types of constituents that a document may include are layout styles (sets of attributes guiding the creation of specific layout structures) and presentation styles (sets of attributes guiding the appearance of the content of the document). ODA documents also include a document profile, whose attributes specify the characteristics of the document as a whole.

Document Application Profiles

In order to use the standard, we have to choose a "Document Application Profile" (DAP). The purpose of a DAP is to define common subsets of ODA to be used in different contexts.

Several DAPs are being defined in the ODA world, mainly by the CCITT and EWOS (European Workshop for Open Systems). EWOS document application profiles are being adopted by the CEN/CENELEC (European functional standardisation body). North-American standardisation institutions (NIST, National Institute of Standards) are also working in the development of DAPs. PAGODA (Profile Alignment Group for ODA) is coordinating the work around the world, and manages the definition of ISO International Standard Profiles (ISPs).

A set of DAPs is currently being defined, with the property of upward compatibility, each of which is a superset of the preceding one. These DAPs are known as Q111 (Basic Character Content) [CEN/CENELEC ENV 41509], Q112 (Extended Mixed Mode) [CEN/CENELEC ENV 41510] and Q113 (Enhanced Mixed Mode) [EWOS 1990]. A document conformant to one of these profiles is also conformant to any of the profiles that follow it in the DAP hierarchy.

Q111 is oriented for the transfer of structured documents between basic word processing facilities; documents such as memos, letters and reports that contain characters only. This DAP is aligned with the CCITT's PM1 (defined in CCITT Recommendation T.502) [CCITT 1988], and it will converge with the ISO ISP called FOD-11 [ISO DISP 10610].

Q112 (or the ISO equivalent FOD-26 [ISO DISP 11181]) allows for the interchange of multi-media documents between advanced document processing systems in an integrated office environment. FOD-26 documents may contain characters as well as raster graphics and geometric graphics.

Q113 (or FOD-36 [ISO DISP 11182]) provides the features supported by Q112 and, in addition, allows more complex logical and layout structures.

Although we initially chose the Q111 profile because it was adequate for our purposes (remote access to an MT-System), we have finally developed Q112/FOD-26 converters in order to take advantage of all the existing word processor facilities.

7.2 Remote Access to the METAL Machine Translation System

For the remote access to machine translation systems, METAL, from SNI, is used as MT-System.

As mentioned before, in order to be open and to follow standards, the communication between the TWB system and METAL is done through standard X.400 electronic mail. For this reason, an X.400 system (based on the results of the CACTUS ESPRIT project [Saras 1988] [Delgado 1988]) has been integrated in both TWB and METAL systems. A special X.400 user agent that interacts with the MT-System has been developed and interfaced with METAL (through "X-Metal"). The role of this user agent, installed in the MT-System side, is to receive X.400 messages from outside, and to generate replies back with the translated document.

The use of ODA/ODIF to send documents to MT-Systems, guarantees the standardisation of the input and output formats, and it allows a translation to be returned with the same structure and format as the source text.

The use of X.400 to access the MT-System provides a widely available standard means to access the service, avoiding the need to define a new access mechanism. Documents (in ODA format) are sent inside X.400 messages.

Once a message has arrived in the MT-System, the following steps are taken:

- The ODA document is extracted from the X.400 message body;
- The content of the document is translated to the required human language;
- One reply message is generated back with the translated document (converted to ODA format) inside its body.

7.2.1 MHS Environment

We have already stated that the X.400 Message Handling System we are using is based on CACTUS, which provides P7 access [CCITT 1988] [ISO 10021] to their users.

A CACTUS user is able to perform a set of distributed operations acting as a client, by means of a mailbox client (MBC), of a CACTUS mailbox server (MBS). The communication between MBC and MBS is made through a logical or physical connection (ie from the same machine or from direct wire, modem, etc).

A mailbox server can support a cluster of different users, each one identified by a mailbox name (the address of a user). But one of the more interesting features of CACTUS is that it allows the server to run special tasks automatically when a message for a particular mailbox is received. These special tasks, called task-mailboxes, are in fact processes that handle messages in the way the designer of such processes dictates.

Therefore, we have the adequate environment to send X.400 messages, using CACTUS, to any machine around the world. We can also activate the suitable tasks on the receiving side of these messages in order to route them to the machine translation system and generate back replies with the translated document.

7.2.2 X-Metal

Fundamentals

The current TWB implementation of the remote access to the METAL machine translation system using the standard X.400 MHS networks, has been made using the CACTUS package, developed by the UPC, as the underlying MHS software, both on the TWB workstation side and on the METAL side. The module, X-Metal, interconnects the MHS system with the METAL system on the METAL side.

Basic Operation of X-Metal

Basically, X-Metal consists of a loop which looks for incoming messages in the MHS inbox and for already translated documents in the METAL output queue.

Should there be an incoming MHS message (sent in ODIF format by a remote TWB user) X-Metal fetches the message, extracts some relevant information (language pair, thematic area, priority, and so on) from the message header. If this information isappropriate for the local METAL installation, X-Metal takes the MHS message body and converts it from ODIF format into MDIF (METAL internal) format. Once the document is in MDIF format, it is sent to METAL for translation.

If there is a document in the output METAL queue, which has already been translated by METAL, X-Metal takes it from the queue, converts it from the MDIF format back to the ODIF format, creates a MHS header, puts the document into the MHS document body and sends the resulting MHS document to the MHS outbox for submission to the message originator.

Error Handling

X-Metal reacts to a number of possible errors which may arise during processing. These errors can be of different types: wrong translations parameters set by the user (e.g. the user specified a language pair which is not supported by the local METAL system), wrong incoming document format (the document is not in ODIF format), malfunction of the converters, malfunction of the METAL system , and so on. In most cases, X-Metal reacts sending a message to the user containing information about the particular error encountered. If possible, X-Metal will retry the operation later (for instance, in those cases where either METAL or the MHS outbox are not accepting documents for some reason).

Portability

Although the current implementation of X-Metal is running on the UPC CACTUS package, it has been designed in such a way that it can be easily ported on top of any MHS package which has an API (Application Programming Interface) similar to the P7 protocol.

7.3 Word Processor <--> ODA Converters

ODA converters have been developed for the FrameMaker word processor, and for several external PC word processors, WordPerfect and MS-Word. These converters between ODA/ODIF and the word processor formats can run in both UNIX and MS-DOS.

Important research work has been undertaken by the UPC around ODA, and an ODA Toolkit ("ODAPSI") has been developed to ease the process of converters development.

7.3.1 ODA Internal Format

An ODA document, according to the standard, is a set of constituents described by attributes. In order for the document to be interchanged, eg as an X.400 message body part, an external format has been defined called the Office Document Interchange Format (ODIF), based on the ASN.1 transfer syntax [ISO 8824/8825]. ISO 8613 also defines another interchange format, Office Document Language (ODL), which conforms to the Standard Generalized Markup Language (SGML) [ISO 8879], but it is not so appropriate to be used in an Open Systems Interconnection (OSI) [ISO 7498] environment.

In order to process ODA documents, it is convenient to store their constituents in a format more suitable for efficient access than ODIF. An ODA processor using a particular internal format must then include modules to parse an ODIF input document into this internal format, and to output a document in this format as an ODIF stream.

The ODA internal format initially used for our word processor <--> ODA converters has been SODA (Stored ODA) [PODA 1988]. SODA is a specification of ODA constituents in C language, and provides a set of library functions to handle these constituents: create/open, read/write attributes, get/add subordinates, close, etc. These functions are easily portable to any system with a 'C' compiler.

However, work is going on to develop a new version of the converters that will be independent of SODA. This new version will be based on the "Intermediate format" (ODAPSI) described below.

7.3.2 Converters Internal Structure

Our approach to the problem of converting documents between different formats consists of dividing the converter into two separate modules, the analyser and the generator, and specifying an interface between them. Apart from these modules, we need converters between ODIF and the stored ODA format.

The analysers scan the input document (in SODA or word processor format) and generate a series of function calls to the corresponding generator, which creates the output document structure. The SODA analyser and SODA generator modules are unaware of any word processor document structure, and so are the word processor modules with the ODA structure.

The function calls constituting the interface between the analyser and generator behave as a sort of "intermediate document format". We call this interface ODAPSI ("ODA Profile Specific Interface"). The ordered sequence of function calls generated by the analyser can be regarded as a (sequential) document description, in the same way as a word processor sequence of formatting commands and text contents, or as an ODA specific structure.

The modules are interchangeable (provided that they generate/accept the same function calls or "intermediate format"). For example, let WP1 and WP2 be two word processor document formats. A WP1 <--> SODA converter can be turned into a WP2 <--> SODA converter by simply replacing the WP1 analyser/generator with a WP2 analyser/generator. Also, the SODA module could be replaced, resulting in a direct WP1 <--> WP2 converter.

7.3.3 The Intermediate Format (Analyser-Generator Interface): ODAPSI

The ODAPSI format describes a document (its logical structure) in terms of the commonly used word processor components, e.g. section, paragraph, style, and so on (these terms are also used by the DAP's). In order to simplify the interface, this description is sequential, and approximately follows the order in which a human user would describe a document from a keyboard in front of a word processor (this order may be different from that of the word processor document's internal structure).

The typical sequence of calls generated by the SODA analyser for every object found in the specific logical structure is:

- create logical object;
- layout style (actually, this is an argument to the 'create' function)
- for composite logical objects:
  - recursive calls for each of the logical subordinate objects
- for basic objects:
  - presentation style attributes
  - content information;
- close logical object.

7.3.4 Results

A very flexible scheme to build word processor <--> ODA converters has been described. Clear internal formats, internal modules and internal interfaces allow a sound basis for the development of converters.

For our initial purposes, the Q111 Document Application Profile was adequate. Experience was obtained in the development of Q111 converters for common word processors, like WordStar, Microsoft Word, WordPerfect or troff.

However, we finally developed software based on Q112/FOD-26 in order to provide more general purpose converters. Work continued to develop Q112 converters for WordPerfect and FrameMaker, the internal word processor of TWB.

7.3.5 MDIF <--> ODA Converters

General Scheme

An ODIF document coming from the network to the METAL system, must first be converted into its static ODA representation (SODA). Next, the SODA document must be converted into an MDIF document, and the corresponding SODA Document structure temporarily stored for further processing. The MDIF document is then segmented into translation units which are sent to the METAL system, which creates an output MDIF file. After this step, the original SODA Document structure is merged with the textual contents of the MDIF output file in order to create the output SODA document. This output SODA document is finally converted into the corresponding ODIF output document and sent to the network.

ODIF -> SODA Conversion

This converter consist of an interpreter which reads the byte stream that makes up the ODIF document and returns the corresponding ODA structures in the form of static structures.

SODA -> MDIF Conversion

The SODA to MDIF conversion is carried out in three steps: content extraction, table handling, and MDIF file creation.

Content Extraction

In this step the SODA document is scanned for text associated with basic objects. This text is extracted and a temporary file is created with it. At the same time, control characters inserted throughout the text and having their 8th bit set to one are detected and converted into mnemonic string sequences. This is necessary in order for the LEX interpreter in the next step to operate properly. Finally, the MDIF file header containing some required parameters is created.

Since Q112 ODA documents may contain graphic content portions, we have to filter them in order to exclude them from the MDIF file. However, the possibility exists to handle graphics described in CGM in order to extract the existing text from it and to insert this text as part of the MDIF file. This is open to further study at the moment.

Table Handling

In this step, the temporary file is scanned for a tabulator character pattern which indicates the presence of tables in the document. Should a table be detected, the temporary file is given explicit information on the table in the form of special string sequences. These string sequences indicate where the table starts, where it ends and its column pattern.

MDIF File Creation

In this step the MDIF file containing the text together with some directives is created from the temporary file. This is performed through an MDIF syntax generator. This generator was implemented using the LEX utility.

Concurrently, a copy of the SODA document is temporarily stored, in order to properly restore the document structure once the text translation has been carried out.

MDIF -> SODA Conversion

The MDIF to SODA conversion is achieved in two steps.

1. MDIF Directive Conversion.

A LEX program, similar to the one mentioned above, performs the conversion from MDIF directives into the corresponding ODA control characters. During this step, a temporal file is also created.

2. SODA Structure and Text Merging.

Finally, a function is called which merges the output text contained in the temporary file and the temporary SODA document, and replaces the text parts of the original SODA document with the new translated text. Thus, as output we get a full SODA document with the same structure as the original plus the translated text.

SODA -> ODIF Conversion

The output SODA document is now converted into its dynamic representation through an ODIF generator.

7.4 Access to a Remote Term Bank: EURODICAUTOM

This module for automatic access to remote term banks allows TWB users to ask for terminological information from a database that is not local to the TWB system.

For this task, the EURODICAUTOM terminological database from the Commission of the European Communities was chosen (it is one of the services offered by ECHO, "European Community Host Organization" [CEC 1991]).

The TWB user is provided, through a user-friendly interface, with automatic access to the EURODICAUTOM terminology database. It should be mentioned that the user does not need to know either the EURODICAUTOM query language, or the use of the network connection and the logon/logoff procedure, since all the dialogue with EURODICAUTOM is handled automatically. In this way, we solve the main problems (the network and the interrogation language) that make remote access to term banks largely unused.

The communication is done through the X.25 public data network with several options available for the installation of the network connection in different hardware environments. For example, we can access the X.25 network from any computer (acting as a client and running TWB) in a local area network, where we have a computer (acting as a server) with the physical X.25 connection. In the case of using Sun machines, Sunlink-X.25 software is what we require to interface to X.25.

Although the current version runs on UNIX, plans are underway to port the remote access to EURODICAUTOM software to PC, with and without the need of an X.25 connection.

7.4.1 The EURODICAUTOM Term Bank

The choice of EURODICAUTOM has two main benefits:

- EURODICAUTOM is an official CEC terminology database;
- It supports all community languages.

Some EURODICAUTOM features are:

- It is a terminological termbank, but not a conceptual one;
- It is not constrained by a particular subject field;
- The intended user group is translators and interpreters.

EURODICAUTOM has the following limitations:

- It does not contain grammatical information about terms (syntactic category, gender, tense, and so on);
- It does not include synonyms and antonyms.
- Depending on a) the language a term pertains to, and b) its subject field, EURODICAUTOM provides a different amount of information, and a different degree of information reliability.

7.4.2 User Query Parameters

The following are the possible user query parameters available in the TWB automatic access to EURODICAUTOM (most of them have default values):

- Word(s) or abbreviation(s);
- Source and target language(s);
- Use of EURODICAUTOM mode:
  * Connection transparent to the user (default);
  * Direct connection to EURODICAUTOM;
- Level of information required: basic (only the main answer) or complete (all possible answers);
- Use of subcodes.

7.4.3 Information Provided by the EURODICAUTOM Database

A terminological unit coming from EURODICAUTOM gives the following information:

I) Administrative information:

- Serial number (identification number of the documentary information);
- Type (or Group. It indicates the symposia, meetings or journals where the question was discussed);
- Originating office (indicates the office or entity which has gathered the terminological information);
- Reference (source of the terminological information);
- Reliability rating (from 0 to 5, being 0=no source, and 5=from a standard);
- Author (term indicating a professor or team of researchers);
- Country (term indicating the country to which the entity asked for belongs to).

II) Linguistic information:

- Phrase (phraseological entry or illustrative context);
- Headword (expression constituting a lexical unit, ie single word or syntagm);
- Abbreviation (term indicating that the question is answered as an abbreviation);

III) Conceptual information:

- Definition (one or more definitions together with one or more contexts);
- Note;
- Subject code or field (code indicating the theme of the answer).

8. General Language Resources: Lexica

Gerhard Heyer, Klemens Waldhör

When dealing with tools for linguistic text processing, the language resources, i.e. dictionaries are necessarily a central issue. In this chapter we will present the idea of reusable lexical resources, as it has been proposed and is being carried out in the ESPRIT project MULTILEX. In the second part we will give more information on a dictionary for the special purpose language of law, commerce, and finance, as it is implemented in the present PC Translator's Workbench.

8.1 The Compilation Approach for Reusable Lexical Resources

8.1.1 Introduction

In order to ensure high quality of lingware, efficient software design, and cost-effective product development, it has generally been recognised during the past years that reusable lexical resources are a key issue. Following Calzolari (1989), we can distinguish two notions of reusability:

(1) transforming already existing lexical resources into a different format, typically transforming printed dictionaries into a machine readable or machine tractable form, and

(2) exploiting already existing lexical resources for different applications and different theories, typically exploiting one lexical database in different applications.

Arguing from a software engineering point of view, we shall present and discuss in the following the idea of compiling application specific lexica on the basis of a standardised lexical database as presently elaborated in ESPRIT II project MultiLex and applied in the project Translator's Workbench. In contrast to work focussing on either one of the two aspects of the notion of reusability, the compilation approach is intended to integrate both aspects, and to optimally support the design of natural language products.

8.1.2 The Compilation Approach

In order to provide a cost efficient basis for all kinds of natural language processing programs, and input for tools by which wholistic natural language processing solutions can be compiled, we imagine an approach that results in multi-functional, reusable linguistic software on all levels of linguistic knowledge, viz. lexica, grammars, and meaning definitions. Let us call this methodology for the construction of natural language processing programs the "compilation approach" (see Fig. 7).

The intuitive idea of the compilation approach is to construct highly efficient and wholistically designed natural language applications on the basis of linguistic knowledge-bases that contain basic and uncontroversial linguistic data on dictionary entries, grammar rules, and meaning definitions independent of specific applications, data structures, formalisations, and theories. To the extent that linguistics is a more than two thousand years old science, there is ample theoretical and empirical material of the required kind available in the form of written texts and studies on the source level of linguistic knowledge, or can be (and is) produced by competent linguists. However, very little of this knowledge is available on electronic media. Thus, the very first task of software engineering for language products, as Helmut Schnelle has recently put it (Schnelle 1991), must be the transformation of available linguistic data from passive media into active electronic media, here called lexica, grammars, and definitions on the linguistic knowledge base level. In terms of implementation, such media will mainly be relational, object-oriented, or hypermedia databases capable of managing very large amounts of data. Clearly, in order to be successful, any such transformation also requires formalisms to be used on the side of the linguists for adequately encoding linguistic data, the linguistic structures assigned to them, and the theories employed for deriving these structures. Moreover, within linguistics, we need to arrive at standards for each such level of formalisation. In reality, therefore, the first task of software engineering for language products is quite a substantial one that can only succeed if the goal of making linguistic knowledge available is allowed to have an impact on ongoing research in linguistics by focussing research on formalisms and standards that can efficiently be processed on a computer (see also Boguraev and Briscoe 1989).

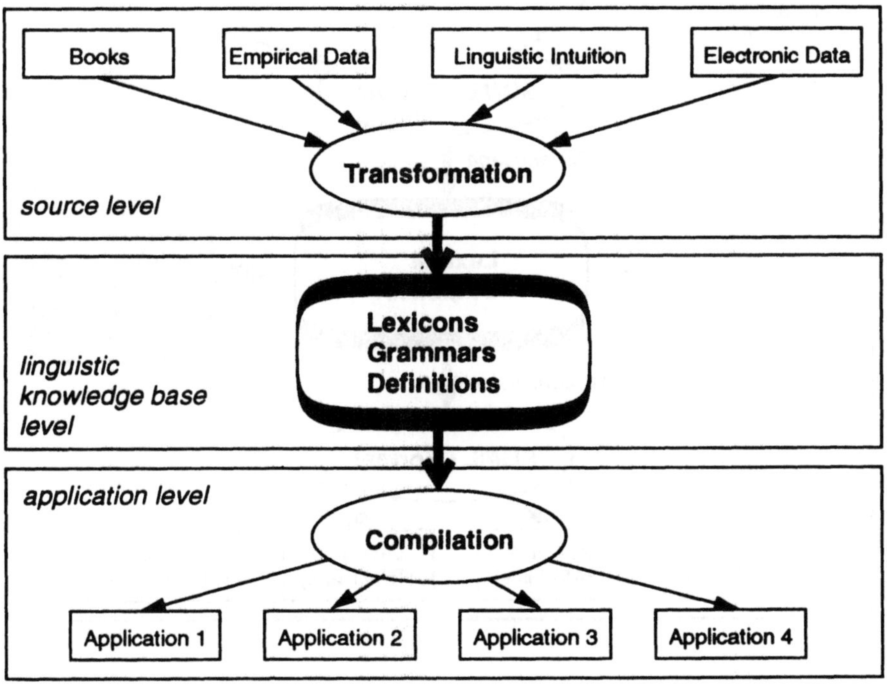

Fig. 7: Multifunctional, reusable linguistic software

8.1.3 Reusable Lexical Resources

Now, to complete the picture, assuming that such linguistic knowledge-bases are available, individual applications are to be constructed, adapted, or modified on the basis of such linguistic knowledge-bases by selectively extracting only that kind of information that is needed for building the specific application, and by compiling and integrating it into the application specific data structures. Details, coverage, and the compiled representation of the linguistic information depends, of course, on the individual applications. The second task of software engineering for language products then consists of providing a general methodology for such a selection of the required linguistic knowledge, and the definition of its optimal data structure representation.

To look at this in practice, let us briefly look at how it can be applied to issues in the area of computational lexicography, as presently discussed in ESPRIT II project MULTILEX (see Fig. 8)

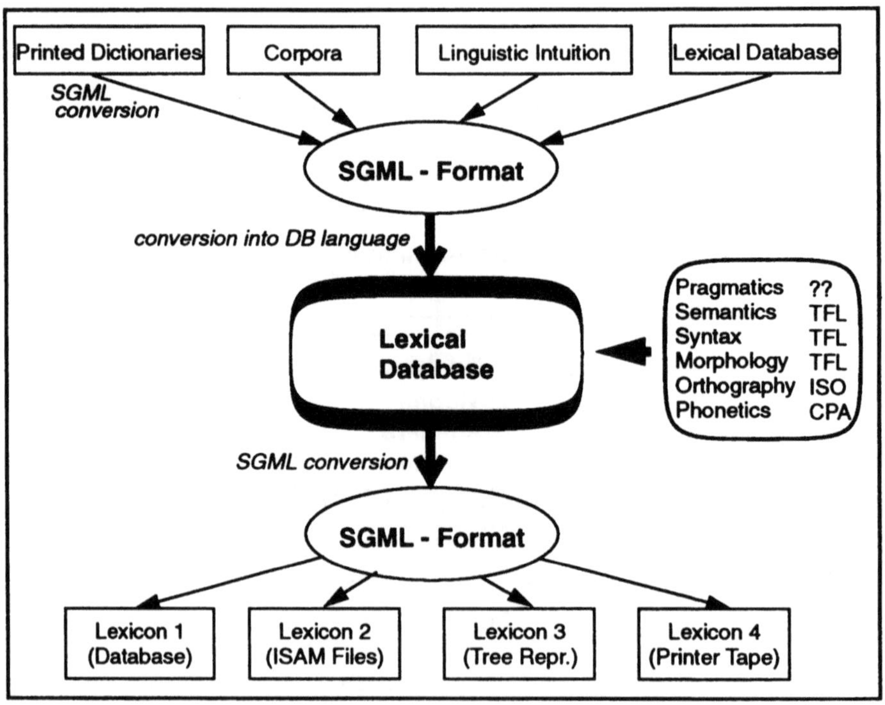

Fig. 8: Multi-functional, reusable linguistic software: Lexicon

On the source level, there are printed dictionaries, text corpora, linguistic intuitions, and some few lexical databases. In order to make these sources available for language products, we first need to transform the available lexical data according to an exchange standard into a representation standard on the level of a lexical database (for each European language). The exchange standard proposed by MULTILEX is SGML, following recommendations from the ET-7 study on reusable lexical resources (Heid 1991). The representation standards proposed for the different lexical levels are the Computer Phonetic Alphabet (CPA) for the phonetic level, the ISO orthographic standard for the orthographic level, and a typed feature logic for the morphological, syntactic, and semantic level. In this functional view, implementation details of the database are irrelevant as long as it allows for an SGML communication.

From a software engineering point of view, when dealing with large amounts of lexical data, a number of problems arise that are similar to choosing an appropriate implementation representation in database systems. The key issue for large lexica here is data integrity. Maintenance operations like updating, inserting, or deleting have to give the user a consistent view on the lexical datebase. All problems that arise in database management system at this level also arise in a lexicon. We therefore suggestthe use of a database system as the basis of our lexicon in order to save work that otherwise would have to be done at the level of the lexical database. The same point also holds for distributed lexical databases, e.g. for lexica that are spread over and maintained in different countries.

Since most existing natural language applications use lexica that have been defined and implemented only to fulfill the application requirements (application specific lexica), the reusability of such lexica is a problem once one wants to use the same lexica in different contexts and applications. With respect to the maintainability of such software systems, we claim that real reusability can only be assured if it is based on a standard representing a general lexical representation. The MULTILEX representation based on the notion of a typed feature logic can be considered such a standard.

In many applications it may be possible to use the MULTILEX format without any change. Typically, such applications are not subject to narrow time and space constraints. If a system has access to a host with a large amount of secondary storage (WORMS, huge disks), and no time critical operations are required, it can use the functions of MULTILEX without modification. Batch systems (e.g. machine translation in a background process) may interact in such a way.

On the other hand, a number of applications are time critical, typically all systems directly interacting with the user, e.g. spelling checking or handwriting recognition. Additionally, such systems havelimited space constraints (e.g. a PC). For such systems it is therefore necessary to provide compilers that select the necessary information from the MULTILEX lexicon and compile this information into a special data structure which supports the operations needed by the application in an optimised way. In general, applications that make use of main memory or memory cards as their lexicon storage medium need other representation formalisms (e.g. AVL trees) than hard disk based systems (which may use binary trees).

Finally, the compilers built for producing application specific lexica not only support an optimised data structure, but also support additional operations like selecting a specific subset of the lexicon entries (one can think of SELECT in relational terms), and selecting a subset of variables of a lexical entry (PROJECT in relational terms). Such operations, for example, may be the selection of verbs or nouns with specific characteristics.

The approach sketched above is presently being used successfully being used to develop specific lexicon based language products such as multilingual electronic dictionary applications for human and machine users in the area of automatic and semi-automatic translation support, highly compressed multilingual spelling correctors and language checkers, and highly compressed lexica for optimising handwriting recognition, as can be seen from the following sections.

8.2 The Dictionary of Commerce, Finance, and Law (HFR-Dictionary)

8.2.1 The Contents

The HFR-Dictionary is a trilingual dictionary covering German, English and French. It contains terms from the area of commerce, law and finance, supporting areas like international organisations (e.g. EC), trade and industry, exporting and importing, manufacturing, distributing and marketing, banking, stock exchange, finance, foreign exchange, taxation, customs, transport, diverse services, insurances, private and public law, public services and so on. The dictionary therefore aims mainly at the user in the office, lawyers and professional translators. It is not intended primarily as a dictionary for private users. The paper version of the dictionary is published in three volumes, each volume covering one source language and two target languages (Volume I: English -> German, French; Volume II: German -> English, French; Volume III: French -> English, German; [see Herbst & Readett, 1985, 1989, 1987 for the different volumes]).

Table 1: Example entry (only one main entry); different languages are seperated by # starting with German, followed by English and French (from Herbst & Readett, 1989; page 1)

abänderlich @adj|alterable;capable of alteration (of being altered)#capable de modification

Table 2: Example entry with more than one meaning; different meanings are given in square brackets "[...]" (from Herbst & Readett, 1989; page 1)

abändern @v (A) | to alter; to modify; to change # changer; modifier | eine Erklärung ~ | to modify a statement # modifier une déclaration

abändern @v (B) [ergänzend ~] | eine Entscheidung ~ | to revise a decision # revenir sur une decision | ein Gesetz ~ to amend (to revise) a law # amender un projet de loi | einen Gesetzesentwurf ~ | to amend a bill # amender un projet de loi | einen Plan ~ | to amend (to modify) a plan # apporter une (des) modification(s) a un projet

abändern @v (C) [berichtigen] | to rectify; to correct # rectifier; corriger

abändern @v (A) #to alter; to modify; to change #changer; modifier #eine Erklärung abändern# to modify a statement #modifier une declaration

abändern @v (B) [ergänzend abändern] | eine Entscheidung abändern#to revise a decision#revenir sur une decision#ein Gesetz abändern#to amend (to revise a law#amender (modifier) une loi#einen Gesetzesentwurf abändern#to amend a

Each volume contains about 100,000 terms which are organised in about 40,000 entries. Each entry contains a main term (source language typed in bold with its translation equivalents plus terms which are related to the main term (see Table 1). Terms also contain a description of the word category (e.g. @adj for adjective, @v for verb and so on). The following examples are taken from the converted printer tapes. They differ from their equivalent printed entries as far as some changes have been made to the printing format (no bold printing, italic printing replaced by the character '@').

Terms which have different meanings are separated as entries and numbered (see Table 2). If more than one meaning exists a description of the special meaning may follow.

8.2.2 Conversion Procedure and Problems Connected with this Conversion

We acquired the dictionary printer tapes from the publishing house OTT-Verlag (Swiss) for the German -> English, French volume (Herbst & Readett, 1989). The raw data were delivered on diskettes which contained each page of the dictionary as a separate file (overall ten disks with about 10 MB of data).

The files contained all the control codes which were generated during the publishing process (based on a LINOTYPE code). The first step was to connect all files and remove the control codes which were not needed any more (e.g. page numbering, page breaks, headers and so on). Some codes had to be kept (e.g. italic printing was used for marking word categories; special character combinations were used to mark different meanings of a word). Control code tables with their meanings with regard to the printing process were given by the publishing company.While parsing the files it turned out that not all control codes (and macros built on them) were available (due to the fact that different type setters worked on one volume and used different macros for the same purpose; which was not documented).

After this processing we had an ASCII-file which contained the same entries as the dictionary (but, of course, also all errors of the dictionary). As a lot of abbreviations had been done in the dictionary (using special abbreviation symbols), in the next step the dictionary was expanded to its full form without abbreviations. The process of converting the raw dictionary data into ASCII format was much more time consuming than originally expected. The expanded version needed about 6 MB of disc space; so about 4 MB of the raw data was made up of control codes.

The next step was to check errors which were found in the lexicon. Two different types of errors were found (which also occurred in the printed version of the dictionary):

- type setting errors: forgetting the separating marks between languages; cutting off entries where continuation text was clearly necessary; insertion of meaningless characters in entries and similar errors; entries used a special abbreviating code and this code was often used wrong or in an unpredictable form. Some of these errors could be recognised by the parser in a purely syntactic way, e.g missing French translation equivalents; intermingling French and English translations)
- linguistic errors: only a few could by found using a parser, which could only check for syntactic errors as mentioned above. This errors were found by manually inspecting the entries and lists when the indexfiles for the Windows applications were generated. As an example "ss" and "ß" were not used correctly.

The process of eliminating these errors was quite costly and had to be repeated several times (in many cases one error hid another error, which could only be detected with the next parser run). Human readers in most cases are able to correct these errors by their knowledge of the language (e.g. if the separation between languages is missing, in nearly all cases it is obvious for a human reader to find and place the separating mark.).

8.2.3 Creating the Database

From the above steps an ASCII file was created containing the information of the printed dictionary in ASCII form. This file preserved the structure of the printed dictionaries.

For all entries of the dictionary, an index file was generated for each language by separating the translation equivalents and building up files which contained pointers to the full entry. We decided to use only the first term of an entry. This created about 40,000 - 50,000 index entries. However, it would be no problem to fully index the whole data file which would lead to about 100,000 - 120,000 index entries. While it was easy to generate the German index files, the creation of the English and French index files was a little bit more tricky. One can use in principle all translation equivalents from the German entries as English or French index entries, but this leads to index entries which one will never find in an English -> French, German dictionary. Thus two criteria were used to generate English and French index entries:

- entries which are longer than 50 characters were ignored (based on the assumption that a native speaker will never search for such long entries which tend to be very complex phrases)
- a linguistic check was made on the remaining index entries manually (comparison with the English->French, German and French->English, German volumes).

This gives a quite reasonable index list. Each index file needs about 500 KB of disk space. The whole database (dictionary file plus indexfiles) needs about 6.5 MB. With full indexing about 8-9 MB of disk space would be necessary.

The database and the accessing functionality were developed inhouse to achieve a maximum performance and compression on the index data. The current version needs about 1-2 disk accesses for the index files and one access to retrieve the whole entry description from dictionary data file. Thus access time could be neglected.

8.2.4 Application HFR-Dictionary

Based on the above data and the database system, an MS Windows version of the dictionary was created.

The aim of the application is twofold:

- the user should be able to use the application as a stand alone program
- the user is working with his or her text processing system, e.g translating a letter or writing some foreign language text and wants to get the translation equivalent for a term. The user can mark the term to be translated and then activate the HFR-Dictionary from within the application (eg Word for Windows; a macro for this text processing system has been implemented). This can be achieved in two ways: a) by using the

standard copy and paste facility of MS Windows and b) by using the DDE approach. The later requires some kind of macro language within the text processing system and the support of basic DDE functionality. For more details please see the chapter on integration of the TWB modules.

When starting the HFR-Dictionary the user gets one source language menu and one to three target language windows. The source language menu contains all the entries for specific single letter (like a printed dictionary; e.g. all entries for the letter "A"). After clicking on the desired entry the translation equivalents are displayed in the target language windows (e.g. one window for English equivalents and one for French equivalents). In most cases the user will only use one target language window. Users can save their preferred settings; when starting HFR-Dictionary again they will have the same user interface environment as the last time the application was used.

Additionally the user may enter terms in an input window and get the translation equivalents in this way. He or she also may copy the contents of the clipboard into the input window. As an additional feature the user can choose to adapt the source language menu to the current input string of the input window (e.g. when entering "qual" the source language menu positions at the words starting with the string "qual" like "qualitativ", "Qualität", "Qualitätskontrolle" ...). As this is sometimes quite time consuming the user can switch off this feature.

When the user is satisfied with the translation equivalent he or she can mark the appropriate parts in the target language window and copy it to the clipboard or transfer it with a special button to the calling application.

8.2.5 Further Application Possibilities

HFR-Dictionary is only a first application with the available data. An MS-DOS version will also be produced which offers exchange possibilities for different text processing systems. Different additional application areas may be found:

- automatic phrase translation: the database contains not only single words but also a lot of phrases. These phrases can be used to support the automatic phrase translation of text. This can be enhanced by adding some facilities to convert target phrases of the text into the canonical form of the dictionary. This can be achieved by different methodologies, e.g. on a linguistic level using special parsers or more simply by a specialized pattern matching routine; using Fuzzy Logic may be another way.
- extracting frequency sorted parts of the lexicon to create sublexica (e.g. the 10,000 most frequently used commerce terms)
- extracting only commerce or law or finance terms
- extracting only language pairs
- usage as language training software
- tagging of the HFR-Dictionary: the different language entries can be parsed and tagged with additional morphosyntactic information; this may be of use when the dictionary is used for phrase translations

As has been described above, within the ESPRIT-Project 5304 MULTILEX a standard representation for lexical resources both multilingual and multifunctional is under development. The HFR-Dictionary will be converted into this format once the standard is defined. This implies that the HFR-dictionary data will also be stored in a relational database (using ORACLE).

8.2.6 Conclusions

The conversion from printer tapes into a computational lexicon is not as easy as it may first look. Thus having only the printer sources is not enough. One also has to invest a considerable amount of time into both syntactically and manually improving the sources.

However, once the dictionary is in an appropriate form various types of applications can be derived from it.

9. Special Language Resources: Termbank, Cardbox

Renate Mayer, Antonius van Hoof

The Commission of the European Communities has recently estimated that 170 million pages of text are translated per year in Europe alone and that this figure will increase to 600 million pages by the year 2000. Despite much useful research and development in the field of machine translation, the fact remains that much of this work is still carried out by human translators, with or without such valuable aids as terminological databases.

Most professional human translators have studied a foreign language and are therefore familiar with language for general purposes. The problem translators have to overcome lies in dealing with language for special purposes. As even experts do not always know all the details of their subject area, one can easily imagine the enormous difficulties translators who in general are not subject experts encounter when translating manuals, reports, announcements, and letters at all levels of detail in several subject fields. Therefore they need support in the special language terminology.

For looking up special language terms, translators use printed resources like lexica, thesauri, encyclopaedias and glossaries. Recently, they have also begun to use the electronic medium. Nowadays, almost all translators make use of computers, especially of wordprocessing software, which supports them in creating, writing, correcting and printing translated texts. In addition to wordprocessors, tools which support terminology work are of increasing interest. These tools comprise computerised lexica, terminological databases and private computer card files.

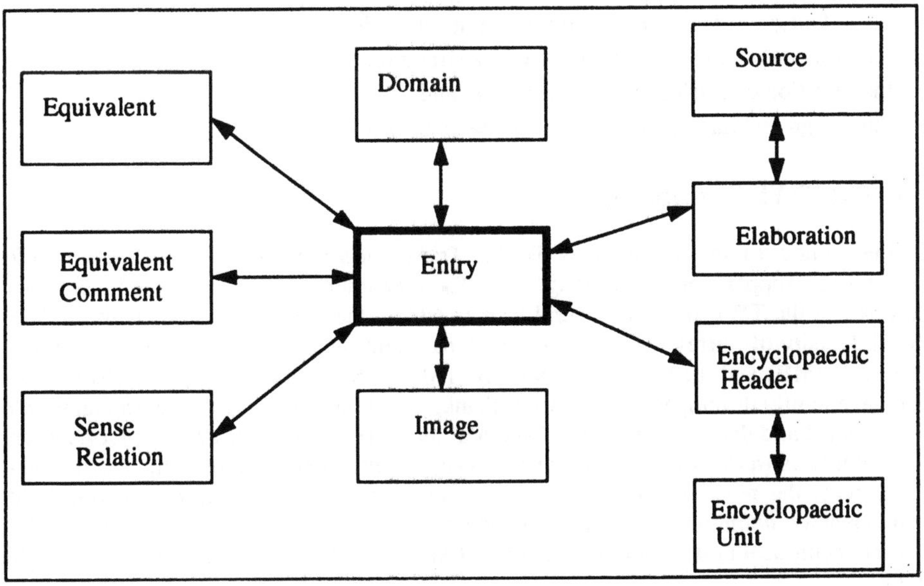

Fig. 9: Conceptual model of the TWB termbank

Terminological databases, or, in short, termbanks, are meant to support translators and experts in their daily work. They contain terminological data on (several) subject fields. Apart from the terms as such, a termbank entry often contains additional information such as definitions, contexts and usage examples, as well as relations between the entries such as 'is-translation-of', 'is-synonym-to', 'is-broader-than' etc. In order to access the stored terminological data, a user interface has to be provided. The user interface has the task of offering the user an easy way to retrieve or modify terminology. Thirty years ago, the first termbanks were introduced in organisations where terminological support is especially needed, like:

- large international companies such as Siemens, Boeing, and Philips;
- organisations like the WHO and the UNESCO; or
- countries where several languages are spoken, like Canada and Switzerland;
- the European Commission where at the moment nine official languages are used.

The first termbanks to be developed were EURODICAUTOM of the CEC, Termium in Canada, and TEAM, which was built by Siemens Munich. They were designed for large computer systems, batch processing jobs, and used non-proprietary software, because no database system was on the market. They comprise a large amount of terminological data in most technical areas and European languages. So far, however, Japanese, Russian, Arabic or Greek terms have hardly been included in the termbanks because of the special character sets. Nowadays, termbanks are used interactively in a network environment; software tools like database systems or multiple window systems improve the functionality and user friendliness of termbanks.

The complete development of a termbank comprises several subtasks such as:

- the definition of the necessary information categories;
- the implementation of the termbank data structure;
- the insertion of entries into the termbank; and
- the design and implementation of the user interface.

9.1 The TWB Termbank

It goes without saying that projects like the Translator's Workbench (TWB) should offer terminology support for special languages. The creation of such a termbank is an important part of the TWB project. Several teams, namely the University of Heidelberg (HD), the University of Surrey (SU), the central department of foreign languages at Mercedes-Benz AG (MB) and the Fraunhofer Society (IAO) in Stuttgart form the term-bank group and have jointly developed the TWB-termbank. As a first step, the user requirements were investigated and discussed by the SU and MB teams (Fulford et al. 1990). Interviews and questionnaires were used to assess the needs and requirements of translators. According to the survey, the most frequently searched information categories beside the translation equivalent are definitions, contexts, and synonyms. Simultaneously, the HD team worked out the theoretical basis of a termbank entry (Albl et al., 1990) (see also the reports in this book).

Based on this information, the SU and IAO teams have jointly developed the prototypical tembank entry and the conceptual, logical and physical structure of the termbank. SU and HD have elaborated terminology for the subject fields "catalytic converters" , "anti-lock braking systems", and "four-wheel drive", and SU entered the data (Ahmad et al., 1990). The IAO has designed and implemented a retrieval interface (Mayer 1990), which was tested and evaluated by translators at Mercedes-Benz AG (Höge et al., 1991).

9.1.1 The Termbank Structure

Most of the well-known termbanks (EURODICAUTOM, TERMIUM, TEAM) use non-proprietary software for the implementation of their database. For the TWB termbank, we decided to use the commercially available database system ORACLE. Using a commercially available RDBMS (Relational Data Base Management System) provides us with the synchronisation of user queries, the management of storage space and a high-level data manipulation language. However, we are faced with some disadvantages: database systems were originally designed for storing business data, which have a standard format and occur frequently, such as data about employees, clients or products. These data differ in some respect from terminological data, which often include long texts and have a variable length depending on the importance of the term entry. Thus neither long texts, as needed for definitions and explanations, nor graphics are supported in today's relational database systems. Due to the enlarged character set, multilingual terminology causes some additional problems. Even the 8-Bit ASCII character set is not sufficient for some European languages such as Russian or Greek.

The structure of the termbank was developed by means of the Entity Relationship approach (Chen 1975). The identified entities (term, explanation, source, domain, grammar, encyclopaedia) and the relationships (equivalent, synonymous, abbreviation, narrower term, etc.) are arranged in several relational tables with their respective attributes. Figure 9 shows the conceptual model of the TWB Termbank which has been elaborated in collaboration with the project partner SU.

The terminological *entry* is the central entity. Other entities are *elaboration* (i.e. textual information about the entry), the *source of the elaboration*, *encyclopaedic units*, the *domain* and *grammar*. The model also comprises relationships between the entities, such

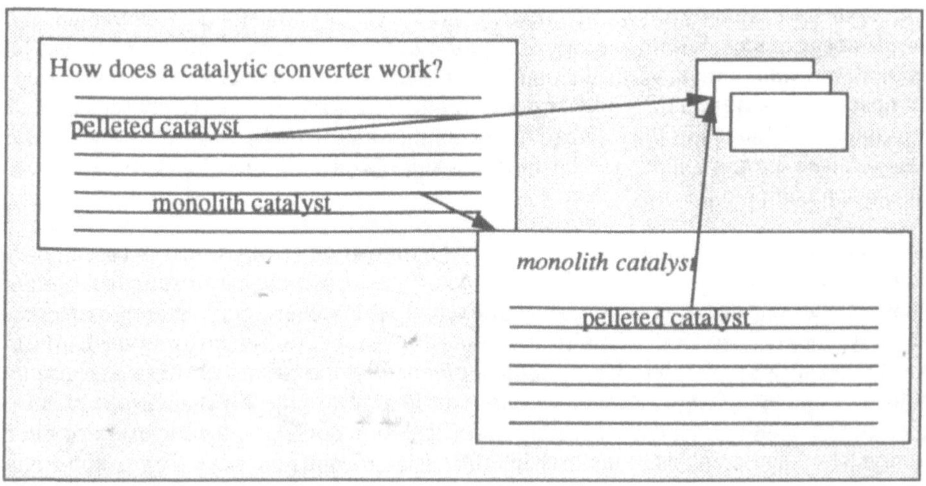

Fig. 10: Example of the encyclopaedic units

as "is-elaborated" between *entry* and *elaboration.* Since the termbank group decided that all entries have the same status, the translation equivalent of an entry, for example, is stored as a relationship between the corresponding language entries.

The entity *elaboration* contains textual information such as definitions, context examples, collocations and usage information. The *encyclopaedic units* are also textual information, but of a special kind. The encyclopaedia was included because translators often need more information on technical terms than a definition can provide. An encyclopeadic explanation gives translators, who normally are not subject experts, insight into the technical background. Several *terms* can be linked to a single *encyclopaedic unit*, which contains information about linked terms. The encyclopaedic units are not isolated but grouped and linked. Every unit has a unique *heading*, which can be accessed via the term. Encyclopaedic units often comprise headers of other encyclopaedic units. The units and the headers form a group; all headers form a non-hierarchical network (see Fig. 10). The user can browse through the network, following the header structure up and down.

Each entity has several attributes. Because the termbank entry is the central entity, its attributes are listed here:

- *entry*, ie a word, a group of words, a phrase;
- *short grammar*, eg indicating gender, part of speech;
- *language*, given in short form: en, es, de, for English, Spanish, German;
- *country*: US, UK, DE, ES for the United States, United Kingdom, Germany, Spain;
- *status*: r, a, g for red, amber, green standing for the term validation (i.e. red = not validated, green = fully validated);
- *termstatus*: eg pre, sta, int for preferred, standardized, internal.

Beside these attributes, the date of insertion or last modification, as well as the name of the responsible terminologist is recorded.

9.1.2 The Termbank Interface

During the last twenty years termbank designers have concentrated on the development of the database model. Within the last few years, however, the main point of interest has shifted more and more towards the problem of interface design (Mayer 1989). Planning a termbank user-interface, the designer has to consider how the user can easily access all the information contained in the termbank. Our solution to the problem was to create a window-oriented interface which can be directly manipulated by means of a mouse and which can be configured to the user's need.

From the human factor point of view, Direct Manipulation (DM), which is based on the graphical depiction of the state of affairs, can be regarded as a well-suited interaction mode for the selected application. In combination with modern programming paradigms (e.g. Hypertext: Bush 1945, Conklin 1987) and conventional software using the hardware and the power of new (Unix based, bitmap oriented) workstations, DM can enhance the efficiency and applicability of such systems considerably. In the TWB-system, which frequently deals with graphically depicted 'wor(l)ds' and 'contexts', the inclusion of direct manipulation and graphics in the user interface is an obvious but nevertheless non-trivial task.'

Having started the termbank by selecting the termbank button in the toolbox, the user first of all has to define the information categories he/she wants to be displayed on the screen. This is done by means of the *specification window* (see Fig. 11).

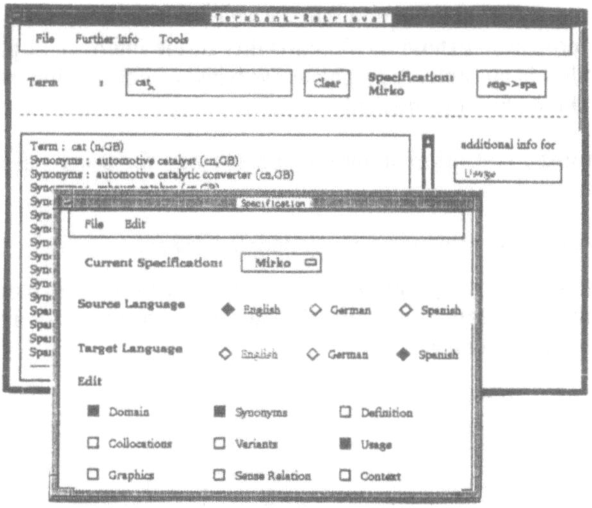

Fig. 11: Termbank and retrieval specification window

The user can save individual specification profiles. After having typed in a search term, the respective information is offered in the *retrieval window*. Additional information can be accessed using the pull-down menu *further info*.

Term access is supported by including spelling variations and wildcard search (see Fig. 12). Then a list of possible mappings is given. The user chooses one of the terms offered by a double-click.

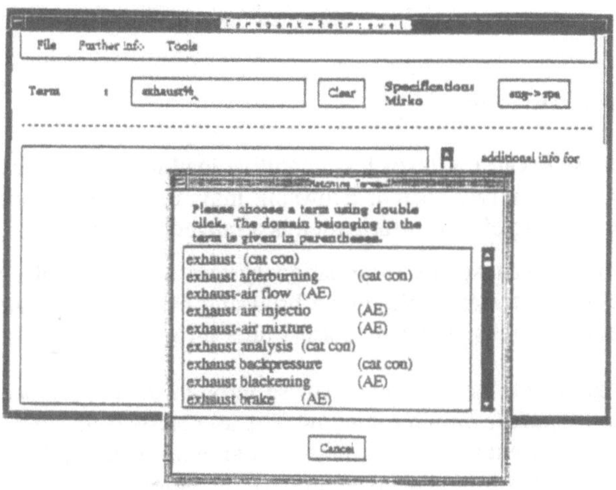

Fig. 12: Termbank retrieval with wildcard

Because most translators usually read the whole text to be translated and mark the unknown terms before starting the actual translation, we provided the tool *list search*. The user can cut and paste all unknown terms into the *list search* window and obtain the retrieved information in a new results window (see Fig. 13). He/she can also print the results, if a hard copy is more appropriate, or save them in a file for later sessionsIn our opinion, it is important to extend the functionality of the interface in places where a kind of browsing facility is possible. A graphical overview of information in connection with a requested term should be implemented.

Browsing is an important information-seeking strategy for users - especially for novice and casual users.

Marchionini 1988 states three reasons why people browse:

- They browse because they cannot define their search objective explicitly. They often proceed iteratively, beginning with a broad entry, browsing for related entries, and looking for additional entry points.

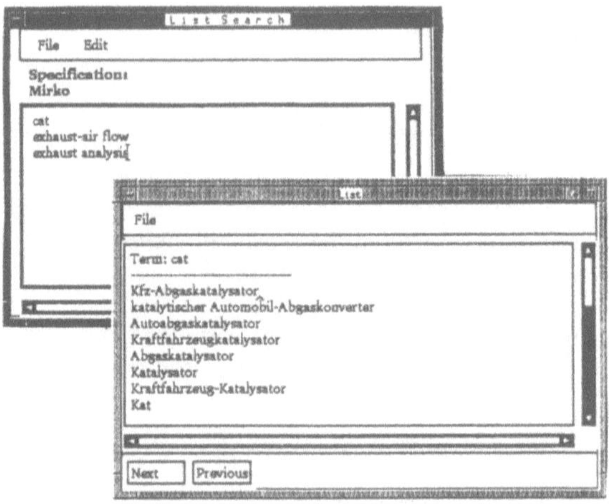

Fig. 13: List search window

- People browse because it takes less cognitive load to browse than to plan and conduct an analytical, optimised search. Browsing may also reflect novice and casual users' poor understanding of how information is arranged in a system.
- People browse because the information system supports and encourages browsing. Electronic books, for example, invite browsing by supplying indexes, outlines, headings, tables and graphs, which help users filter information quickly.

In the TWB termbank the user may browse through the encyclopaedic units. Figure 14 shows the *encyclopaedic browser* window. The user starts from a term and obtains a list of headers of all linked encyclopaedic units (where more than one unit is linked), or if only one unit is linked, it will be displayed directly. The user selects one of the headers and is shown the text corresponding to this header. It is possible to get to all headers of the upper units (units where this unit is mentioned) and lower units (mentioned in the actual unit) as

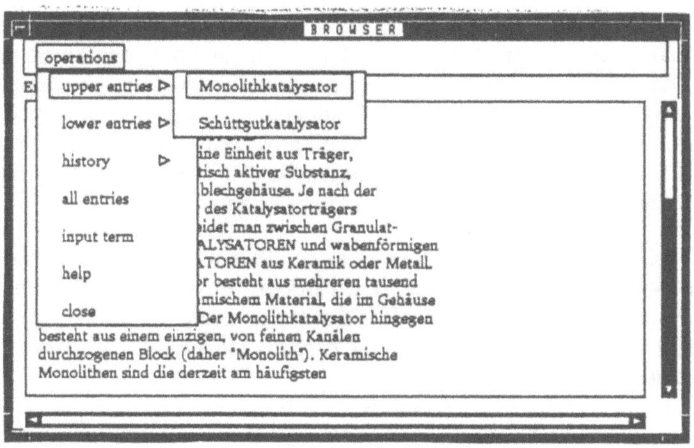

Fig. 14: Browswe interface

well. Selecting one of these headers brings on the corresponding text in the text area. The user can also list all headers in alphabetical order and obtain a history list of all headers of all units he/she has accessed in the session.

9.2 The Cardbox

Translators show a tendency towards individual strategies and a personal style in translation. They have some strategies in common, but it is impossible to describe exhaustively how translators approach their work or how they work with a dictionary and organise the terminological work.

The design of an overall Translator's Workbench should take this variety of working styles into account and provide a working environment which is as flexible and as adaptable to individual working styles as possible, although the termbank is intended and designed as a static tool. The information categories and the content of the termbank were provided by the termbank group and not by the users themselves. The interface allows partial flexibility providing features like browsing and determining a personal translator's profile. This approach doesn't appear to be hospitable to the individual translator; however, we have proceeded in this way in accordance with the requirements of many translation offices and other commercial and industrial enterprises. These bodies express a preference for a common terminology collection, fixed access permission and a standardised working environment. The right to create new entries or to update existing ones is a right reserved for the few translators or professional terminologists responsible for maintaining the common terminology collection.

By interviewing professional translators, we have been able to determine that many of them still maintain their private card file. Most translators start collecting terminology and relevant information concerning a specific subject during their training at university. Later on, during their professional career, this private term collection is revised and expanded and grows over the years to a considerable number of cards. Some translators informed us that they often create a special stock of cards for a single translation job comprising information relevant to the work at hand. The specific arrangement of the cards, then, is crucial, because it usually has a unique order, tailored to the job and only obvious to the creator of the system. Other translators have several hundred cards organised in a single batch and ordered alphabetically. Often English and German term definitions are mixed with names of companies, experts, abbreviations, etc. The cards cover a wide range of information from straight monolingual definitions, bibliographic hints, short graphics, mathematical symbols, and idiomatic expressions to translation equivalents.

Therefore, the *Cardbox*, which functions as a private termbank, was planned to cater for individual working strategies and styles. The cardbox allows the translator to define individual cards online. The advantage of this is that the translator does not have to change the working medium since the termbank and the cardbox (as a kind of private termbank) can be accessed simultaneously.

9.2.1 The Cardbox Structure

For the definition of the cardbox, we investigated HyperCard, which is a product of Apple Computers, running on Macintosh (Williams 1987). The main characteristics of HyperCard are that it allows stacks of cards and the establishment of links between them to be defined. We designed a direct manipulative interface for the implementation of the cardbox which resembles the possibilities offered by HyperCard.

The most important objects and features of the cardbox are (Longhurst et al. 1991):

Card Stacks: Definition of any number of card stack *templates*, where the number and name of attributes may be chosen freely. Creation, addition, and deletion of templates or any *attributes* of a defined template are possible.

Cards: Writing cards (insertion of new cards), manipulation of cards (replacement of a card), and the deletion of any entry on a card, as well as the deletion of whole cards.

Links: Linking cards by specifying a link *name* and the name of the card to be linked. Any link may be deleted. Any number of links can start from any card. Conversely, a card may be the destination of any number of links.

9.2.2 The Cardbox Interface

If the user selects the Cardbox button from the TWB Toolbox, then the cardbox window appears (see Fig. 15). The user can now proceed to create, modify, and retrieve cards and templates. The definition of a mask for a card stack (see Fig. 16), called template, involves selecting a suitable title for the template, defining its attributes, and optionally determining the order in which these attributes appear (a layout function).

Unlike paper cards, computerised cards do not have to be arranged in a fixed order but can be sorted according to changing criteria without the need for duplication.The retrieval or modification of cards includes the production of new cards. The user has to pick out an existing template in the cardbox window.

With the command *"Retrieve/Modify"* the user is able to search in a stack of cards which belong to the chosen template, or to create a new card (see Fig. 17). Typing a search term

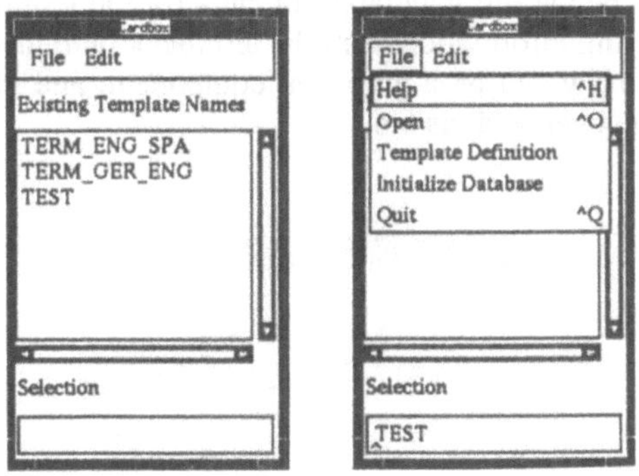

Fig. 15: Cardbox window

in any of the attribute fields causes the respective cards to be displayed. Wildcards can also be used. The number of selected cards is displayed.The user can browse through the selected cards using *next* and *previous.*

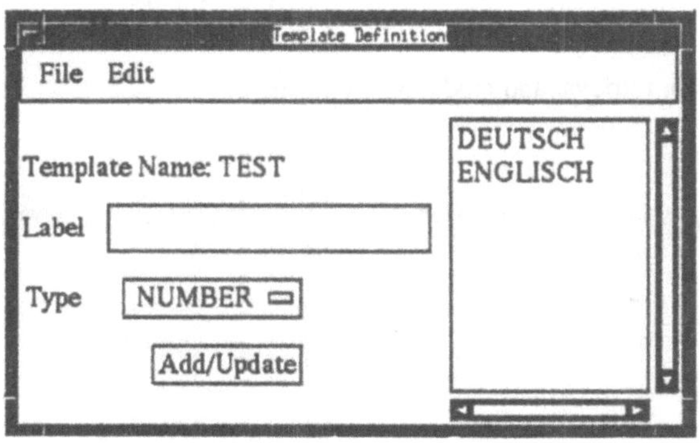

Fig. 16: Template definition window

The links between cards can be traced and followed in the *link* menu (see Fig. 18).

Additionally, the user can produce a hard copy of any number of cards using the print function and can determine the order in which cards are displayed using the order function.

Outlook

How can we make the interface of a termbank more attractive? In the area of user interface development, additional multi-media tools like video, animation, sound, pictures etc. are being investigated on a large scale. Interpreters or learners, for example, may be interested in the correct pronunciation of a term. Experts could be supported by an animation component which explains the functions of a machine.

Another addition may be the full integration of cardbox and termbank. Users should have the possibility of copying information from the termbank onto their cards. Another useful addition to the cardbox would be a graphical component, and the possibility of having more than one card file open and visible.

Fig. 17: Window for retrieval and modification of cards

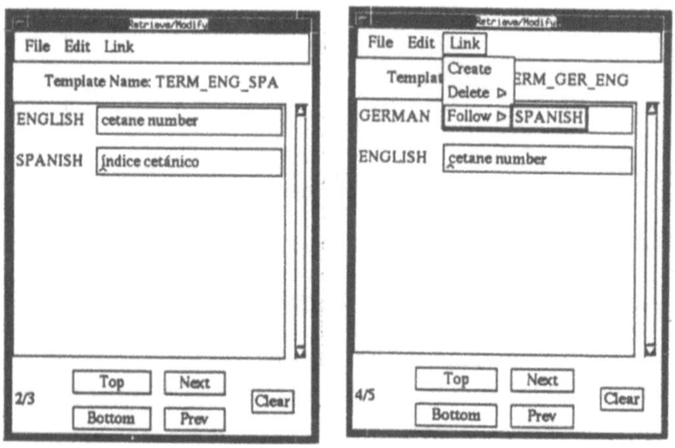

Fig. 18: Links between cards

10. Creating Terminology Resources

Khurshid Ahmad, Andrea Davies, Heather Fulford, Paul Holmes-Higgin, Margaret Rogers

This section describes a terminology management methodology for creating multilingual terminologies of emerging multidisciplinary domains for use by translators, developed at the University of Surrey. The term "Terminology management" denotes the modern methods of creating, organising, and exploiting terminology resources, i.e. of compiling text corpora on computer systems together with software programs which can be used with WIMPS (Windows, Icons, Menus and Pointers), (proprietary) database management systems and information retrieval software systems for the formalised elicitation and elaboration of terminology (a collection of terms) of a specialist domain. We have demonstrated how terminology can be identified, organised and disseminated using corpus-based computer-assisted methods drawing on text analysis, Artificial Intelligence (AI) and data base systems within the linguistic framework of Language for Special Purposes (LSP).

A prototype terminology in a selected LSP, also referred to by some experts as sublanguage (for example, see Kittredge and Lehrberger 1982), terminology has been identified, organised and disseminated using our terminology management methods and tools: a four-phased, corpus-based methodology of term elicitation and elaboration. A set of software tools (the MATE - Machine-Assisted Terminology Elicitation - environment) has been developed to operationalize the methodology. To demonstrate the terminology management methodology, a terminology from three sub-domains of automotive engineering - catalytic converters, anti-lock braking systems and four-wheel drive systems - in three major European languages, German, English and Spanish, has been created. Six text types have been selected with the aim of representing as extensively as possible the range of documents and terminology encountered by translators. The texts form a corpus of over 772,000 words. The prototype database currently contains over 4,000 terms and related terminological data comprising over 300 texts in each of the three languages.

The methodology is transferable to other domains and to other lesser-used languages; to demonstrate the multidisciplinary and multilingual nature of our terminology management methodology, we have tested it in a number of other domains (e.g. radioactive chemicals) and with other languages such as Welsh and Greek.

This section begins with a definition of LSP and LSP terminology (Sect. 10.1). Next we describe a four-phased elicitation and elaboration of terms (Sect. 10.2), and assess current terminology management resources (Sect. 10.3). We then describe the TWB's specification of a term bank record format for terminology storage (Sect. 10.4). Section 10.5 outlines progress monitoring procedures and their role in the management of terminology elicitation and elaboration. In Sect. 10.6 the corpus-based approach is discussed. Finally, Sect. 10.7 gives an outline of the progress made and problems encountered in the development of the prototype terminology of automotive engineering.

10.1 Background

A special language, or a LSP, is the language of experts in a narrowly defined domain. It is a specialised, monofunctional, subject-specific language in which words or "terms" are used in a way peculiar to that domain lexically, semantically, and also in some cases, morphologically and syntactically. The study of LSP is a well-established (academic) discipline complete with its repertoire of academic departments, journals, books, and so on. LSP terms - usually nouns - are used to encode different aspects of the knowledge of a domain including abstract concepts, sense-relations, nomenclature, and process-oriented or device-related descriptions.

A **terminology** is a collection of such LSP terms within a particular domain, in which the terms are defined and the interrelationships between them explained.

The knowledge of a specialised domain evolves according to a life-cycle paradigm, i.e. inception, currency, refinement and obsolescence of knowledge; this is reflected in the evolution of the terminology of the domain. Terms are used by experts and technical writers for communicating the knowledge of the domain to other experts, novices and in some cases laypersons.

Generally, text is used as the medium for this communication and can be classified into a range of text types as described later. Given the aim of closer cooperation between linguistically diverse nation states, such as those within the EC, and the establishment of a multi-national corporate culture, specialised knowledge has to be transferred across communication barriers. This transfer takes place through the medium of language, and notably, text. Note that, as the nature of an LSP may be defined at a number of linguistic levels, the terminology of a specialised domain and the use of terms in a given language will reflect the lexical organisation of the language, its morphology and its syntax.

10.2 The Systematic Elicitation of Terms: A Life-Cycle Model

Our work focused on developing a scientifically-based working model for building term banks - the engineering of term banks with clearly defined phases of specification, design, implementation and testing of terms and their potential utility. We stipulate that the model should have synergy and reflect the fact that terms are used for encoding (communicating) and decoding (interpreting) the knowledge of specialised domains. This communication, primarily text-based, manifests itself in a range of text types (e.g. informative, instructional, persuasive) in different languages for a varied audience comprising experts, novices, students, laypersons, etc.

Within our model, the development of term banks - the organised collection of terms of a domain for identifiable target users - is simulated as a continual process of term elicitation and elaboration. This process involves the execution of four consecutive phases (see also Fig. 19):

Phase 1: **acquisition** - the conceptual organisation of the domain and the creation of a corpus; the identification of specialist terms in texts, glossaries or dictionaries.

Phase 2: **representation** - the linguistic description of the term (words/phrases), including identification of grammatical category, category-specific morphological and syntactic information, and linguistic variants.

Phase 3: **explication** - the elaboration of the term including its descriptive definition and descriptive contextual use.

Phase 4: **deployment** - the exploration of the sense relations between the term and other (pre-stored) terms, including the establishment of cross-linguistic equivalence.

The successful execution of each phase of term elicitation is delineated with clearly identifiable data: e.g. the acquisition phase data include an overview of the domain or subdomain and a list of terms together with archival data. The representation phase follows the acquisition phase and is deemed complete for a term (or a list of terms) with the provision of specified linguistic data. The explication phase involves the procurement of definitions, generally from domain experts, and of examples of contextual use from a carefully selected corpus of texts. In the deployment phase, both experts and the corpus can be used to identify and quantify sense-relations such as synonymy and hyponymy.

The term data can be refined by repeatedly executing one or all the phases mentioned above. As each phase generates its own data, it becomes clear that data associated with each term can be categorised as acquisitional, representational, etc. These data require different data structures to be effectively stored in (or retrieved from) a computer system. Once stored, the requirements of maintaining and updating these data will be different. The retrieval of the different data items will depend on the given user - e.g. the TWB User Requirements Study (Chap. 4) identified that a translator will generally require deployment data (foreign language equivalent, etc.), representational data (grammatical information, etc.) and explicatory data (context, etc.).

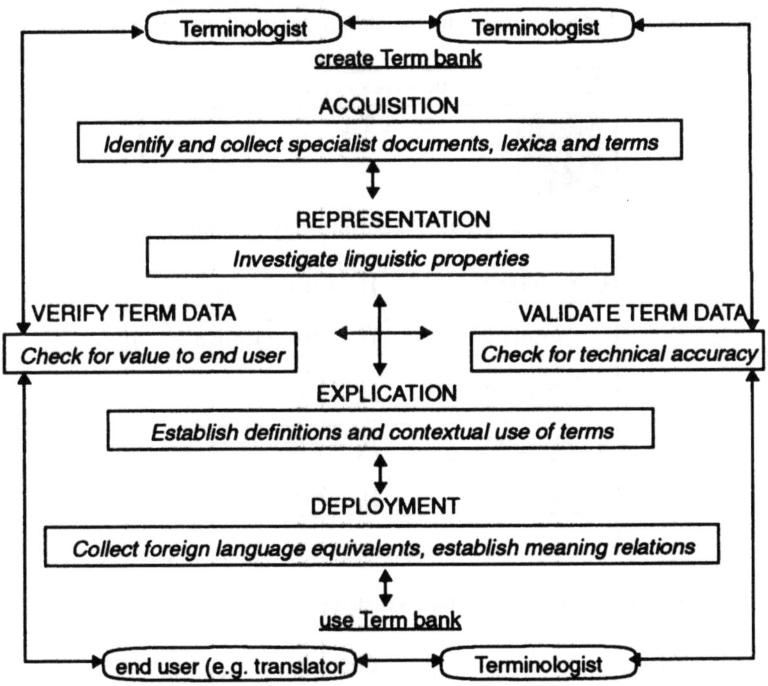

Fig. 19: Life cycle model of term elicitation (Ahmad and Rogers, forthcoming)

The different data structures required to encode the data from each of these phases is as follows. Acquisitional data need 'simple' data structures (records and lists); representational data need data structures with predicative power; explicatory data require network data structures; and deployment data require network and list structures.

10.3 The Life-Cycle Model of Term Elicitation: Outline of Computing Resources

For the successful execution of each of the phases of the term elicitation cycle, the terminologist will require different sets of computer programs for the following tasks:

- creation of corpus, including its organisation in terms of data files arranged according to language (variety) and text type - this can be satisfied by most operating systems utilities (e.g. DIR, etc.);
- browsing and (literary) concordance facilities for scanning texts, listing concordances and collocations either file by file or globally within a concordance, or according to a specific language variety and/or a special text type;
- document creation facilities for selecting ('highlighting') 'chunks' of a selected file, and facilities for 'cutting and pasting' these chunks into a file for incorporation into term banks (particularly in the 'explication' table or cluster); also, facilities for date-stamping and for the name attribution of the terminologist by using the system's time clock and user's login name.

At the University of Surrey a custom-made computer-based terminology toolkit called MATE has been developed to assist the terminologist in all of the above tasks (Fig. 20):

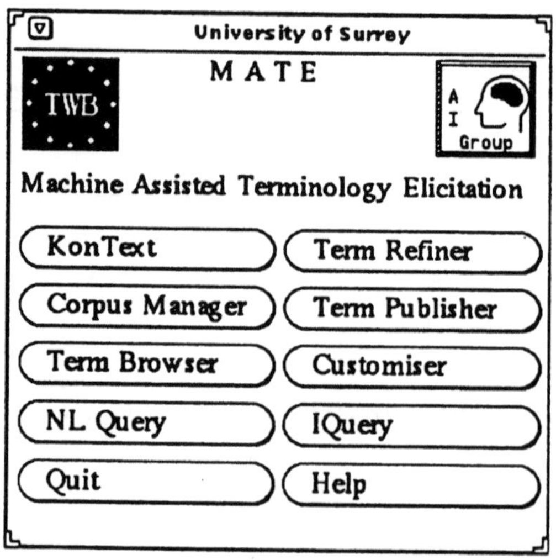

Fig. 20: The University of Surrey's machine assisted term elicitation environment

Using the MATE (Machine Assisted Term Elicitation) environment, developed by Holmes-Higgin (see, for instance, Holmes-Higgin and Griffin, 1991, Holmes-Higgin, 1992, Ahmad et al. 1990, Ahmad et al. 1991) terminology can be elicited from a corpus of LSP texts, elaborated, disseminated and retrieved interactively or off-line in a variety of formats. The toolkit comprises:

- **Corpus Manager**: enables the user to organise texts in a structured hierarchy;

- **KonText**: generates word lists, indexes, KWIC lists, and concordances for use in acquiring terms and related terminological data from texts. Sophisticated search facilities are provided;
- **Term Refiner**: allows the user to design and create mono- or multilingual term banks. Automated guidelines provide assistance when data is being entered, ensuring consistency and accuracy;
- **Term Browser**: provides hypertext-like term bank browsing and navigation facilities for rapid data retrieval;
- **Term Publisher**: prints the contents of term banks in a variety of formats, including terms lists, dictionaries, and full term bank records;
- **Customiser**: allows each user to set up a personal installation and working profile.

The MATE system is written in QUINTUS-PROLOG, a logic programming language available on a SUN-SPARCstation, running under the UNIX operating system. The user interface was written using ProWindows and the bulk terminology data was stored in ORACLE, a proprietary database management system. Recently, supported by Mercedes-Benz AG, a smaller version of MATE has been ported onto PC-compatible hardware: the PC-MATE. PC-MATE is written in C++, a procedural programming language on an IBM-compatible PC running under DOS (see Fig. 21). The user interface for PC-MATE was written using MS Windows 3 and the bulk terminology data was stored in COMFO-BASE, a Siemens database system.

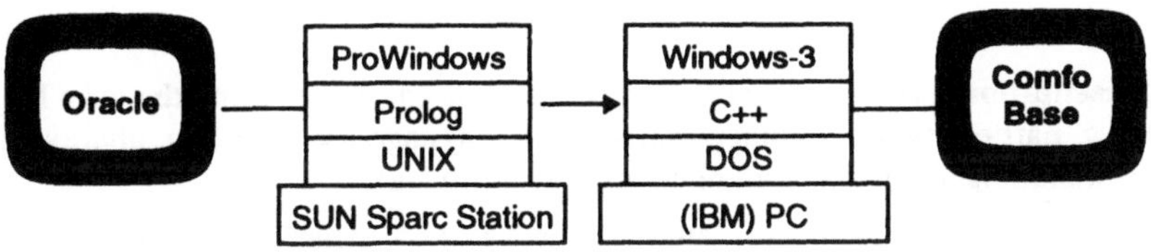

Fig. 21: MATE and PC-MATE

10.4 Term Bank Record Format

The organisation of LSP vocabulary requires a format whereby over 20 different fields (e.g. headword, definition, administrative details, etc.) of terminological data can be organised for storage, retrieval and updating purposes: the term bank record format.

Figure 19 showed that each phase of the term elicitation cycle yields clearly identifiable data which delineate that phase. We have developed a record format which records the acquisition, representation, explication and deployment data items in four clusters respectively. Each cluster has been simulated on the computer system as a 'relational' table. Figure 22 shows the record format diagrammatically, reflecting the internal architecture of the term bank, not necessarily the view available to the terminologist.

The record format devised by the University of Surrey has the following clusters:

a) **Acquisitional data:** typically axiomatic data, comprising the term, archival data (such as the name of the terminologist or expert who identifies terms and the data on which the identification was based) and references (or, more precisely pointers) to other descriptive or relational data exemplifying the term and its usage;

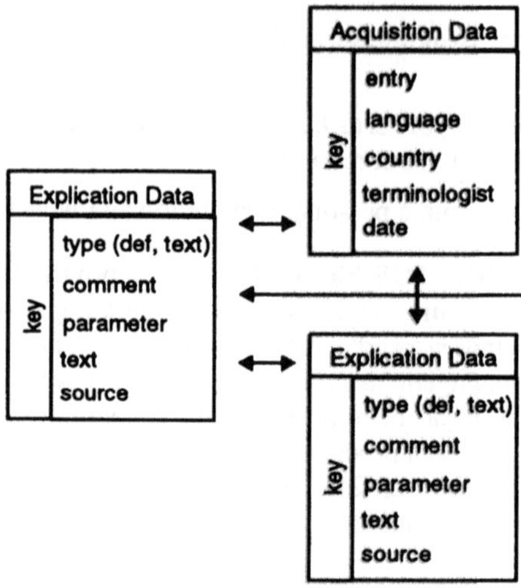

Fig. 22: Knowledge-based record format (Ahmad et al. 1990)

b) **Representational data:** generally descriptive data for categorising the term linguistically (e.g. part of speech, number, gender) and language use data (e.g. abbreviations, variants, including chemical and mathematical formulae);

c) **Explicatory data**: descriptive data with the focus on meaning (e.g. definitions and illustrations of contextual use);

d) **Deployment data:** data which signify the semantic or knowledge-based content of a term and its relationship to other terms and their contexts, including foreign language equivalents, synonyms, etc.

The record formats presented below were created for a multilingual (English, Spanish, German) term bank of automotive engineering and for a bilingual (Welsh, English) term bank of chemistry. In both cases, the fields of the record formats have been specified uniquely in order to meet the needs of translators. The data contained in the record formats was collated from a multilingual corpus of LSP texts (catalytic converter technology and radiation chemistry), using the MATE (Machine-Assisted Terminology Elicitation) environment. The record format (only a few fields of which are shown in Fig. 23) can be specified according to users needs in other domains and language combinations.Examples of entry records.

DOMAIN:	cat con
TERMINOLOGIST:	khw
ENTRY DATE:	11-sep-90
LANGUAGE:	en
COUNTRY:	GB
ENTRY:	A/F ratio
GRAMMAR:	NOUN + NOUN + NOUN
GERMAN EQUIVALENT:	Kraftstoff-Luft-Verhältnis
SYNONYM:	air/fuel ratio
DEFINITION:	Mass ratio of air to fuel inducted by an engine.
DEFINITION SOURCE:	enGB00487
CONTEXT:The dual substrate catalyst was an essential compromise for obtaining simultaneous conversion of HC, CO and NOx over a wide A/F ratio range.	
CONTEXT SOURCE:	enGB00481

DOMAIN:	radioactive chemicals
TERMINOLOGIST:	AED
LANGUAGE:	cy
COUNTRY:	GB
ENTRY:	arbrawf
ENGLISH EQUIVALENT:	experiment
GRAMMAR:NOUN masc	
WELSH DEFINITION:	Ymgais i brofi rhywbeth megis damcaniaeth.
ENGLISH DEFINITION:	A test or investigation, esp. one planned to provide evidence for or against a hypothesis.
DEFINITION SOURCE:	enGB00003
CONTEXT: Sail yr arbrawf CMN yw cyflwyno yr ynni cywir ac, i ddilyn, mesur sut y caiff ei dderbyn gan y niwclysau.	
CONTEXT SOURCE:	cyGB00001

Fig. 23: Examples of entry records

10.5 Monitoring the Life-Cycle Phases

Progress Monitoring: A literature review failed to reveal the cost of developing terminology data-banks (our own target figure of 4000 terms in each language was based on the classical studies of Alford 1971). Given that we were able to design a phased approach to the term elicitation process, we decided to 'monitor' the use of human and machine resources during the process as a facet of overall terminology management. TWB's Term Record Statistics Log is a record maintained each week of the number of terms and terminological data acquired and elaborated by terminologists. Some typical results of term elicitation for German, English and Spanish terms are shown in Fig. 24.

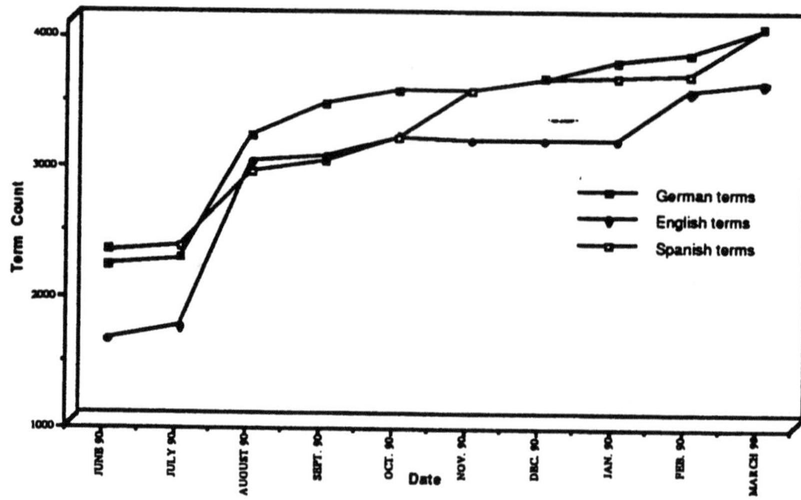

Fig. 24: Progress of term elicitation

Term Validation: The systematic verification and validation of terminology, i.e. comments and criticisms made by domain experts, is logged in two ways: a) by regular consultation with domain experts - preferably native speakers who are domain experts, b) by the terminologist filling in a questionnaire ('log') of the validation process - the 'Term Validation Form' (see Appendix B) in the presence of the expert(s) validating the term. The form comprises three major sections: i) archival notes (e.g. names of the terminologist and domain expert(s), the time and place of validation), ii) representation, explication and deployment data printed on the form directly from the term bank, and iii) comments on each of the data clusters by experts. This form systematically records under the appropriate sub-headings all the details and suggestions given by experts: conceptual, linguistic and administrative data. Further controls are implemented as new terms are identified and elaborated.

Guidelines for the selection of contextual examples (see Fulford and Rogers 1990): Two principal purposes can be identified for including contextual examples of use in a terminology. The first is to clarify the meaning of a term for purposes of both comprehension and production by the end user. The second is to establish how the term is used stylistically and grammatically in running text (production only) (see also Sinclair 1988:xv). Contextual examples of the term in use provide descriptive information for the user, in so far as the terminologist is recording and following current language use in this aspect of term elaboration (see also Sinclair 1988:xii for general purpose lexicography). Contextual examples may also help the translator to distinguish between use of the term in different text types. A definition is unable to fulfil this need.

The selection of contextual examples needs to proceed on a principled basis. Given the current size of, for example, Surrey's automotive engineering corpus - c. 195,000 words (British English), c. 161,000 words (American English), c. 126,000 words (German) and c. 290,000 words (Spanish), a number of examples of contextual use of a term can be found when an exhaustive search of the automotive engineering corpus is undertaken.

The University of Surrey has developed a set of guidelines designed to help the terminologist identify those contextual examples which are most appropriate to the needs of the end user. The guidelines are divided into a) 'Introductory' criteria for recommended texts, b) 'Comprehension' guidelines (decoding) based on text-linguistic and semantic considerations, and c) 'Production'

guidelines (encoding) based mainly on grammatical criteria. The division of the guidelines can be shown diagrammatically as in Fig. 25.

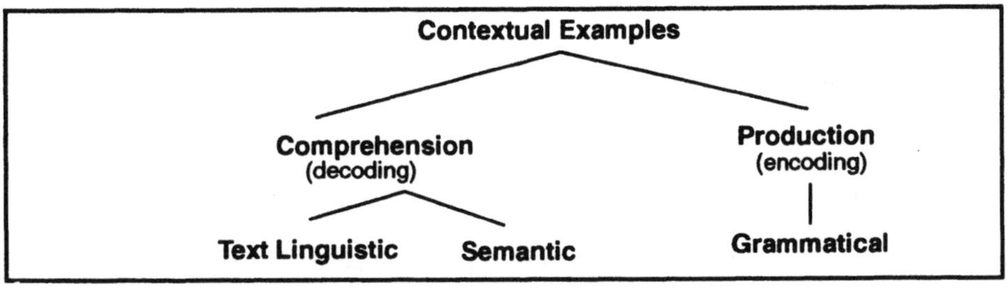

Fig. 25: Criteria of contextual guidelines (Fulford and Rogers 1990)

There are currently 16 guidelines in all, just under half (n=7) based on text linguistic measures (e.g. avoid examples containing pronouns, avoid examples containing table headings, or in text titles); semantic criteria (n=4) (e.g. avoid advertising material or examples containing proper nouns, avoid examples with two or more technical terms) and grammatical criteria (n=4) (e.g. if the entry term is in the singular [plural], find an example of when it appears in the singular [plural]), and text types to search (n=1) (see Ahmad, Fulford and Rogers forthcoming for more details).

10.6 Corpus-Based Approach

In accordance with current lexicographical practice (COBUILD, 1988; Longman's Dictionary of Contemporary English (LDOCE), 1987), the methodology developed by TWB for terminology management is corpus-based. Texts are collected in the selected languages and are stored in machine-readable form. The corpus is used in at least three of the term elicitation phases. In the acquisition phase, it is used to help identify terms. In the representation phase, it is used to identify various linguistic characteristics. In the explication phase it is used to support the construction of definitions, and is a source of examples of contextual use. The corpus of automotive engineering texts is currently 772,567 words. It contains over 350,000 words of English (194,828 British English and 160,487 American English words), over 126,000 words of German and over 290,000 words of Spanish. Figure 26 depicts the distribution of texts across the respective languages and language varieties.

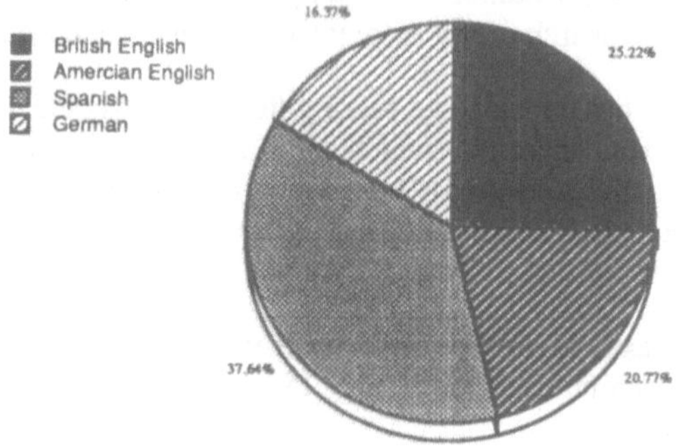

Fig. 26: Distribution of texts in German, English and Spanish

Over 300 texts from the sub-domains of automotive engineering, namely catalytic converters, anti-lock braking systems and four-wheel drive, in the languages and language variants listed above have been converted into machine-readable form.

Figure 27 shows the structure and sizecof the corpus according to language and sub-domain.

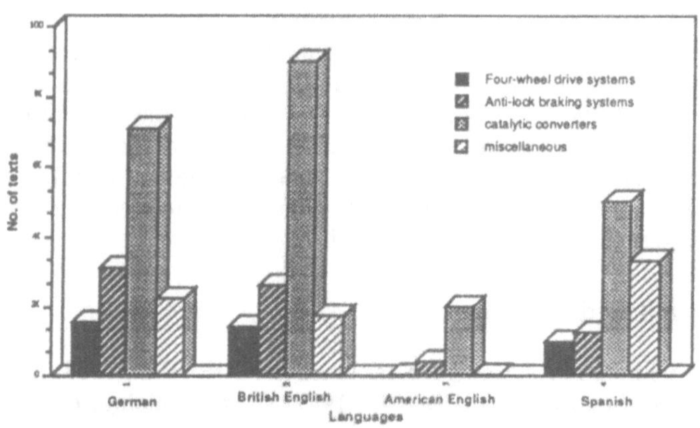

Fig. 27: Structure and current size of corpus according to language and sub-domain (Surrey's automotive engineering corpus)

Text monitoring of this kind allows the user to gauge the balance of texts across languages and across text types.

Six text types have been identified as representative of the range of texts encountered by end users. Books and learned journals can be classified as informative, workshop manuals are instructional, and newspaper articles and advertisements are broadly persuasive. One other informative text type is that of official documentation. By official documentation we understand patents, legislative articles, regulations and standards. The information such texts contain is highly descriptive and precise, and is often the first source of terminology of a new domain. These texts are also frequently found to contain definitions. To maintain control over and identify the differences between texts, 'headers' have been inserted at the beginning of each text to indicate sub-domain, language, text type and date of publication. A full bibliography of texts is also maintained and is accessible to the user.

A corpus-based approach enables the terminologist to identify, study and record terms in their natural habitat, and translators, as users of the term bank, to have customised access to a full set of information about all the terms and related terminological data of a domain.

10.7 Language-Specific Issues: Progress and Problems

In the creation of a prototype termbank of automotive engineering progress was shown to be good (see Fig. 24). However, a small number of difficulties have been identified in each of the four phases of term elicitation. In the acquisition phase, the lack of textual data in Spanish has set - and will continue to set - real constraints on the identification of Spanish terms. The paucity of textual material available in Spanish can be attributed to the relative newness of catalytic converter technology in Spain, compared to the Federal Republic of Germany, where the use of less pollutant cars is a topical issue, and to the UK, where car manufacturers have begun producing vehicles equipped with catalytic converters. In the representation phase, i.e. when representing grammatical and language-use data, it has been established that the knowledge of a domain expert is required, particularly since the sub-domains in question (especially catalytic converters) are still undergoing technological development. There are, for instance, problems with regard to variants, more so because developments are taking place in countries which are not necessarily English speaking. The explication phase has problems associated with finding an accurate definition suited to the needs of a non-domain-expert (i.e. a translator) and a suitable contextual example. Experts have been consulted for definitions, especially where such definitions are not available in reference literature. In the deployment phase, the chief problem has been to match equivalents across languages - the problem lies in the fact that Germany, for example, is more technologically advanced than other countries such as Spain. Attempts at cross-linguistic matching of terms serve to highlight terminological lacunae.

10.8 Conclusions

The main results achieved by the TWB project at the University of Surrey may be summarised as follows:

A four-phased methodology has been established for creating and maintaining corpora of LSP texts and for eliciting terms from such text corpora and validating them and their associated data with the help of domain experts. This terminology management methodology provides the basis for terminographical work using computer-based resources. Its artifacts comprise a text corpus and a term bank for use in translation. Our work is therefore of relevance to the terminologist/terminographer and the translator.

A prototype termbank of automotive engineering has been created using the four-phased methodology. The methodology has been refined to optimise progress and to counter language-specific problems which occurred during the creation of the prototype termbank. The four phases of term elicitation have also benefited from the monitoring procedures established during the project for quantifying the work of terminologists and from providing them with a Machine-Assisted Terminology Environment (MATE) for managing and searching corpora and terminological data banks.

10.9 Appendix

TERM VALIDATION FORM

Term Bank Name: TWB

Sub-Domain: Catalytic Converters

Terminologist

Date:

Place:

Verifier Name

Verifier Address

Term to be verified; its definition, foreign language equivalent and an example of contextual usage

klopfen [00214 nnt; =Klingen

Premature ignition of the air/fuel mixture in the combustion chamber of an internal combustion engine, causing damage to the engine.

Mithin konnten effizientere Motoren mit höherer Kompression gebaut werden, ohne gefahr zu laufen, daß das Luft/Kraftstoffgemisch unter hohem Druck zu früh explosionsartig verbrennt; dadurch entsteht das berüchtigte Klopfen oder Klingeln des Motors.

Verifier's Comments on: (Add x or as appropriate)

(a) CONCEPTUAL Data in the Record :

Definition Current

Extra (indicate attached sheets)

Context Current

Extra(indicate attached sheets)

(b) LINGUISTIC Data in the Record:

(c) ADMINISTRATIVE Data of the Record:

III. Translation Processes

Tools and Techniques

11. Currently Available Systems: METAL

Gregor Thurmair

METAL is a system which follows the approach of "computer integrated translation"; i.e. it tries to integrate tools needed in translation and to group them around a machine translation kernel. It follows the same approach as TWB: allow for integration of the software tools in the process of documentation and translation.

The first prototype was developed in Austin, Texas; product development has been based in Munich since 1986; the system has development sites in Austin, Spain, Belgium, Denmark, and Germany. Languages treated are English, French, German, Spanish, Dutch, Danish, and Russian. Others, like Chinese, are being investigated.

The system is described in more detail in Thurmair 1991.

11.1 System Architecture

METAL consists of the following components:

- In order to be able to import text, and to connect the system to the outside world, METAL offers an interface for document handling; it is called "**METAL Document Interchange Format**" (MDIF). This is a markup language which allows for identification of layout information inside texts (like font changes, anchors, foreign characters, etc.). All further linguistic treatment is based on the MDIF formats. MDIF is not just used for machine translation but also for human translation (as it saves the formatting of the original text processor), as well as for other linguistic processing tools (like Term Bank comparisons).

  In order to support the MDIF format, METAL offers several **converters** into MDIF, like FrameMaker, Interleaf, Viewpoint, Word, WordPerfect, and ODIF (see below). Converters parse the original document format in order to identify the text elements and their formatting information, and mark them up in MDIF.

- The MDIF files are then deformatted. **Deformatting** performs the following tasks:

  - Identification of text blocks (e.g. in a multi-column ASCII layout),
  - identification of sentences
  - identification of certain constructions (like acronyms)
  - calling the Intelligent Pattern Matcher (see below)

  The deformatting is controlled by a set of parameters which the users can set (eg: "undo hyphenation Y/N"? This is necessary for Ascii based editors, but it is not needed for more sophisticated word processors).

  The result of this step is a file in Plain Text Format (PTF) which contains only the text. This interface is again used for more purposes than just MT: all linguistic components of SNI are based on this format.

- The next step is a **lexicon lookup**. Every word in the input is looked up in the lexicon. The result is a glossary of the known terms, a list of unknown terms (together with the contexts they occur in), and a list of default translations for compounds.

As the translation of a term is often dependent on its context, the lexicon lokup must do a full parse of the input to determine its translation; this holds also for multiword entries. Users can control this by parameters.

Missing terms must be **coded** in the lexicon. For this reason a comfortable coding tool (called Intercoder) has been created.

- After the lexicon has been updated, the text can be **translated**. METAL uses an augmented phrase structure grammar for morphological and syntactic analysis. It is parsed with an active chart parser using a middle out control strategy and a scoring mechanism (Caeyers/Adriaens 1990).

  The parser produces a canonical interface structure called "METAL Interface Representation" (MIR). It describes the linguistic properties of the input sentence in terms of tree structures and features; but it has words on its leaves. Therefore it is not a pure transfer approach (as the original METAL prototype was) and not an interlingua, but a combination of both, which can be called "Transfer interstructure" (Alonso 1990).

  On this MIR representation, transfer is performed which produces MIR structures again for both simple and complex lexical transfer (Thurmair 1990). And finally, generation rules produce the proper target text from a MIR input.

  This approach allows for easy combination of new language pairs from existing components at relatively low cost.

- After translation, the text must be **postedited**. Users are supported here with several postediting and search-and-replace tools, as well as a special editor. Postediting time is critical for the machine translation process.

- After postediting, the text is **reformatted** (i.e. brought into a MDIF format from a PTF format), and then it is reconverted (i.e. brought into the user's native text processing format from an MDIF format).

This process can be split into two parts, following a client-server philosophy: Conversion, text processing, and postediting can be done on a client; translation, which needs massive computing power, can run on a server in the network. Of course, both client and server can run on the same machine as well (a standard UNIX platform).

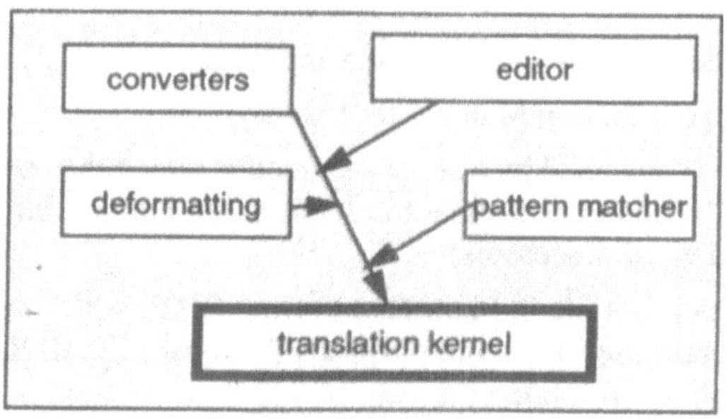

Fig. 28: Productivity Tools

11.2 The Translation Environment

The translation environment consists of a set of productivity tools which can be used even if the translation proper is not done by machine. The idea is, again, to create a set of tools to be configured according to users' needs. The following productivity tools are available:

11.2.1 Converters

METAL offers a set of converters to allow for text import into the system. Converters parse the external word processing formats (like ODIF, Word/RTF, FrameMaker/MIF, and others) into a standard markup format. This can be used by human translators or by the machine for translation. The converters create two files, one containing the irrelevant document parts (graphics, global layout etc.), the other containing the text and some layout information in MDIF format. Only the latter file is relevant for the translation process.

The common platform of the converters is defined to be ODA/ODIF; this is what the TWB converters are based on (see the chapter on document access above).

11.2.2 Document Version Comparison

METAL has developed a tool which compares versions of a document, and produces a delta file of new text. This tool is based on the PTF format. It compares sentences with previously translated ones, and if they match, it searches for the target language equivalents. The result is a bilingual file where only the new parts of a document remain in the source language.

11.2.3 Intelligent Pattern Matcher

Users are able to define their own search-and-replace patterns. The pattern matcher accepts regular expressions, searches the input for them and replaces them with the appropriate output pattern. (The challenge is to deal with the formatting markups in such patterns).

The pattern matcher is used in several places in the system:

- For the identification of acronyms and expressions not to be translated (like file names, variable names, and others);
- For normalisation of some input patterns (e.g. "5%" -> "5 %") to make the job of word segmentation and morphology easier;
- For automatic pretranslation of some frequently used patterns (e.g. "Sehr geehrter Herr" -> "Dear Mr.), without using the full translation machinery;
- For correction of frequently occurring errors in the target language, depending on the output of the system (e.g. "does not be" -> "is not").

The users can specify their patterns in files which are hierarchically organised (text specific - user specific - site specific); they are supported by system-defined classes of patterns. The can call the Intelligent Patterm Matcher at different stages of processing, using the parameter files.

11.2.4 Editor

METAL uses a special editor (MED: Metal editor) for internal purposes. It is based on an extension of EMACS and is designed particularly for translation and postediting purposes:

It is based on the ISO 8859/1 character set. Care was taken to support easy handling of foreign characters.

It is completely transparent with respect to control sequences: As the escape sequenes of a foreign system could enter METAL (as part of the MDIF files), the editor must not react to them in a strange way. As a result, even binary files can be edited with MED.

It uses function keys for the most frequent postediting operations (collecting words, moving them around in sentences, etc.), as well as special editing units like "translation unit".

It is not designed, however, for comfortable layouting, text element processing, etc., as it is assumed that this has been done outside METAL already (in the documentation department). It offers everything needed to (post)edit a text coming from outside, without damaging it by adding additional / new editing control sequences.

11.3 The Translation Kernel

While the tools mentioned above can be used with or without automatic translation, the present chapter concentrates on the translation kernel proper. It consists of a language-independent software kernel which processes the analysis and generation components, and language-(pair)-specific lingware, in particular lexica and grammars.

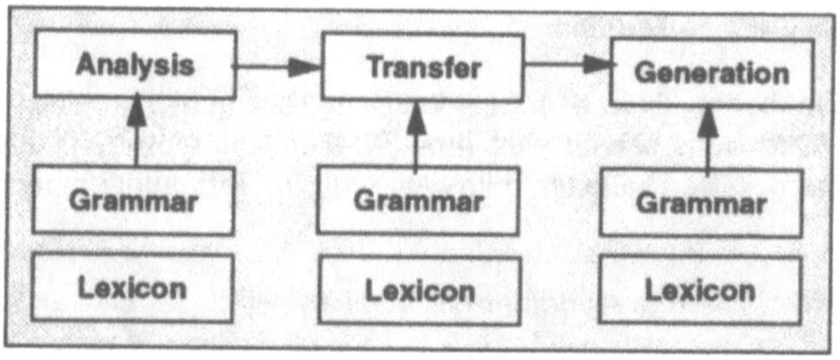

Fig. 29: The translation kernel

11.3.1 Lexica

The METAL lexica are organised according to two major divisions. First, they consist of monolingual and bilingual dictionaries. Monolingual dictionaries contain all information needed for (monolingual) processing. METAL uses the same monolingual dictionaries for analysis and generation; and the monolingual lexica can be used for purposes other than machine translation (like, in the case of TWB, verification of controlled grammars). Bilingual lexica contain the transfers. The METAL transfer lexica are bilingual and directed (i.e. the German-English transfer lexicon differs from the English-German transfer lexicon; this is quite natural in the case of 1:many transfers (see Knops/Thurmair 1992).

The second division of the lexica follows the subject areas. The lexica are divided into different modules to specify where a term belongs . The modules are organised in a hierarchy, starting from function words and general vocabulary, then specifying common social and common technical vocabulary, and then specifying different areas, like economics, law, public administration, computer science, etc. These subject areas can still be subdivided further, according to users' needs. This modular organisation does not just allow for interchange of lexicon modules; it also allows for better translations. Users can specify the modules to be used for a given translation, and the system picks the most specific transfers first.

Internally, the monolingual lexica are collections of features and values. Features describe phonetic, morphological, syntactic, and semantic properties of an entry. The transfer lexica describe conditions and actions for a given transfer entry to be applied. The number of entries of the lexica varies for the different languages; it lies between 20,000 and 100,000 citation forms.

It must be kept in mind that an MT lexicon entry differs considerably from a terminological entry which is basically designed for human readers (see Knops/Thurmair 1992 for a comparison). The challenge is to find common data structures and lexicon maintenance software to support both applications.

11.3.2 Analysis

METAL is a rule-based system. It applies rules for morphological and syntactic analysis.

The METAL rules have a phrase structure backbone which is augmented by features. Rules consist of several parts. A test section specifies under what conditions a rule can fire; conditions include tests on the presence or absence of features or structures or contexts. A construction section applies actions to a given structure; they consist of feature percolations, putting new features to a node, changing tree structures, and producing the canonical MIR structure for a given subnode. There are other rule parts as well, including rule type (morphological or syntactic), maintenance information (author, date, last editor) and comment and example fields.

The grammar itself uses a set of operators which perform the respective actions; it is a kind of language in itself. The operators are described in Thurmair (1991). METAL grammars comprise between 200 and 500 rules depending on their coverage.

The rules are applied by a standard active chart parser for the different grammars. If the grammar succeeds it delivers a well-formed MIR structure; if not, it tries a "fail soft" analysis and combines the most meaningful structures into an artificial top node.

There are three special issues to be mentioned:

Verb Argument treatment is always a critical issue, as often a verb can have several frames which have optional elements. It is difficult and time consuming to calculate all possible combinations between different frames and potential fillers. METAL uses special software to do the calculation. The frames for a verb are specified in the monolingual lexicon in a rather general way (which allows for interchanging this information with other lexica, cf. Adriaens 1992. Analysis uses sets of morphosyntactic and semantic tests to identify potential fillers for a given verb position (e.g.: verb takes an indirect object filled with a "that"-clause). Usually there are several candidates for a role filler; the computation of the most plausible is done by software. Again, all language-specific aspects are part of the lingware and maintained by the grammar writer; the software only does the calculation and is language independent.

Another area where METAL uses software support is **anaphor resolution**. Anaphors are identified following an extension of the algorithm of Hobbs, taking into account the different c-commanding relations of the different pronoun types. The anaphor resolution is called whenever a sentence could be parsed. It is also able to do extrasentential resolution. The anaphor nodes are marked with some relevant features of their antecedents.

With rather large grammars as in METAL, the danger exists that the system produces too many hypotheses and ambiguities which cause the system to explode. METAL avoids this danger by applying a preferencing and **scoring mechanism** which processes only the best hypotheses at a time. The score of a tree is calculated from the scores of its son nodes and the level of the rule which was fired to build it. Scoring is controlled by linguistics, by attaching levels to rules (indicating how successful a rule is in contributing to an overall parse), and by influencing the scores of trees explicitly in rules (see Caeyers 1990). During parsing, the scores are evaluated, and only the best hypotheses are processed further.

Robustness is always an issue for a system like METAL. It is tackled at several stages in the system:

- Unknown words are subject to special procedures which try to guess the linguistic properties of that word (like category, inflectional class, etc.). This is done using an online defaulting procedure (see Adriaens 1990).
- Ungrammatical constructions are partly covered by applying fallback rules for certain phenomena (like punctuation errors in relative clause constructions); the respective rules have lower levels than the "good" ones.
- If the parser fails, the system still tries to find the best partial interpretations of the input clause; this is under control of the linguists: they can apply default interpretations, basic word ordering criteria, etc.

The result of the analysis is a MIR tree which is defined in terms of precedence and dominance relations, and in terms of (obligatory and optional) features.

11.3.3 Transfer and Generation

This tree is transferred into the target language. Transfer contains three steps: Structural transfer transforms source language constructions into target language constructions; lexical transfer replaces nodes on the leaves of the tree by their target equivalents; and complex lexical transfer changes both structures and lexical units (e.g. in cases of verb arguments mappings, or argument incorporation; see examples in Thurmair 1990. Transfer again creates MIR trees.

These trees are the input to the generation component. Generation transforms them into proper surface trees, using the same formalism as the analysis component, in particular the tree-to-tree transformation capabilities. As a result, properly inflected forms can be found at the terminal leaves of the trees; they are collected and transformed into the output string.

11.3.4 Productivity Tools

In order to support the translation kernel, METAL has developed sets of tools for lexicon and grammar development and maintenance.

The basic coding tool is called **Intercoder**. It allows for fast and user-friendly coding of new entries. It applies defaulting strategies to pre-set most parts of lexical entries; it presents the entries via examples rather than abstract coding features. As a result, users need only click on the items to select or deselect them. Internally, the intercoder consists of a language-independent software kernel; the language-specific coding window systems are controlled by tables which are interpreted by the software kernel.

In addition to the Intercoder, METAL offers several tools for **lexicon maintenance**. Among them are consistency checking routines (does every mono have its transfer and target entry?), import/export facilities, merging routines which resolve conflicts between lexical entries, lexicon querying facilities, and others.

For grammar development, a system called **METALSHOP** has been developed. It allows for editing, deleting, changing rules, for inspection of the chart during analysis, for rule tracing and stepping, for tree drawing and comparison, for node inspection, and others. It also supports suites of benchmark texts and automatic comparison of the results.

These productivity tools are indispensible in an industrial development of large-scale natural language developements. Otherwise there will never be a return on investment for this kind of system.

11.4 METAL and TWB

Although METAL was not developed inside TWB, the interrelations are numerous.

11.4.1 System Architecture

From a strategic point of view, a real translator's workbench will have an MT system as one of its components. The workbench will be flexible enough to decide when MT can be used effectively (there are many cases where it is superiour to human translation both in speed and accuracy), and when other ways of translation have to be preferred. From this point of view, distinctions like HAMT, FAMT, MAHT, etc. are obsolete. The translators have a collection of tools, an MT system being one of them, and decide themselves when to apply which tools. In this respect, a system like METAL is logically a part of TWB.

11.4.2 Remote Access

In TWB itself, a **remote access facility** to METAL has been implemented. This shows that the project is aware of the fact that MT must be an integral part of a translator's workbench. METAL was chosen as an example because it fitted best to the overall TWB philosophy, because it was available, and because of its embedding into the document production environment.

In order to be open and to follow standards, the communication between the TWB system and METAL is done through standard X.400 electronic mail. For this reason, an X.400 system (based on the results of the CACTUS ESPRIT project) has been integrated in both TWB and METAL systems. A special X.400 user agent that interacts with the MT-System has been developed and interfaced with METAL (through "X-Metal"). The role of this user agent, installed in the MT system side, is to receive X.400 messages from outside, and to generate replies back with the translated document.

The use of ODA/ODIF to send documents to MT systems guarantees the standardization of the input and output formats, and it allows a translation to be produced with the same structure and format as the source text (see Chap. 7 for more detailed information).

As a result, it turned out that remote access has its obstacles and requires additional efforts to deliver productive translations:

- There must an operating service at the other side of the line, i.e. a translation office which runs the remote translations effectively, deciding which translations should be done how, controlling the process, etc. To set up such a service was beyond the intentions of TWB.
- A problem for remote access is lexicon update. Users want to use their own terminology which is often customer- or even product-specific. Standard translations from a mass term lexicon usually do not suffice. A remote service must be able to offer at least some lexicon downloading functionality; but this also means offering local lexicon coding tools. This kind of organisation needs further considerations.
- Finally, the restriction to X.400 lines and ODIF converters is an obstacle to a remote service as it restricts the number of potential clients considerably.

In conclusion, for casual users, a remote translation facility can be attractive. In a professional Translator's Workbench, however, a MT system should be integrated locally (or as a server in a local network), both for reasons of availability of such a tool and of integration into the documentation and the terminological environment. Nobody can accept a situation where different lexica have to be maintained for human and machine translation processes.

11.4.3 Re-use of METAL components

Moreover, the METAL analysis components have been re-used in other TWB components, like in a grammar checker for Spanish, and in a Verifier of Controlled Grammars for German. This shows that well-developed natural language resources can effectively be ported to other applications; it is an encouraging example of the re-usability of lingware.

Those components are described below in more detail.

The availability of a system like METAL has improved the productivity of TWB, both in terms of functionality and in terms of re-usability. Instead of writing yet another grammar and lexicon, we were able to concentrate on tasks which presupposed the existence of those components.

12. Translation Memory

Antonius van Hoof, Bernhard Keck, Renate Mayer, Marianne Kugler, Cornelia Menzel

12.1 Introduction

The development of fully-automatic high-quality machine translation has a long and chequered history. In spite of the extensive amount of protracted research effort on this topic the ultimate goal still lies very far beyond the horizon, and no substantial break-throughs are in the offing.

Today's machine translation (MT) systems have a reasonable performance in very restricted subject areas, translate texts with a restricted grammatical coverage. However, most of the existing MT systems cannot live up to the needs and expectations, both in quality and costs, of an ever growing market for translations. In Europe alone, several million of pages per year are being translated. The future European integration, through the EC, will certainly lead to an impressive increase of this figure, making translation more and more a serious cost factor in product development and sales.

The translation of technical documentation, manuals, and user instructions comprises the bulk of work in most translation departments and bureaus. One of the most striking characteristics of such texts is that there is a degree of similarity amongst this type of text. Moreover, as we found out in a specially commissioned survey by TWB (Fulford et al. 1990), many of these texts are translated more than once, because new versions of these texts become necessary as the documented product alters. The original version of the text is often difficult to locate, and even when traced, pin-pointing the differences between both versions and the appropriate editing of the translation is a labourious and time-consuming task. There are no tools that effectively support translators in this task and very often a completely new translation is considered to be a reasonable alternative.

The frequent translation of documents which are similar in content clearly indicates the need for a translation aid system which makes previously translated texts or parts of texts directly available, without the user having to expend much effort. We claim the Translation Memory to be such a system.

Translation Memory is more than a system that just stores and retrieves texts. It collects and applies statistical data from translated text, builds stochastic models for source and target language (SL and TL), and for the transfer (the translation) between these SL and TL models. The Translation Memory system displays a 'cumulative learning behaviour': once the stochastic models have been developed on a small sample of texts, the system's performance improves as it is exposed to more text. This exposure helps the stochastic models to automatically expand their coverage. Due to this approach the system can not only retrieve/re-translate old sentences, but can even translate sentences that never have been input before, provided that their components (words or phrases) have already occurred in previously stored texts. As a result, system performance is dependent on the scope and quality of the existing database and is expected to improve as the database grows.

In the following we will discuss the state of the art in statistical machine translation and will then present our approach. Next we will describe the implemented system followed by first results of the system in use.

We will conclude this chapter by briefly discussing future work on the Translation Memory.

12.2 State of the Art

The first studies in the field of machine translation (MT) were conducted in the late 1940s. Early research in this field had been influenced by information theory, an area which Claude Shannon and Warren Weaver were developing at that time. One of the historically important documents is the "Weaver's Memorandum" of 1949 (Weaver 1949), in which Warren Weaver expressed the opinion that a large number of problems of machine translation could be solved by the application of statistical methods. He believed that word ambiguities might be resolved by taking into account the immediate context of the words.

Weaver's optimism was partly confirmed in the years following. In the 1950s, a number of research groups concentrated on the application of statistical analysis to MT. Their success was very limited, particularly due to the rather slow and limited computer hardware and due to a lack of large machine readable text corpora, which act as a source of statistical data vital to such an approach.

The statistical approach was to become practical non-existant (until quite recently) after the publication of Chomsky's revolutionary work on transformational generative grammar (Chomsky 1956 and Chomsky 1957). In (Chomsky 1956) Chomsky proved that no finite state grammar - a category to which statistical models like Markov models belong - is capable of generating a language containing an infinite set of grammatical strings while excluding the ungrammatical ones. He argued that a grammar unable to generate all and only the grammatical sentences of a language would be of no further empirical interest.

In the 1970-80s, the use of statistical methods became a broadly accepted and successful practice in the field of speech recognition. A good example of a statistics based system is the well-known speech recognition system developed at the IBM T.J. Watson Research Center, which is probably the most advanced system today and employs a Markovian language model that is an order three approximation to English (Bahl et al. 1983).

The process of speech recognition can be viewed as a translation of symbols of one language (acoustic signals) to symbols of another (character strings). Therefore, it is not surprising that the same research group around F. Jelinek recently started the investigation of applying these statistical methods to machine translation. The general conditions for it are favourable as well: today, computers are several orders of magnitude faster and with larger memories than those in the 1950s, and large bi-lingual text corpora are available as well.

The approach and first results of the IBM research group have been presented by Brown (1988 and 1990). It appears that translation is regarded as a three-staged process:

1. partitioning of the source text into a set of fixed locutions;
2. using a glossary plus contextual information to select the corresponding set of fixed locutions in the target language;

3. arranging the words of the target fixed locutions into a sequence that forms the target sentence.

"Fixed locutions" may be single words as well as phrases consisting of contiguous or non-contiguous words. Although the papers present many fruitful ideas with regard to stage 1 of the process, they do not (yet) describe to the same extent their ideas and solutions for the further stages.

An important aspect of Brown et al.'s approach is that all the statistical information is extracted fully automatically from a large bi-lingual text corpus. Brown et al. have argued that it is possible to find the fixed locutions by extracting a model that generates TL words from SL words. Such a model uses probabilities that describe a primary generation process (i.e. production of a TL word by a SL word), a secondary generation process (production of a TL word by another TL word), and some restrictions on positional discrepancy of the words within a sentence. This gives rise to a very large number of different probabilities, and the automatic extraction of these probabilities seems to be computationally very expensive and requires highly advanced parameter estimation methods and a very large amount of corresponding translated training text. For the construction of the contextual glossary for stage 2, one would need all these probabilities plus, of course, some new ones, all of which result in the production of glossary probabilities.

Despite the large number of unsolved problems, first experiments of French to English translation of the IBM group have shown promising results. With a 1,000 words English lexicon and 1,700 words French lexicon (the most frequently used words in the corpus) they estimated the 17 million parameters of the translation model from 117,000 pairs of sentences that were fully covered by the lexica. The parameters of the English bigram language model were estimated from 570,000 sentences from the English part of the corpus. In translating 73 new French sentences from the corpus they claimed to be successful 48% of the time. In those cases where the translation was not successful, it proved to be quite easy to correct the faulty translation by human post-editing, thus all in all reducing the work of human translators by about 60%.

12.3 The TWB Approach

Following the approach of the IBM research group, we divide the translation process into three stages: (i) analysis of the input SL sentence; (ii) transfer to the target language; (iii) synthesis of the TL sentence. For all three stages we apply statistical models. But our models differ from theirs in complexity: this is due to our strategy of not going for fully automatic parameter extraction. We did not start from a large corpus, but expect the user (the translator) to "train" the system in the course of inputting freshly translated texts into the Translation Memory. The system thus relies to some extent on the user to resolve the potential word ambiguities that the system might encounter in the analysis of the input SL and TL sentence equivalences. In our opinion, this interaction is acceptable, provided the number of such problems is kept at a low level. Our expectation is that this number will decrease as the number of trained input translations grows.

12.3.1 The Language Models

The Translation Memory creates and makes use of identical language models both for modelling the source language and the target language. These language models consist of:

- the single probabilities for each word $P(s_i)$,
- the digram probabilities $P(s_i \mid s_j)$, that the word s_i follows immediately after the word s_j, and
- the trigram probabilities of the form $P(s_k \mid s_i, s_j)$, that the word s_k follows immediately after the sequence s_i, s_j.

These probabilities can be estimated by counting the respective relative frequencies from the trained input sentences. Note that a model which is defined by trigram-probabilities is in fact a Markov model of order three. The digram-probabilities and the single probabilities define Markov models of order two and one respectively.

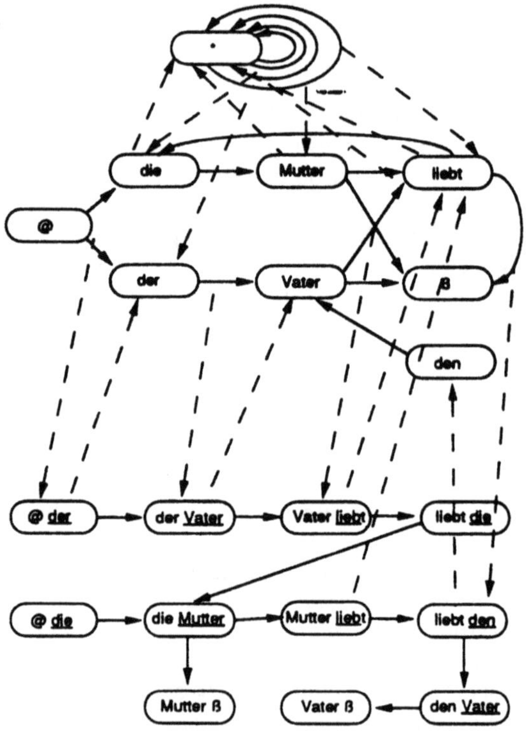

Fig. 30: Language model by integration of Markov models of different order

Thus the language models of the Translation Memory are in fact models that are an integration of Markov models of different order. The connections between the models of different order are equivalent to the application of two rules:

(1) After a transition in a Markov model of order m, the process changes state to the Markov model of order m+1 without producing additional output, provided that there is a Markov model of order m+1. This state in the Markov model of order m+1 is uniquely defined by the transition in the Markov model of order m.

(2) If a proper path in a Markov model of order m (that corresponds to a given sentence, for example) cannot be found for reasons of lack of training data, the process changes state to the Markov model of order m-1. The state in the Markov model of order m-1 is defined by cutting off (deleting) the first word of the string that defines the state in the Markov model of order m.

Figure 30 shows the principle of a model that integrates a Markov model of order three with a corresponding model of order two and one of order one (The figure only shows the transitions, not the probabilities attached to them). The order-one model indicates that any transition from some word in the lexicon to any other word in that lexicon is possible in this order model. The special symbols α and β are markers for begin and end of string. The dashed arrows indicate some of the possible state transitions that do not produce output but are used to change the order of the model.

If we would have to find the path in this integrated model that corresponds to the string

"α *die Mutter liebt der Vater* β",

we would find that the word "*der*" cannot be produced by a transition to any successor state of the order-3-state defined by "*Mutter liebt*". Thus we have to decrease order and change to the state in the Markov model of order two that is defined by the word "*liebt*". We find once more that "*der*" cannot be generated by any transition from the order-2-state "*liebt*". Therefore we change state to the only state of the order-one Markov model. Now, there is a transition in the order-one-model, that produces "*der*", because this word is contained in the lexicon. After this production the process automatically changes state to the order-2-state defined by the word "*der*". This state has a transition to produce "*Vater*" and, moreover, leads to a non-productive state transition to order-3-state "*der Vater*". Since there is no corresponding transition from this state to produce "β", we have to reduce order again and go back to order-2-state "*Vater*", find from there an order-2-transition to "β", and end with an order transition to order-3-state "*Vater* β".

12.3.2 The Transfer Glossary

The connection between SL and TL models is provided by the transfer glossary, the entries of which take into consideration not only the context of SL words but also possible contexts of the corresponding TL words. The defined structure of the glossary will be seen to excellently fit to the structure of the integrated Markov models of source and target language as proposed above.

The transfer glossary is based on both single word and multiple words unit probabilities. The first are of the form

$$P(t_i, \psi[t_i, T] \mid s_i, \psi[s_i, S])$$

that the SL word s_l, which meets the contextual conditions defined by $\psi[s_l, S]$, is translated by the TL word t_i, provided that t_i complies with the TL contextual conditions defined by $\psi[t_i, T]$, where S denotes the SL sentence we are translating and T the corresponding TL sentence we are generating as a translation for S. This first form is valid for the most frequent case that one TL word corresponds to one SL word. The second form of probabilities, treating multi-word correspondences, consists of entries

$$P(t_i, \psi[t_i, T], ..., t_k, \psi[t_k, T] \mid s_l, \psi[s_l, S], ..., s_n, \psi[s_n, S])$$

that the SL words $s_l, ..., s_n$ are translated by the TL words $t_i, ..., t_k$, provided that the respective contextual conditions are satisfied. Since SL and TL units do not have to contain the same number of words, we are thus in a position to appropriately align SL and TL sentences of unequal length.

The contextual conditions of a word s_l or t_i are defined by zero, one or two predecessor words. Thus the glossary establishes connections between the single, bigram and trigram probabilities of the connected language models.

Figure 31 illustrates the transfer in a rather simplified model. Having an order-2 model for both SL (English) and TL (German), some of the transfer probabilities are indicated by the dashed arrows (or rather, that such probabilities are contained in the transfer glossary, since we did not indicate quantities on those arrows)Generating a TL sentence from a SL sentence thus amounts to solving a complex constraint satisfaction problem. This will be relatively easy for sentence pairs that the Translation Memory has been trained with in the past, since the "correct" applicable probabilities are already contained in the complex translation model. But the same procedure can be used to translate completely new sentences (i.e. strings the Translation Memory has not been trained with). Given a well-trained model, these translations will turn out to be quite acceptable, although a human translator might need to post-edit them.

12.4 A Brief Description of the Implemented System

The Translation Memory has been implemented, like the other programs within the TWB project, on a SUN workstation running UNIX and OSF-MOTIF. The Translation Memory comprises a number of autonomous modules (this autonomy allows the stand-alone use of the modules):

(1) **sth:** the standard program by which a user can interactively make translations or train/update the system's databases;
(2) **sthback:** a program for batch mode translation of texts;
(3) **sthtra**: similar to sth, but comprises interactive translation only;
(4) **sthlearn**: similar to sth, but comprises training/data aquisition only.

There are two other programs:

(5) **sthini**: to initialize the databases for a language pair, and
(6) **sthunlock**: to unlock databases when the system did not terminate in the ordinary way.

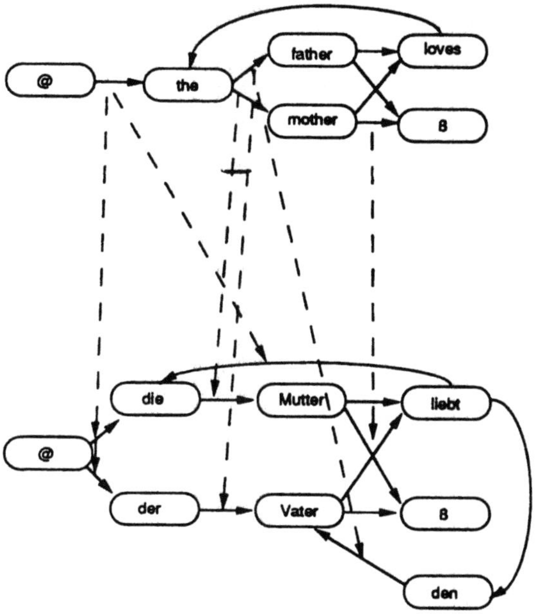

Fig. 31: Transfer glossary - an integration of SL and TL Markov models

Since the databases containing all the statistical information are of vital importance for the system, extreme care was taken to secure them against data loss, owing to unexpected system terminations.

In the following, we will briefly discuss the **sth** programm, since it shows the basic functionality (translation and training) of the system.

When starting the program, the user uses a window in which he or she has to specify some basic information: the databases to use for training/translation; the SL and TL textfiles he or she wants to operate on. If needed, the user can get access to a further parameter settings dialogue, in which he or she can set parameters both concerning the editor (initial cursor position, window width, scrollbars, highlighting of non-input-focus areas, and automatic selection/highlighting of the next sentence after a call to the tranlation or data aquisition routines) and can access information concerning the behaviour of the translation routine (whether to prefix unkown words with "*", whether the program is allowed to shift the order of SL or TL model, the number of search steps is maximally allowed, and whether or not it should ignore context in the transfer phase, thus providing the user with the possibility to generate a poor, but extremely fast word-by-word translation) and thus the quality of the translation. All these settings can be saved and be used as defaults for future program calls.

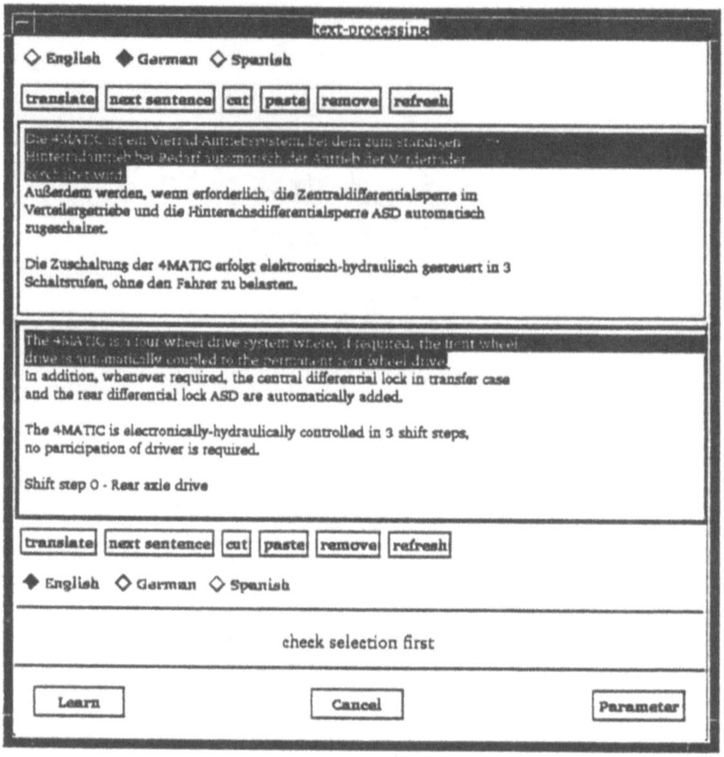

Fig. 32: The translation memory built-in editor

After this confirmatory dialogue, the user interacts with an editor (see Fig. 32) that is split into two areas, each of which contains the chosen SL or TL textfiles respectively. The editor is WIMPS based and has a number of buttons. With the button "*next sentence*" the user can select/highlight the next sentence from the actual cursor position in that area.When a sentence is selected and the "*translate*" button is pushed, the system generates a translation for this sentence that will be inserted in the text of the other area at its cursor position. The other buttons have standard editorial functionality. The "*Parameter*" button leads to the additional parameter settings dialogue discussed above. "*Cancel*" terminates the program.The "*Learn*" button can only be used when a string (not necessarily a sentence) is selected in both text areas. This button is located outside the above areas because the data acquisition routine performs parameter estimation in both directions, thus building and refining - apart from the integrated models for both languages - a *transfer glossary for both directions*. Thus, the Translation Memory can perform translations in both directions on the basis of the very same databases.

When the "*Learn*" button is pushed, the data acquisition routine first refines the data models for the SL and TL on the basis of the changed relative frequencies. If the data acquisition routine encounters unknown words it asks the user whether it should store the words in the database.

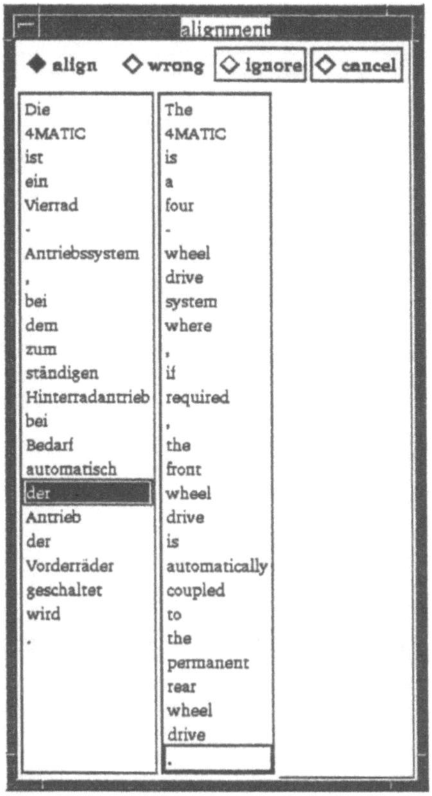

Fig. 33: The alignment window

After the refinement of the language data models, the routine has to estimate the transfer parameters. To be able to do this the system has to align the respective selected strings. To the extent that it has information on previous aligments of words occurring in the strings, the data acquisition routine can do this automatically. Where this information fails, the routine interacts with the user in a so-called alignment dialogue (Fig. 33), in which the user can indicate both single-word and multi-word correspondences. Before updating the databases the routine presents the user with a confirmation dialogue (Fig. 34)that shows the unit correspondences in both translation directions. The user can confirm these, in which case the databases will be updated accordingly, or the user can indicate that the correspondences are wrong, in which case he or she will again be presented with the alignment dialogue. During the execution of the program the database updates have a temporary status. Only when the user wants to exit the program these updates are made permanent. Thus, the user has the possibility to "undo" the data aquisition of a given session. Furthermore, in case of an unexpected system termination the databases will not be corrupted, something which is of vital importance for a stochastic system.

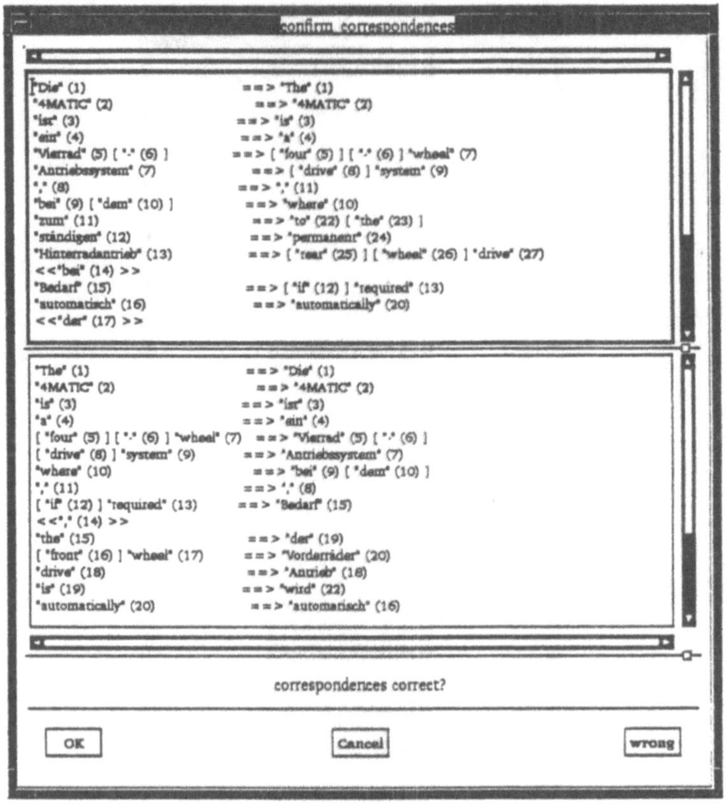

Fig. 34: The confirm correspondences window

12.5 Evaluation of the Translation Memory - First Results After Training Spanish-German, Spanish-English, German-English

12.5.1 Training the Translation Memory

At the time of this evaluation, the Translation Memory had been trained with eight texts from the book *Wie man mühelos in fünf Sprachen korrespondieren kann* (Heidelberg: Decker & Müller). Training was carried out on all the three language pairs German-English, Spanish-German and Spanish-English.

In order to understand differences in training, some characteristics of each language will be discussed before dealing with different aspects of training for these three pairs and for translating with the resulting databases .

Characteristics of the languages trained

German is a highly inflected language. Nouns are inflected and there are four cases. There are a great number of compound nouns. In German, compounds of originally two separate nouns are written as one word, thus constituting a new noun. The usual order of adjectives and the nouns they modify is: adjective-noun.

Verbs are conjugated into a number of tenses and moods. There also are separable verbs. They consist of the verb proper and another part, which can become separated from the verb, forming a bracket. Thus there may be other parts of speech occurring between the verb and the other part (e.g. "einlladen -> ich lade meine Freunde ein"). The same may happen between a modal verb and a full verb.

German phrasing in business matters is characterized by verbosity and complication in certain phrases, especially some of those used in touchy situations.

Spanish also is inflected, but to a lesser degree, since nouns are not subjected to inflections. Instead of relying on inflection, Spanish employs prepositions. Being the members of a closed set, there are only a few prepositions, so each can occur in a great number of situations and contexts. The order of adjectives and the nouns they modify is more often noun-adjective, rarely adjective-noun.

Spanish has one interesting feature the two other languages, ie English and German, do not have. The personal pronoun has to be connected with the infinitive of the verb in certain cases. Example: "No es posible facilitarles ..." which means: "It is not possible to give you ..." The indirect object ("you = les") is written as one word with the infinitive "to give".

Verbs are inflected as much as German verbs. However, in Spanish "complicated" tenses and moods, like the subjunctive and future are used much more than in German and British English/American English. Compared to German, the Spanish language also offers a high number of verbose phrases in addition to some complications, such as the use of the gerund which is rather typical for a language so closely related to Latin.

English is less inflected than Spanish or German. Like Spanish, it relies heavily on the use of prepositions. Composite nouns are written as two words, whereby each retains its own character. The usual order of adjective and noun is adjective-noun.

English verbs, theoretically, know the same number and almost the same kinds of tenses and moods as those of the other two languages. But in English the "excessive" use of the more "complicated" tenses and moods is avoided. In the English texts there were less phrases of great verbosity, phrases were shorter compared to the other two languages.

12.5.2 Comparison of Training the Different Languages

Training the Spanish-English pair was much easier than that of the Spanish-German and English-German pairs. The reasons for this lie in the differences between the languages some of which were explained above. One of the problems encountered with the Spanish-German pair was that some phrases were too verbose to be encoded in a meaningful way. In order to judge on "meaningful" training the following strategy was taken: grouping of source and target language words/word groups should be done in a way that would yield only acceptable translations when the word/word group should occur in another environment.

One problem was, that the Translation Memory in its present implementation can only handle so many secondaries to a "kernel" word, ie the length of a phrase to be used as a undividable unit is restricted. In some cases a sentence had to be changed slightly in order to obtain one that would not force the user to encode it in a meaningless way. The new sentences probably were not quite as polite as the original ones but still represented the same meaning.

In training the Spanish-English pair, it was often very easy to establish one-to-one correspondences. This situation was pleasing but a note of caution is due here. It leads one to encode the sentence or phrase with one-to-one correspondences right away before considering which words it would be sensible to encode in groups first. This leads to some severe errors later when actual translations are made. Some adjectives just occur often with certain words and some nouns often combine to make a composite noun. If these adjectives and nouns are not at first encoded as fixed combinations, they turn up in the wrong order in the translations or, even worse, a different word is chosen which usually should not occur in this particular combination. Thus it is better to first encode phrases as phrases and later break them down into smaller parts if necessary. This will ensure better quality of translation.

12.5.3 The Optimal Translation Parameters

In order to determine the translation behaviour of the system, and the degree to which it is influenced by its parameters, two fairly extreme sets of parameters were tested. The idea was to test the translation quality of the database on the same text(s) and look for changes, newly introduced errors etc. with the different parameter sets. When doing test translations in between the training of two texts, the following two sets of parameters were applied:

Simple:

simple method,
no check of neighbours,
max length of list: 20,
no context reduction,
max number of search steps: 2000.

Complex:

standard method,
check one neighbour,
max length of list: 30,
reduce context once,
max number of search steps: 5000.

The "simple" parameters represent a fairly limited search space, i.e. a short list, and comparatively small number of search steps. The complex parameters have a larger search space, and additionally more context information to check.

English-German

For the pair English-German only one test text was used. It contained sentences which were almost entirely taken from the phrases of the annual report of an enterprise but were a little modified and contained some unknown words.

Looking at the simple parameter translation, we see that the quantity of translation improved: that is to say, more of the unknown words were translated with growing size. On the other hand, there was a decrease in the quality of the translation.

One problem is the use of the determiner. In English there is only "the" and "a", but in German there are "der, die, das, dieser, diese, dieses, ein, eine" and so on. Therefore, with the growing size of the database the use of determiners became more often incorrect.

Comparing the translations under simple parameters with those under complex parameters, word order seems to come out with a higher degree of correctness under the simple parameters.

Spanish-English and Spanish-German

For the pairs Spanish-German and Spanish-English, two test texts were employed. The first one ("sptest1.txt") was like the test text for English-German. The second test text ("sptest2.txt") was a letter containing words, phrases and sentences from all eight texts listed above. It contained at least one sentence or phrase from each text.

By and large, there were no big differences between the translations offered under the two different sets of parameters. But each set has its own virtues and drawbacks. Under the simple parameters the syntax followed that of the source language, whereas the complex parameters often turned out a sentence structure that was more appropriate in the target language. The complex parameters, for example, were able to handle the distance between a modal verb and the main verb that we often find in German sentences. On the other hand, sometimes the complex parameters could not find a rather simple word like "hemos = we have" which had occured often enough in training, although maybe not in this particular combination.

So while the simple parameters sometimes turn out sentences that are a little jumbled, the complex parameters tend to be "overcautious" and rather turn out nothing at all for seemingly simple words.

As the training proceeded, certain changes appeared. A rather complex phrase "Las actas fueron levantadas por Sr. Meyer" (German:"Für die Protokollführung war Herr Meyer verantwortlich.") which had been trained with the first text was forgotten as soon as the second text was trained. It probably was too complex to be recognized even under the complex parameters. Prepositions and articles tended to change as more texts were trained which, of course, is due to the quantitative approach that is employed in the TM. So "an order" became "a order", "at the moment" became "by the moment", and so forth. This happened in both language pairs respectively. These "mistakes" will probably have to be detected by a grammar checker.

There should be some more experimentation with different parameter configurations before final judgment is passed on. Maybe, there is an even better configuration yet to be found.

There does not seem to be any grave difference of quality between the translations from Spanish to German and from Spanish to English. The quality of the translation naturally depends on the quality of the training the database has received. And, of course, it depends on how close the text to be translated is to what the database has been trained with.

12.5.4 Improvements in the New Releases

Suggested Improvements of the User Interface

The user interface of the translation memory is still very minimal. As it is a prototype to be reimplemented on the DOS platform, the user interface will be rewritten completely. Therefore, critical points like use of scrollbars, user interface language, etc. will be treated properly in the new environment.

Essential facilities for correct training

The missing UNDO facility is crucial and critical to TM's operation. It very easily leads to severe mistakes in the databases. The following two functions are vital for good training:

- Undo-function to remove a correspondence from the database, which has been entered by mistake, or to correct one that has turned out to be impractical.
- A kind of delete-from-storage function to delete words that were wrongly stored, contain typing errors, or are not needed.

Still, in the planned DOS network version only properly qualified people should be allowed to add to the databases to prevent uncontrolled expansion and insertion of untested material. The distinction between public and private terminology should thus be carried into the area of the translation memory as well.

Functional Improvement

The lack of morphological and grammatical information is a serious limitation of the system in its present state. The relevant knowledge about the grammatical structure of sentences is already available, (see Chap. 16). As the cohesion of words within phrases, e.g. within a noun phrase, is much stronger and thus statistically much more significant than the cohesion at phrase boundaries, a restriction of training to phrases only could lead to a considerable reduction of data base size with very little loss of performance. The integration of morphological information can provide a fall-back position for the translation where the inflected word is not known. In the follow-up project we will try to follow one or more of these strategies of optimization.

12.6 Future Outlook

The future of Translation Memory as a marketable product appears promising. To this end there are a series of actions that we plan to undertake to make it into such a product.

First, since most potential users of the system (both translation bureaus and freelance translators) work on PC platforms, the Translation Memory will be ported to DOS and be integrated into a standard word processing environment. For this we envisage an integration into Word for Windows. We will also use this opportunity of porting the system to MS Windows for redesigning the user interface of the system, especially to ease the process of data-acquisition.

Second, since well trained Translation Memory databases are expected to accumulate up to Gigabytes of probabilistic data, we think that it is important to look for ways for compressing this information considerably, notwithstanding the fact that cost of external computer memory is falling steadily.

Third, although the synthesis of target language sentences is quite reasonable in many cases, the percentage of reasonable productions decreases as SL and TL are more different in the way they organize their word order. The linguistic issue of so-called long distance dependencies plays here a role as well. To improve the quality of translation we want to look into possibilities to integrate information on these issues into the models. As a further help to the user the system might provide him with translation alternatives from which he then can choose the (most) adequate one.

All these issues were brought into the proposal for a continuation of the TWB project in the new phase of ESPRIT.

12.7 Annex A: Growth of the Databases

After the training of each text the current values of the databases were saved.

The databases of all three pairs of languages grew in a similar fashion and would show almost identical curves. The sizes of the databases (in Bytes) were:

after 1 text (M, 79 sentences = ca. 13%)

	ge_en:	en_ge:	sp_en:	en_sp:	sp_ge:	ge_sp:
.com:	68096	68096	68096	68096	68096	68096
.dbm:	30720	26624	30720	26624	32768	32788
.nod:	9208	9280	10112	9480	9792	9296
.wor:	2226	1525	1877	1516	1893	2230

after 4 texts (287 sentences = ca. 48%)

	ge_en:	en_ge:	sp_en:	en_sp:	sp_ge:	ge_sp:
.com:	172544	172544	172544	172544	172544	172544
.dbm:	63488	53248	67584	47104	65536	63488
.nod:	31192	30592	34136	31264	33632	31288
.wor:	6326	4615	5849	4540	5934	6383

after 8 texts (597 sentences = 100%)

	ge_en:	en_ge:	sp_en:	en_sp:	sp_ge:	ge_sp:
.com:	311808	311808	311808	311808	311808	311808
.dbm:	90112	67584	92160	75776	92160	81920
.nod:	57568	55504	61208	56488	59920	57064
.wor:	10128	7193	9613	7103	9679	10079

12.8 Annex B: An Example of Training

Some examples of how the training is performed:

E: we must reckon with a slight decrease in production.

S: debemos contar con una ligera disminucioxon en la produccioxon.

In the first round the following correspondences were made:

("we")must("reckon")("with")	=	debemos("contar")("con")
("a")("slight")decrease	=	("una")("ligera")disminucion
("in")production	=	("en")("la")produccion
.	=	.

Then some phrases and words were trained on their own:

a)("we")must	=	debemos
b) with	=	con
c) slight	=	ligera
decrease	=	disminucion

E: Please let us know the maximum quantity you can supply immedately.

G: Bitte teilen Sie uns die größte Menge mit, die Sie sofort liefern können.

First round:

Please	=	Bitte
let("us")("know")	=	teilen("Sie")("uns")("mit")
("the")("maximum")quantity	=	("die")("größte")Menge
("you")("can")supply("")immediately	=	("die")("Sie")("sofort")liefern("können")
.	=	.

Then:

a) maximum	=	größte
b) quantity	=	Menge

c) supply	=	liefern
d) immediately	=	sofort
d) können	=	can

S: parece que Vds. conocen la empresa desde hace tiempo.

G: wir glauben, daß Sie die Firma seit einiger Zeit kennen.

First round:

parece("que")	=	("wir")glauben(",")("daß")
Vds.	=	Sie
conocen	=	kennen
("la")empresa	=	("die")Firma
("desde")("hace")tiempo	=	("seit")("einiger")Zeit
.	=	.

Then:

a) empresa	=	Firma
b) tiempo	=	Zeit

13. Extended Termbank Information

Kurt Kohn, Michaela Albl

A terminological database aiming to be relevant for translation purposes has to be designed to meet the specific needs translators have when trying to solve terminological problems of source-text comprehension and target-text production. Otherwise, it will be of only limited use, as is evident from the sometimes harsh criticism termbanks and specialist dictionaries provoke among professional translators (cf. Lothholz 1986). Considering the procedural complexity of the translation task, the diversity of LSP-conventions, and the strategic creativity of real-life communication, the specific demands on a translation-oriented termbank cannot be accommodated by the rigid and narrow termbank structures developed for standardization purposes. What is needed is a termbank design reflecting the descriptive needs translators have when being confronted with terminological problems of source-text comprehension and target-text production (cf. Albl et al. 1990; Albl et al. 1991; Kohn 1990b).

13.1 Unilingual and Language-Pair Specific Information

A term bank for translation purposes clearly needs to be language-pair specific and uni-directional; but it should also allow for efficient extension procedures with respect to languages and language directions. These seemingly conflicting requirements can be met if a distinction is made between unilingual information and transfer information.

Unilingual terminological information is not specific to a particular language-pair nor indeed to translation at all. It refers to the knowledge of a competent speaker who knows the language, the domain and the textual conventions of the relevant LSP texts, and it is relevant for anyone who needs to use terms in the comprehension and production of texts. Transfer information, in contrast, refers to language-pairs; it is uni-directional and translation-specific in that it is information required for making the transition from one language to the other. It consists of transfer equivalents, i.e. suggestions for translating the source language term, and transfer comments providing additional information to assist translators' in making an appropriate translational decision between alternative transfer equivalents.

In order to add new transfer directions for existing language-pairs, the unilingual information remains intact, and only the relevant transfer information has to be adapted anmd extended. In the case of the inclusion of additional languages, both the language-specific unilingual information pertaining to the new languages and the respective language-pair specific transfer information have to be integrated.

13.2 Types of Terminological Information

Developing a termbank intended to cater for the informational and procedural needs of a translator is a rather complex process which should better be broken down into managable steps. During a first phase of the project, development and implementation concentrated on the core termbank basically covering the following categories: domain, grammar, elaboration (i.e. meaning definitions and context examples), usage, collocation, and equivalents (i.e. synonyms, transfer equivalents). The extended termbank, further developed and implemented during the second phase of the project, includes additional information categories considered to be of particular relevance in the translation context: transfer and synonym comment, encyclopaedia, hierarchy, and word family.

As the main burden of developing and implementing the extended termbank version is in connection with the integration of transfer comments and encyclopaedic information, these categories will be discussed at greater length.

13.3 Transfer Comments

Transfer comments are linked up to source language terms by means of a many-to-many relation; they appear automatically whenever the user looks up a source language term and asks for transfer equivalents. Transfer comments help the translator to bridge the translational gap between the source language/text and the target language/text. They draw the translator's attention to subtle and/or confusing differences in the meaning and usage of transfer equivalents, they explain culturally bound pecu?liarities, and they also provide warnings of common mistakes and false friends.

Transfer comments are sensitive to the direction of translation. This is illustrated by the English term control and the various compound terms for which it can stand in a text, e.g., control system, feedback control (system), closed loop control (system), open loop control (system).

TRANSFER COMMENT related to the English terms control and control system (simplified version):

Transferäquivalente:

engl. feedback control (system)	dt. Regelung (Regelkreis)
engl. closed loop control (system)	dt. Regelung (Regelkreis)
engl. open loop control (system)	dt. Steuerung (Steuerkette)

Wird im englischen Text eine der Mehrwortbenennungen durch die Kurzform control ersetzt, so kann es bei der Übersetzung ins Deutsche zu einem Transferproblem kommen. Aus dem (Text-) Zusammenhang muß erschlossen werden, ob eine Regelung oder eine Steuerung gemeint ist.
(-> EU: REGELUNG UND STEUERUNG DER GEMISCHBILDUNG BEI OTTOMOTOREN) Im Falle von control system ist entsprechend zu klären, ob es

Fig. 35: Transfer comment example ("control system")

What is crucial here is the distinction between closed loop (or feedback) control (dt. Regelung) and open loop control (dt. Steuerung). In a German text it is either Regelung or Steuerung; therefore, the translation into English should create no particular problem. This is quite different, however, when translating from English into German. In English texts, the short form control is used quite often without any precise indication of the type of control (open or closed loop). The direction-specific transfer comment provides information to help the translator, first to become aware of the problem, second to determine the intended reference, and third to select an appropriate equivalent.

Stylistic discrepancies between the two languages may also call for a transfer comment. The English term stoichiometry, for instance, does not belong to the same part of speech as its German transfer equivalents. An appropriate translation may therefore require an extensive restructuring of the original phrase.

TRANSFER COMMENT related to the Englisch terms stoichiometry, lambda (simplified version) (cf. Fig. 36):

Transferäquivalente:

engl. stoichiometry	dt.	stöchiometrischer Punkt
	dt.	bei stöchiometrischem Mischungs-verhältnis,
	dt.	bei einem Luft-Kraftstoff Verhältnis von lambda = 1

Der Terminus stöchiometrie gehört zur Fachsprache der Chemie und wird im Deutschen in der Fachsprache der Katalysatortechnik nicht als Äquivalent für stoichiometry verwendet.

Übersetzungen auf der Basis von lambda = 1 können allerdings grammatikalische oder stilistische Probleme aufwerfen, da lambda = 1 nicht modifiziert werden kann. Adverbiale Modifikationen wie in

(1.1) to operate the catalyst slightly rich of stoichiometry
(1.2) to operate the catalyst rich of stoichiometry for short periods of time

können daher nicht mit

(2.1) * etwas/leicht lambda = 1
(2.2) * kurzzeitig lambda = 1

Fig. 36: Transfer comment example ("stoichiometry")

The transfer comment related to stoichiometry focuses on the various grammatical and stylistic problems involved, and on the consequences and problems that could arise in specific textual environments. In addition, the translator is warned not to use the term stöchiometrie, which is a "false friend" and does not exist in this domain.

Regarding the language in which transfer comments should be written, in the target or the source language, there are no principle arguments which would favour the one over the other. Assuming, however, that in most cases the target language is the translator's native language, the target language solution seems to have a slight advantage. It is certainly easier for translators to grasp the sometimes rather intricate aspects of meaning and usage explained in a comment if these are presented in their mother tongue. In addition, the problems discussed in a transfer comment arise from the specific translation direction. A transfer comment is related to a source term, but it is about the transfer step and the correct use of the transfer equivalents. For this reason, it is often easier to explain certain transfer problems in the target language.

In general, transfer comments tend to be quite heterogeneous, which is hardly astonishing considering the fact that they are about terms in relation to the interacting conditions and complex problems of translational text processing. Transfer comments draw on various types of terminological information, especially on meaning definitions and usage, and they often contain references to encyclopaedic units (see below) in order to direct the user's attention to relevant subject information. In many cases, therefore, one particular comment can assist the translator in solving different transfer problems. Because of this varied and multi-faceted nature of transfer comments, their production requires a careful coordination of the various types of information contained in the termbank.

13.4 Encyclopaedia

The translational relevance of the encyclopaedia derives from a close interaction between term-oriented encyclopaedic information and other types of terminological information, such as meaning definitions, grammatical properties, collocations, and conditions of use. Encyclopaedic units are written with a view to the special needs of translators; they embody terminologically relevant information in a concise and customized way. It is, in fact, the interplay of both types of information - domain-specific and language-specific - that makes the encyclopaedia a particularly useful instrument for the translator.

Other than in a textbook, the presentation of encyclopaedic information in connection with a termbank is not a goal in itself. Rather, the information is selected, organized and presented with a view to the specific terminological problems of text comprehension and production. One major function of encyclopaedic information, in this context, is to supplement the meaning definitions of terms by illustrating particular aspects of the subject area under consideration, thus placing terms in a wider context, without which an adequate interpretation would be difficult, or even impossible.

Translators are not confronted with terms in isolation. The terms they are dealing with occur in texts, where they are bound together by cohesive ties on the basis of their participation in a common knowledge frame. Some of the terms which are in a frame relation to stöchiometrisch are given below together with their meaning definitions:

> stöchiometrisches Luft-Kraftstoff-Verhältnis (stoichiometric air/fuel ratio): Ein stöchiometrisches Luft-Kraftstoff-Verhältnis ist das für die Verbrennung ideale Verhältnis von Kraftstoff und zugeführter Luftmenge. Es liegt vor, wenn 1 kg Kraftstoff mit 14,7 kg Luft gemischt wird.
>
> Luftverhältnis Lambda (air ratio of lambda): Das Luftverhältnis Lambda ist das Verhältnis zwi-schen der tatsächlich dem Kraftstoff zugeführten Luftmenge L und der für die vollständige Verbrennung des Kraftstoffs erforderlichen Luftmenge Lth (theoretischer Luftbedarf).
>
> stöchiometrischer Punkt (stoichiometry): Der stöchiometrische Punkt ist erreicht, wenn für das Luftverhältnis Lambda gilt: Lambda =1, d.h. wenn die für die vollständige Verbrennung des Kraftstoffs erforderliche Menge Luft zugeführt wird.

Sauerstoffüberschuß (excess of oxygen): Man spricht von Sauerstoffüberschuß im Luft-Kraft-stoff-Gemisch oder im Abgas, wenn 1 kg Kraftstoff mehr als die zur Verbrennung ideale Luftmenge von 14,7 kg zugeführt wird.

Sauerstoffmangel (deficiency of oxygen): Man spricht von Sauerstoffmangel im Luft-Kraftstoff-Gemisch oder im Abgas, wenn 1 kg Kraftstoff weniger als die zur Verbrennung ideale Luftmenge von 14,7 kg zugeführt wird.

mager (lean): Man spricht von einem mageren Luft-Kraftstoff-Gemisch, wenn 1 kg Kraftstoff mehr als die zur Verbrennung ideale Luftmenge von 14,7 kg zugeführt wird.

fett (rich): Man spricht von einem fetten Luft-Kraftstoff-Gemisch, wenn 1 kg Kraftstoff weniger als die zur Verbrennung ideale Luftmenge von 14,7 kg zugeführt wird.

It is quite obvious that these definitions only provide partial and isolated information. They are not intended to integrate terms in the context of their domain, and to display them in their natural textual habitat; meaning definitions alone are hardly sufficient for someone not familiar with the subject.

STÖCHIOMETRISCHES LUFT-KRAFTSTOFF-VERHÄLTNIS

[fett; ideales Mischungsverhältnis; Lambda; Lambda = 1; Lambda > 1; Lambda < 1; Luft-Kraftstoff-Gemisch; Luft-Kraftstoff-Verhältnis; Luftmangel; Luftüberschuß; Luftverhältnis; Luftzahl; mager; Sauerstoffmangel; Sauerstoffüberschuß; stöchiometrisch; stöchiometrisches Luft-Kraftstoff-Verhältnis; stöchiometrischer Punkt; überstöchio-metrischer Bereich; unterstöchiometrischer Bereich]

Der im Tank von Kraftfahrzeugen in flüssiger Form mitgeführte Kraftstoff muß für die Verbrennung im Ottomotor aufbereitet, d.h. mit einer bestimmten Menge Luft gemischt werden. Das mit dem griechischen Buchstaben **Lambda** bezeichnete **Luftverhältnis** (auch **Luftzahl** genannt) beschreibt das Verhältnis zwischen tatsächlich zugeführter Luftmasse und dem für die vollständige Verbrennung des Kraftstoffs theoretisch notwendigen Luftbedarf (Lambda = L:Lth). 1 kg Kraftstoff (ca. 1,4 l) benötigt zu seiner vollständigen Verbrennung etwa 14,7 kg Luft (11,5 m3). Dieses **ideale Mischungsverhältnis** von 1 : 14,7 wird als **stöchiometrisches Luft-Kraftstoff-Verhältnis** bezeichnet. Für das Luftverhältnis Lambda gilt in diesem Fall **Lambda = 1**. Dieser **stöchiometrische Punkt** muß möglichst genau eingehalten werden, da bei Lambda = 1 die Konversionsrate für die im Abgas enthaltenen Schadstoffe am höchsten ist. Für eine möglichst genaue Einhaltung des stöchiometrischen Punktes sorgt die GEMISCHREGELUNG.

Je nach Betriebszustand des Motors weicht das praktische Mischungsverhältnis vom stöchiometrischen Punkt ab. Wird mehr Luft zugeführt als zur vollständigen Verbrennung benötigt wird (**Sauerstoffüberschuß**), ist also **Lambda > 1**, spricht man von einem **mageren Luft-Kraftstoff-Gemisch**; der Motor wird dann im **überstöchiometrischen Bereich** betrieben. Bei **Sauerstoffmangel**

Fig. 37: Encyclopedic entry example (1)

The encyclopaedic unit STÖCHIOMETRISCHES LUFT-KRAFTSTOFF-VERHÄLTNIS provides the required additional information. It sheds light on the interpretation of terms by presenting the whole cluster of thematically related terms within the relevant knowledge frame.

In addition to and beyond the semantic exploitation of the factual information given, an encyclopaedic unit can be useful in that it implicitly provides terminologically relevant linguistic information about, say, grammatical properties and appropriate collocations (e.g. dem Kraftstoff Luft zuführen; den stöchiometrischen Punkt einhalten; vom stöchiometrischen Punkt abweichen; die Einhaltung des stöchiometrischen Punktes), and about the actual use experts make of terms when conveying technical knowledge.

GEMISCHREGELUNG

[abmagern; anfetten; Gemischregelung; Katalysatorfenster; Lambdafenster; Lambdaregelung; Restsauerstoffgehalt; Sauerstoffanteil; Totzeit]

Zur Einhaltung des STÖCHIOMETRISCHEN LUFT-KRAFTSTOFF-VERHÄLTNISSES findet beim Drei-Wege-Katalysator eine **Gemisch- bzw. Lambdaregelung** statt (REGELUNG UND STEUERUNG DER GEMISCHBILDUNG BEI OTTOMOTOREN). Mit Hilfe eines Meßfühlers, der LAMBDASONDE, wird dabei der **Sauerstoffanteil** im Abgas (Regelgröße) vor Eintritt in den Katalysator gemessen. Der **Restsauerstoffgehalt** ist in starkem Maße von der Zusammensetzung des Luft-Kraftstoff-Gemisches abhängig, das dem Motor zur Verbrennung zugeführt wird. Diese Abhängigkeit ermöglicht es, den Sauerstoffanteil im Abgas als Maß für die Luftzahl Lambda heranzuziehen. Wird nun der stöchiometrische Punkt (Lambda = 1; Führungsgröße) über- oder unterschritten, gibt die Lambdasonde ein Spannungssignal an das elektronische Steuergerät der Gemischaufbereitungsanlage. Das Steuergerät erhält ferner Informationen über den Betriebszustand des Motors sowie die Kühlwassertemperatur. Je nach Spannungslage der Lambdasonde signalisiert das Steuergerät nun seinerseits einem Gemischbildner (Einspritzanlage oder elektronisch geregelter Vergaser), ob das Gemisch **angefettet** oder **abgemagert** werden muß (vermehrte Kraftstoffeinspritzung bei Sauerstoffüberschuß, verminderte bei Sauerstoffmangel). Da vom Zeitpunkt der Bildung des Frischgemisches bis zur Erfassung des verbrannten Gemisches durch die Lambdasonde einige Zeit vergeht (**Totzeit**), ist eine konstante Einhaltung des exakten stöchiometrischen Gemisches nicht möglich. Die Luftzahl Lambda schwankt vielmehr in einem sehr engen Streubereich um Lambda = 1. Dieser Bereich wird als **Katalysator**- oder **Lambdafenster** bezeichnet und liegt bei einem Wert unter 1%.

In zwei Fällen wird die Gemischregelung abgeschaltet: zum einen nach

Fig. 38: Encyclopedic entry example (2)

The encyclopaedia is constructed as a modular part of the termbank accessible both from within terminological entries and from the outside. The information presented is broken down into encyclopaedic units of manageable size describing a particular aspect of a given domain; compare the encyclopaedic unit GEMISCHREGELUNG.

Each encyclopaedic unit consists of a well-motivated encyclopaedic header (or title), an alphabetical list of encyclopaedic terms in square brackets for whose contextual understanding it is relevant, and a free text. The link-up between terminological entries and the encyclopaedia is established by means of a many-to-many relation between terms and headers; that is, one unit refers to several terms, and the same encyclopaedic terms can be covered by more than one unit. Characteristically, the encyclopaedia provides information only where information is needed. That is, it neither caters for all the terms in the termbank, nor does it cover every single aspect of the subject area under consideration. For this reason, links to the encyclopaedia are only established for terms for whose translational processing the intended user might need additional encyclopaedic information.

Encyclopaedic units need to be organised within larger knowledge structures. A structure suggesting itself from a traditional point of view of classification is a hierarchical one. But such an approach is faced with a serious problem. Depending on the angle from which a subject area is looked at, it presents itself with a different structural organisation. When viewed from one perspective, a particular unit may seem to be subordinate to others, and superordinate when looked at from a different point of view. What at one time seems to be closely related can at others be wide apart. In this sense, any subject area is multidimensional, and this should be reflected by its encyclopaedic structure. A rigid hierachical structure does not meet this requirement.

The links between thematically related encyclopaedic units established by means of their headers (in capital letters) provide the basis for an alternative approach. Starting from any unit, the user is able to access all other units, or a selection of them, whose headers occur within this unit either contextually or as explicit references, e.g. the headers STÖCHIOMETRISCHES LUFT-KRAFTSTOFF-VERHÄLTNIS, LAMBDASONDE and REGELUNG UND STEUERUNG DER GEMISCHBILDUNG BEI OTTOMOTOREN in the encyclopaedic unit GEMISCHREGELUNG. Exploiting these header-links, the user can thus move along an indivual path to create an **encyclopaedic grouping** of units reflecting the specific perspective from which the encyclopaedia is accessed, and providing an individual answer to individual information needs.

With the initial unit GEMISCHREGELUNG as its focal point, for instance, the ensuing encyclopaedic grouping spreads out to embrace more and more units, containing general or specific information, as chosen and specified by the user through the headers. In this way subordinate, superordinate, and coordinate units are grouped together forming a tailor-made overview on individually selected aspects of the issue in question.

An encyclopaedic grouping represents a dynamic structure containing the encyclopaedic information which is of relevance in the current retrieval situation. Starting from a given term and searching for individually needed subject information, an ad hoc organisation of the relevant units is created via the flexible interplay of encyclopaedic terms, headers, and units. Such a dynamic structuring of encyclopaedic units through freely generated groupings is a reflection of the multi-faceted and multi-dimensional thematic make-up of a subject area.

IV. Translation Post-Processes

The 'Output' Resources

14. Proof-Reading Documentation - Introduction

Marianne Kugler

Checking natural language for errors can be subdivided into several levels of complexity. A well known kind of checking is the conventional word-based spelling checking. Nearly every text processing system has an integrated spelling checker (differing, however, in quality, especially where languages other than English, French, and German are concerned). Only a large dictionary is needed against which the text can be matched. But not all spelling errors, nor any grammatical errors or stylistic errors can be found out with these checkers.

Some progress has been made in the last decade to cover this lack of checking: Special dictionaries have been developed to solve misleading spelling, statistical algorithms have been used to give the author information about word, sentence length and readability score, new algorithms have been found to check with a minimum of effort sophisticated mistakes and last not least parsers have been developed to check grammatical mistakes which could not be checked up to now.

In order to deal with the different kinds of errors found in texts, several layers of proof-reading tools are used in a cascade in the TWB project:

- word-based spell checking in languages where no spell checker of acceptable quality is available (-> Greek, and Spanish);
- extended spell checking, i.e. context-sensitive checking as an intermediate between word-based and grammar based checking (German, and to some extent English)
- simple grammar checker for detecting errors in noun phrase agreement
- elaborated grammar and style checker for preparation of documents for automatic machine translation

The following chapters deal with these aspects of proofreading and give some insight into language-specific problems.

15. Word- and Context-Based Spell Checkers

15.1 Spanish Spell Corrector

Montserrat Meya

Spell correctors are today standard tools integrated in commercial word processors. However, commercial products usually apply the same algorithm or correction strategy over different language data. These strategies are in the majority heuristically oriented although the linguistic data of the different languages would obviously require different linguistic treatment.

The Spell Corrector developed for Spanish within the TWB is, like all the integrated tools, "language specific". Spanish graphemics are phonological and therefore there is a restricted set of phonotactics with easy graphemic rules that generate the allomorph variants. Word structure relies on the syllabic structure; therefore a solid syllable design serves both for word segmentation and for hyphenation purposes, and for capturing misspellings due to incorrect syllabic structures.

15.1.1 Spell Corrector Strategy

Both error detection and error correction follow the same strategy. The system checks first for legal syllables within the word. If the word is wrong the system generates word candidates that are validated against syllable occurrences within word positions. Here we have considered three positions: initial, middle, and final. Syllables are checked against syllable occurrences within word positions in Spanish.

According to the list of allowable syllable occurrences in words, the system positions the corrections within word pools (dictionary). The correction module generates word candidates applying the four standard strategies for each syllable:

- delete grapheme
- insert grapheme
- exchange graphemes
- reorder graphemes

Each correction strategy generates a certain syllable type. Given the fact that each pool is consistent with its syllable typology, each new generated candidate must belong to a restricted subset of word pools. From each word pool there is a link to the corresponding word pools related to the four possible corrections for the first syllable; then the correction strategy is applied to the second word syllable and so forth.

The system generates only syllables that are permitted in the language for a given position.

Syllables consist of the possible combination of:

- initial cluster (present or not)
- vocalic core
- coda (present or not)

Figure 39 shows the architecture of the Spanish Speller.

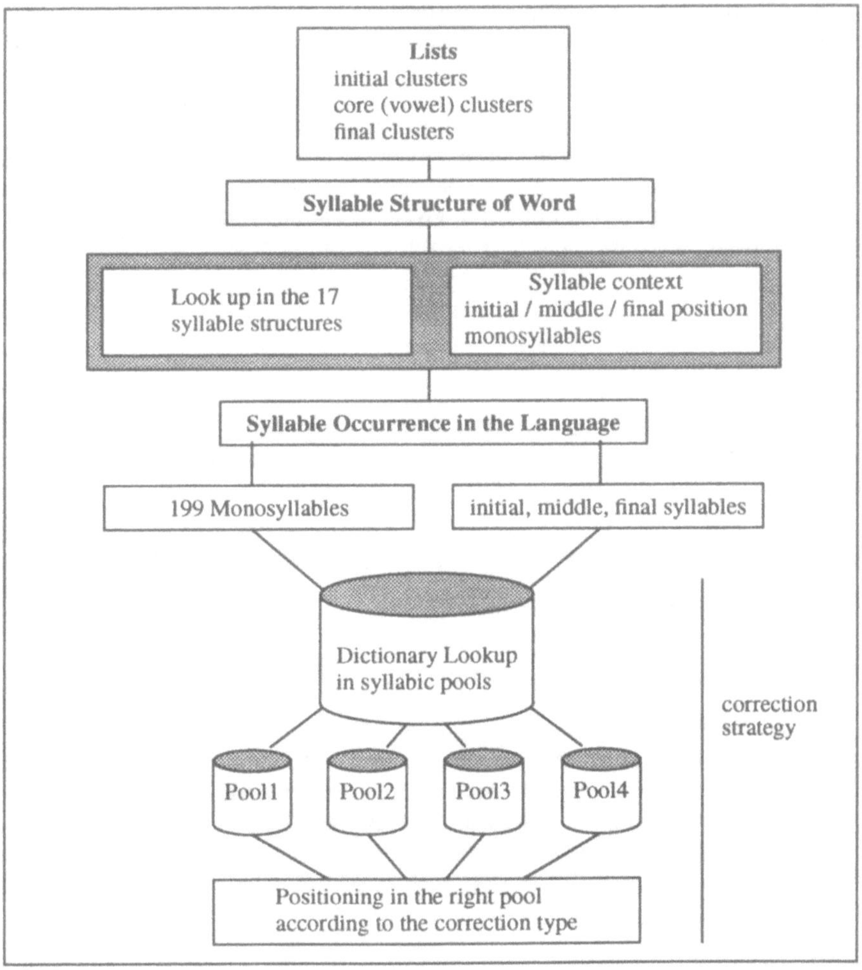

Fig. 39: Architecture of the Spanish spell checker

15.1.2 Error Typology and Speller Evaluation

Spelling mistakes made by native speakers are mainly typing errors. This can be attributed to the simple syllable structure of the language and to the fact that Spanish is spelt phonologically. With the exception of some "b/v" and "-/h" orthography cases, misspelling errors depend on typing skills and mechanical factors: key disposition (adjacent keys) and simultaneous keystrokes. The most common mistake is adding a letter by inadvertently pressing the adjacent keys.

The TWB Spanish Spell Checker when measured against other Spellers (Proximity, Word, Wordperfect) upon the same documents, offers a higher correction accuracy. Accuracy is defined in terms of the average of word candidates offered to misspellings.

Commercial spell checkers presuppose correctness in the first word graphemes, therefore whenever this is not the case, the amount of correction candidates may grow considerably and may not even contain the right correction.

Therefore, not surprisingly, better results are obtained with a spell corrector that supports the phonological structure of a language. Given the fact that Spanish has phonologically oriented graphemics and an easy-to-handle syllable structure, spelling correction can be done with a syllabic approach. Moreover, given the nature of the data (syllable inventory) and the algorithm; there are spin-off applications of this approach:

- hyphenation
- speech recognition support
- OCR recognition support

The present implementation runs on SUN Sparc; it works with 220.000 word forms organised in 5712 pools according to their syllable typology; the syllabic discrimination is made upon 17 different syllable types.

15.2 Extended Spelling Correction for German

Ralf Kese, Friedrich Dudda, Marianne Kugler

15.2.1 Motivation

As indicated by Maurice Gross in his COLING 86 lecture (Gross 1986), European languages contain thousands of what he calls "frozen" or "compound words". In contrast to "free forms", frozen words - though being separable into several words and suffixes - lack syntactic and/or semantic compositionality. This "lack of compositionality is apparent from lexical restrictions" (at night, but: *at day, *at evening, etc.) as well as "by the impossibility of inserting material that is a priori plausible" (*at {coming, present, cold, dark} night) (Gross 1986).

Since the degree of 'frozenness' can vary, the procedure for recognizing compound words within a text can be more or less complicated. Yet, at least for the completely and almost completely frozen forms, simple string matching operations will suffice (Gross 1986).

However, although this clearly indicates that at least those compound words whose parts have a high degree of 'frozenness' are accessible to the methods of standard spelling correction systems, it is true that these systems try at best to cope with (some) compound nouns while they are still ignorant of the bulk of other compound forms and of violations of lexical and/or co-occurrence restrictions in general.

As Zimmermann (1987) points out with respect to German forms like "in bezug auf" (=frozen) versus "mit Bezug auf" (= free), compounds are clearly outside the scope of standard spelling correction systems due to the fact that these systems only check for isolated words and disregard the respective contexts.

Following Gross (1986) and Zimmermann (1987), we propose to further extend standard spelling correction systems onto the level of compound words by making them context-sensitive as well as capable of treating more than a single word at a time.

Yet even on the level of single words many more errors could be detected by a spelling corrector if it possessed at least some rudimentary linguistic knowledge. In the case of a word that takes irregular forms (like the German verb "laufen" or the English noun "mouse", for example), a standard system seems to "know" the word and its forms for it is able to verify them, e.g. by simple lexicon lookup. Yet when confronted with a regular though false form of the very same word (e.g. with "laufte" as the 1st/3rd pers. sg. simple past ind. act., or with the plural "mouses"), such a system normally fails to propose the corresponding irregular form ("lief" or "mice") as a correction.

Following a suggestion in Zimmermann (1987), we propose to enhance standard spelling correction systems on the level of isolated words by introducing an additional type of lexicon entry that explicitly records those cognitive errors that are intuitively likely to occur (at least in the writings of non-native speakers) but which a standard system fails to treat in an adequate way for system intrinsic reasons.

15.2.2 Overview of new Phenomena for Spelling Correction

As there are irregular forms which are nevertheless well-formed, i.e.: words, there are also regular forms which are ill-formed, i.e.: non-words. Whereas words are usually known to a spelling correction system, we have to add the non-words to its vocabulary in order to improve the quality of its corrections.

On the level of single words in German, non-words come from various sources and comprise, among others, false feminine derivations of certain masculine nouns (*Wandererin, *Äbtin), false plurals of nouns (*Thematas, *Tertias), non-licensed inflections (*beigem, *lila(n)es) or comparisons (*lokaler, *minimalst) of certain adjectives, false comparisons (*nahste, *rentabelerer), wrong names for the citizens of towns (*Steinhagener, *Stadthäger), etc. Some out-dated forms (e.g.: Preißelbeere, verkäufst, abergläubig) can likewise be treated as non-words.

It is on the level of compounds that words rather than non-words come into consideration again, when we look for contextual constraints or co-occurrence restrictions that determine orthography beyond the scope of what can be accepted or rejected on the basis of isolated words alone.

For words in German, these restrictions determine, among other things, whether or not certain forms (1) begin with an upper or lower case letter; (2) have to be separated by (2.1) blank, (2.2) hyphen, (2.3) or not at all; (3) combine with certain other forms; or even (4) influence punctuation. Examples are:

1)	Ich laufe eis.	versus
	Ich laufe auf dem Eis.	
	Er dürfte Bankrott machen.	versus
	Er dürfte bankrott sein.	
2.1)	Sie kann sehr gut Fahrrad fahren.	versus
2.3)	Sie kann sehr gut radfahren.	
2.1)	Es war bitter kalt.	versus
2.3)	Es war ein bitterkalter Tag.	

2.2) Er liebt Ich-Romane. versus
2.3) Er liebt Romane in Ichform.

3) Betonblöcke vs. *Betonblocks versus
Häuserblocks vs. *Häuserblöcke

4) Er rauchte, ohne daß sie davon wußte. versus
Er rauchte ohne, daß sie davon wußte.

15.2.3 Method

The extensions proposed in (1) above are conservative, in the sense that their realization simply requires widening the scope of the string matching/comparing operations that are used classically in spelling correction systems. No deep and time-consuming analysis, like parsing, is involved.

Restricting the system in this way makes our approach to context-sensitivity different from the one considered in Rimon/Herz (1991), where context sensitive spelling verification is proposed to be done with the help of "local constraints automata (LCAs)" which process contextual constraints on the level of lexical or syntactic categories rather than on the basic level of strings. In fact, proof-reading with LCAs amounts to genuine grammar checking and as such belongs to a different and higher level of language checking than the extensions of pure spelling correction proposed here.

Now, in order to treat these extensions in a uniform way, each entry in the system lexicon is modelled as a quintuple <W,L,R,C,E> specifying a pattern of a (multi-) word W for which a correction C will be proposed accompanied by an explanation E just in case a given match of W against some passage in the text under scrutiny differs significantly from C and the - possibly empty - left and right contexts L and R of W also match the environment of W's counterpart in the text.

Disregarding E for a moment, this is tantamount to saying that each such record is interpreted as a string rewriting rule

W --> C / L___R

replacing W (e.g. Bezug) by C (e.g. bezug) in the environment L___R (e.g. in___auf).

The form of these productions can best be characterized with an eye to the Chomsky hierarchy as unrestricted since we can have any non-null number of symbols on the LHS replaced by any number of symbols on the RHS, possibly by null (Partee 1990).

With an eye to semi-Thue or extended axiomatic systems one could say that a linearly ordered sequence of strings W, C1, C2, ..., Cm is a derivation of Cm iff (1) W is a (faulty) string (in the text to be corrected) and (2) each Ci follows from the immediately preceding string by one of the productions listed in the lexicon (Partee 1990).

Thus, theoretically, a single mistake can be corrected by applying a whole sequence of productions, though in practice the default is clearly that a correction be done in a single derivational step, at least as long as the system is just operating on strings and not on additional non-terminal symbols.

Occurrences of W, L, and R in a text are recognized by pattern matching techniques. Since the patterns for contexts allow L and R, in principle, to match the nearest token to be found within an arbitrary distance from W, we have to restrict the concept of a context in a natural way in order to prevent L and R from matching at non-significant places. Thus, by having the system operate sentencewise, any left or right context is naturally restricted to some string within the same sentence as W or to a boundary of that sentence (e.g.: a punctuation mark).

In case a correction C is proposed to the user, an additional message will be displayed to him or her, identifying the reason why C is correct rather than W. Depending on the user's knowledge of the language under investigation, he or she can take this either as an opportunity to learn or as a guide for deciding whether to finally accept or reject the proposal.

15.2.4 Problems and Limitations

A first prototype of the system described above has been developed in C under UNIX within the ESPRIT II project 2315 "Translator's Workbench" (TWB) as one of several separate modules, checking basic as well as higher levels (like grammar and style; see Thurmair 1990 and Winkelmann 1990) of various languages. A derived and extended version has been integrated into the TA SWP text processing software under DOS in which it runs independently of the built-in standard spelling verifier.

On both these implementations, some problems have received practical solutions to an acceptable degree.

For example, the problem of mistaking an abbreviation for the end of a sentence (because both end with a period), which could prevent a context from being recognized, is solved by having the sentence segmentation routine always read beyond a known abbreviation. This might result eventually in taking two sentences to be one, but would, of course, not disturb intra-sentential error correction. Nothing, however, prevents the system from stopping at an unknown abbreviation and thereby falling short of a context it would have otherwise recognized. From this it is clear that the system should at least know the most frequent abbreviations of a given language.

Likewise, the formatting information of a text is preserved to a very high degree during correction, as it should be. Nevertheless, there are naturally cases in which some such information will get lost as is clear from the simple fact that there can be shrinking productions reducing differently formatted elements n on the LHS to m elements on the RHS, with $m < n$. But these are borderline cases.

What is less acceptable, for each of the implementations mentioned above, is the lack of integration of the checking on the various levels. Thus, for a complete proof-reading of a given document, a user has to first run the standard checker over the whole document and then start again with each of the non-standard ones in turn.

Beside being a user's nightmare, this situation is also inadequate for theoretical reasons: for, on the one hand, it may be that the checkers - running one after the other over the same text - disturb each other's results by proposing antagonistic corrections with respect to one and the same expression: within the correct passage "in bezug auf", for example, "bezug" will first be regarded as an error by the standard checker which then will propose to rewrite it as "Bezug". If the user accepts this proposal he will receive the exactly opposite advice by the context sensitive checker.

On the other hand, checking on different levels could go hand in hand nicely and produce synergetic effects: for, clearly, any context sensitive checking requires that the contexts themselves be correct and thus possibly have been corrected in a previous, eventually context free, step. The checking of a single word could in turn profit from contextual knowledge in narrowing down the number of correction alternatives to be proposed for a given error: While there may be some eight or nine plausible candidates as corrections of "Bezug" when regarded in isolation, only one candidate, i.e. "bezug", is left when the context "in___auf" is taken into account.

Thus, there is a strong demand for arriving at a holistic solution for multi-level language checking rather than for just having various level experts hooked together in series. This will be the task for the near future.

15.2.5 Portability

The software of the system described is modular in the sense that it can be integrated into any word processing software. We have already ported the German prototype from the TA SWP word processing program into Microsoft's WinWord 1.1, for example.

As concerns the lingware, we take it that a similar approach is also feasible for languages other than German. Although in comparison with English, French, Italian, and Spanish, German seems to be unique as regards the relevance of the context for upper/lower case spellings in a large number of cases, there are at least, as indicated in (Gross 1986), the thousands of compounds or frozen words in each of these languages which are clearly within reach for the methods discussed.

16. Grammar and Style Checkers

Introduction

Gregor Thurmair

Grammar Checkers today cover corrections that deal with misspellings that can only be captured within the sentence context. Some can deal with complex grammar errors that concern verbal arguments or normative cases set down in academic books.

Spell Checking tools differ greatly from language to language. Here we could compare the approach of the "Extended TWB Speller for German" (loaned from the Duden Norm), or the commercial "Grammatik II".

Different users, according to their profile, make different mistakes. For instance, Spanish native speakers almost never make agreement mistakes; even non-native speakers do not have many problems with this. When writing technical documents, the most usual mistake is wrong tenses, wrong appositions and problems with reflexive forms or with marked prepositions. All these cases can only be captured by means of parsing and with a robust lexical grammar.

In a wider approach to be presented in Sect. 16.3 on **Verification of Controlled Grammars**, the effort not only concentrates on getting rid of wrong grammatical sequences, but rather on presenting an integrated framework of controlling the user's language and thus aiding a full grammar and style analysis. To this respect, the first two approaches give a more limited, agreement-based view on grammar checking, which is comparatively faster and has been shown to be portable to PCs, whereas the full-fledged style checking provides the in-depth analysis. Thus the two approaches are complementary, depending on the task and the time available.

16.1 German Grammar Checker: Efficient Grammar Checking with an ATN-Parser

Günter Winkelmann

Within Translator's Workbench (TWB) TA developed a grammar checker. This paper summarises the main efforts done in commercial grammar checking in the last decade and describes the results of an empirical study on orthographical errors in German. In the second part requirements for the architecture of an efficient grammar checker are given and main features of the TA grammar checker are described.

Commercial Checkers / Grammar Checkers

When we first look at available commercial checkers, two approaches, Writer's Workbench and EPISTLE/CRITIQUE have been very successful in the way that they served as input for several commercial software systems.

Writer's Workbench (Cherry et al. 1983) has influenced the development of commercial software such as Rightwriter, PC-Style, Electric Webster, Punctuation and Styel and several versions of Grammatik (all this software is restricted to English). Writer's Workbench, a sample of 30 computer programs that perform many of the functions of human editors, has been under development at AT&T since 1979. Target machines are computers with a UNIX operating system. Beyond well known facilities such as spell checking, Writer's Workbench does style and grammar critiquing, though it cannot do critiquing that requires a parser output. Thus, its style critiquing is restricted to phenomena which can be analysed with the help of small dictionaries, simple patterns of phrases and statistical methods. Errors which can be checked by software using this approach are errors like split infinitives, wordy phrases, wrong word use, jargon, gender-specific terms, etc. The user can be provided with information about frequency of passive voice, wordiness, frequency of abstract words and often readibility scores.

EPISTLE (Heidorn 1982; Jensen et al. 1986) and its successor CRITIQUE have been developed by IBM as a mainframe text-proofing system. They are based on concepts and features of Writer's Workbench. Unlike those of Writer's Workbench, the checking tools of EPISTLE use an integrated parser. This allows EPISTLE to cover a wider range of grammatical and stylistic errors. In addition to the features described in Writer's Workbench above, EPISTLE is able to check grammatical phenomena like errors in agreement (between subject and verb, noun and premodifier), improper form of the infinitive, etc.

What about commercial successors of EPISTLE? There seems to be one, looking at Microsoft's Word for Windows. The Beta-Version of Word for Windows 2.0 includes a grammar checking facility covering most of the features of EPISTLE - a very remarkable fact. This would be the first time that an enhanced grammar checking utility including a parser is integrated in a very common text processing system thus reaching a larger number of people.

AT&T, IBM and Microsoft as pioneers of grammar checking - this looks like a snapshot of a book "who's who in the American computer industry". Are there any efforts to do grammar checking for other European languages - others than English? Aren't there any non-American, say European efforts in this area?

To answer the first question: It must be admitted that most commercial software is restricted to English. Concerning the second question: There are some efforts - namely the Chandioux group released in 1990 GramR Le Detecteur, a DOS based grammar checker for French. But this is too little compared with the efforts spent by American researchers.

Checking tools in TWB

On this background checking tools for European languages are very important. Partners of several European countries (Greek, Spain, Germany, Great Britain) and thus the corresponding linguistic knowledge is concentrated in the Translator's Workbench project. With respect to German, we can summarize that although simple spelling checkers for German are already integrated in standard text processing systems, there is a lack in checking more complex errors. While the context-sensitive spell checker has been described in the previous section, this paper will focus on the grammar checker developed at TA Triumph-Adler AG.

Empirical Study

Is there in German really a need for such a sophisticated tool like a grammar checker? Is the percentage of grammatical mistakes significant compared to the total of mistakes occurring in German texts? To answer this question a study was carried out by the University of Heidelberg, Department of Computer Linguistics (see Hellwig/Bub/Romke 1990). The corpus includes 1000 errors and the most frequent errors can be classified in errors of

- Illformed words: stems, compunds (15.8%)
- Illformed words: upper, lower case (8.7%)
- agreement in NPs (18%)
- choice of words (6.2%)
- prepositional phrase (5.3%)
- syntax of determiner (4.8%)

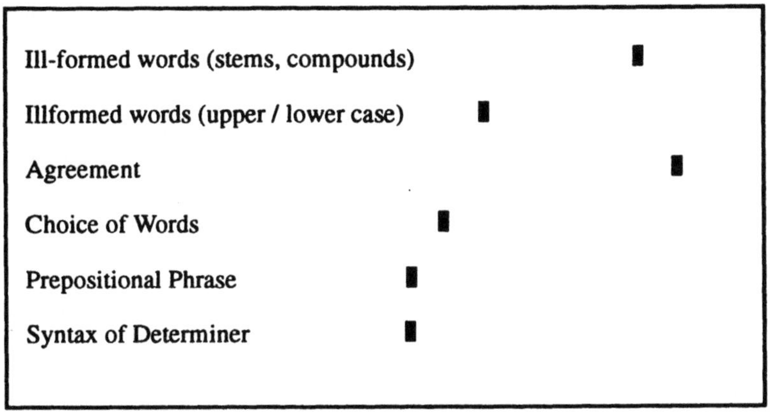

Fig. 40: Error distribution in the Heidelberg corpus

As shown in Fig. 40, the orthographic errors are the most frequent (totally 25.5%), but also errors of agreement occur very often. In addition to errors of agreement within noun phrases (18%) there are errors of agreement between subject and verb (3.5%).

Examples of agreement errors in German

Agreement in German noun phrases is an agreement between number, gender and case. Very often noun phrases are not restricted to a simple structures as (a) or (b).

(a) Die Neuerung (...)	DET N
(b) Die innovative Neuerung (...)	DET ADJ N

More complex structures as (c) and (d) have the problem that they not only consist of terminal symbols (DET N ADJ) but also of nonterminals (NP, PP, Rel.-Clause, ..), i.e. a recursive algorithm is needed to parse the structure correctly.

(c) Die innovative von TA eingeführte Neuerung (...)	Det ADJ PP PARTCPL N
(d) Die Neuerung, die von TA eingeführt wurde, (...)	Det N Rel.-Clause

Checking correct agreement between subject and verb leads to another problem. Subject and verb agree in number and person. There are no problems if the subject consists of a single noun as in (e). And there are even no problems if the subject consists of coordinated plural nouns. Difficult cases are the cases in (g) and (h) where two singular nouns are coordinated resulting in a plural noun phrase.

(e) Ich bin (...) NP(1.person) V(1.person)

(f) Die Drucker und die Laufwerke sind (...)NP(plural) KOORD NP(plural) V(plural)

(g) Der Drucker und das Laufwerk sind (...)NP(singular) KOORD NP(singular) V(plural)

(h) Ich und Du sind (...) NP(1.pers/sg) KOORD NP(2.pers/sg) V(1.pers/pl)

Looking at these examples we see that recursivity and a certain complexity of algorithms is necessary to parse the structure of NPs and to check agreement. But how can we avoid the expensive recursivity (expensive concerning both time and space) and where should algorithms checking (g) and (h) occur?

Requirements for the Architecture

A checking tool has to fulfill several conditions to be accepted by the user. It has to be

- fast
- small (little disk space)
- covering the most of the language
- robust
- not overgenerating

and with respect to the TWB project to a large amount

- adaptable to other languages

A last requirement concerns the interface to the user: Agreement errors should be shown, recommendations should be given, but a correction seems not to be useful, as there are usually several correction possibilities. This ambiguity can only be solved by using a full-fledged parser, which is not advisable on a personal computer.

Let us have a closer look to the requirements and how they can be resolved.

Architecture, Robust Parsing

A parser used in research laboratories is not fast because researchers try to describe the whole language. Is this necessary for a commercial grammar checker? We think not and have decided to restrict ourselves to a lower degree of complexity of parsing. Thus we can avoid time- and space-intensive recursions at least for the first prototype. We do not intend to parse relative-clauses and very complex subclauses within NPs, but we intend to extend the parser in the future in order to find the right compromise between sophisticated functionality and time- and space-saving simplicity. The question is: What will we do with the complex subclauses within NPs? We make parsing on two levels: In the first step we build a simple phraselist from the tokenlist which includes the lexical information, i.e. we build simple phrases (coordinated ADJs, PPs, simple NPs). In a second step we build complex phrases (coordinated NPs, coordinated PPs, participles within NPs, and so on). Another advantage of the division between simple phrase list and complex phrase is that we can avoid recursivity.

Architecture, Small and Fast Lexica

A small lexicon which allows a rapid access is one of the central features of the grammar checker. The lexicon is small because we use

- bitwise coding of grammatical data
- prefix trees for the tokens.

The lexicon is very fast because we use

- trees for the structure of the lexicon
- assembler routines for the access.

A small dictionary with 2.500 entries has been implemented. We estimate that we can code 400.000 words including grammatical information using 1.5 MByte. The average access to the lexicon is at the moment less than 20% of the total time using for checking and for providing the user interface.

Architecture, User Interface

At the moment the grammar checker runs as a standalone application under MS-DOS but we intend to integrate it in the proofreading tools of TA running under MS Windows.

16.2 Spanish Grammar Checker

Montserrat Meya

The implementation of the Spanish Grammar Checker was seen as an opportunity to develop grammar rules to start with the analysis of Spanish strings. It only covers NP structures. The implementation uses the METAL parser and the standard grammar formalism.

The grammar checker applies the rules of the standard parsing unification mechanism to the features and values. If the mechanism fails, the system tries to relax the unification assigning an identifier to each relaxed/ weakened unification type. These relaxed rules are the "peripheral rules".

A peripheral rule is PSR with a "liberalisation" of the feature restrictions.

Once a rule triggers off a relaxed unification, the system tags it, then recovers it and assigns a correction together with a message.

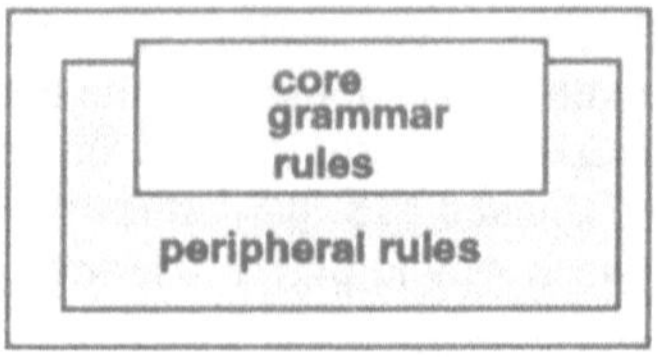

Fig. 41: Grammar rule types

The Spanish Grammar Checker as mentioned before only covers nominal constructions (with adjectival phrases, participles and all sorts of appositions, e.g. acronyms, abbreviations, etc.). We do not cover grammatical relative clauses.

The model behind the implementation is very simple. It can be applied to any grammar model; it simply adds the possibility of allowing additional "paths" as well-formed strings in the agenda during parsing.

The system applies unification gradually but on different feature sets, and each time upon a smaller set of restrictions. The rule triggered off (PSR) is the same, but obviously with a wider scope, so that it can accept incorrect input.

This mechanism is contained in each rule. However, if the Grammar Checker were implemented table driven, users could select options that would internally trigger off the application of different feature unifications. In that way users could tune the scope of the grammar checker according to user types (foreigner/ native) or document type (technical/ administrative).

Both Spanish checkers (Grammar and Speller) run on SUN Sparc and run separately.

The Grammar Checker uses the METAL Spanish dictionary (20,000 entries) and 40 analysis rules (for nominals and restricted sentence constructions).

16.2.1 Coverage

The most common grammar errors are mispellings that concern the gender and number agreement of words. However, most of these errors can be cought via spelling correction. The grammar checker mainly deals with the agreement of determiners or adjectives because in the romance languages, there must be agreement for both features.

Moreover, native speakers will never make such mistakes because they have clear competence in assigning the correct gender and number of words, and the keyboard layout makes it very difficult to type the key for "o" instead of that of "a".

Within TWB we developed a reduced grammar for Nominals that handles two types of phenomena: easy copula sentences with predicate agreement, and nominal appositions.

Appositions were divided into: narrow appositions, namely defining modifiers, and wide appositions (non defining modifiers).

Narrow appositions cope with the following contructions:

- Noun with Proper Names (acronyms or not)
- Common noun and common noun

By default when the parser finds an unknown string, it is tagged as a noun. Then the rules concerned with apposition can be triggered.i.e.:

"memoria RAM" or " memorias RAM"

The system offers correction for Gender and Number as far as proper nouns are concerned, or the right corrections for number when two common nouns are involved.

"directorios races" vs. " directorios raz"

"pruebas pilotos" vs. " pruebas piloto"

"el rey Juana" vs. " el rey Juan"

The next group of appositions covers the wide appositions or non defining modifiers. These cases are always between commas. Non defining appositions and relative clauses (parenthetical constructions) are at the same level.

" el oxgeno, fuentes de vida,..." vs "el oxigeno, fuente de vida,.."

" Juan, mi hermana,..." vs "Juan, mi hermano,..."

For computational purposes appositions are all treated as XP. However, given the fact that the narrow and wide appositions are at different Bar-levels, this fact can be cought by the feature that specifies the apposition type. Here the system blocks the occurrence of determiners or other forbidden adverbial modifiers.

Presently, the Spanish grammar checker is implemented in the METAL environment, and for that reason it was not integrated as a complementary part to the Spanish spell checker.

16.3 Verification of Controlled Grammars

Gregor Thurmair

This TWB component is the result of trying to optimise the documentation process. Considerations of how to improve the input of machine translation were compared with guidelines for technical authors, and large overlaps were detected. This resulted in a common effort to improve both the readability and the translatability of texts, by setting up styleguides for authors. Since they define a sublanguage of their own, in that they restrict the grammar of a language, they are called controlled languages.

There are several reasons for setting up controlled grammars:

- corporate identity requires the use of certain terms and expressions instead of others;
- ease of readability and understanding also for non-native speakers require very limited grammar usages (e.g. in the case of AECMA);
- ease of translatability also restricts the language (e.g. in Xerox' adapations for SYSTRAN translation).

Our task was to implement software which compares texts with those guidelines and flags the deviations. This is the content of the Controlled Grammar Verifier in TWB.

16.3.1 Architecture

There are two possible architectures for a Controlled Grammar Verifier. Either only the subset described by the Controlled Grammar is implemented; anything that cannot be parsed is considered to be ill-formed. Or a full parser is implemented and deviations are flagged. The former apporach is easier to implement but has some drawbacks:

- It is correct that deviations lead to parse failures. But no other parse failures must occur; else a parse failure is not meaningful anymore. This cannot be guaranteed, however.
- No error diagnosis can be given, as a parse failure gives no hints where or why the parser failed. This is not considered to be user-friendly.

We therefore decided to implement the latter strategy in TWB. Here, the overall architecture of the system looks as described in Fig. 42.

In this approach, a Controlled Grammar Verifier basically consists of four components:

- an input sentence analyser which produces linguistic structures of the sentences to be checked;
- a collection of linguistic structures which are considered to be ill-formed (according to some criteria);
- a matcher which matches the input structures with the potential ill-formed structures and flags the deviations;
- an output module which produces useful diagnostic information. We do not, however, intend to produce automatic correction. This is too difficult at present

16.3.2 The Input Sentence Analyser

In order to do diagnostics on linguistic trees, it is presupposed that these trees are available; i.e. a parser and lexicon must be available which produce these structures.

For a number of reasons, described in Thurmair 1990, we chose the METAL analysis components.

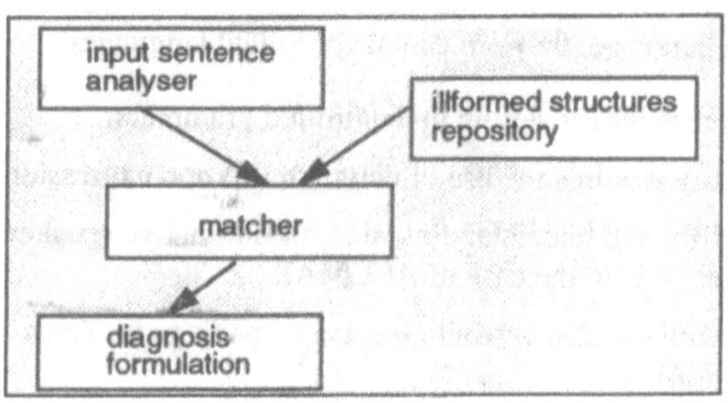

Fig. 42: Verifier Components

However, as a Controlled Grammar Verifier deals with a subset of the grammar, it should be implemented such that the grammar is not touched at all. The only thing needed should be a description of the trees the grammar produces; then any parser and grammar can be used as long as it produces the kind of trees specified.

In TWB, this was the guideline for the implementation. Nothing was changed inside the METAL analysis components to perform the diagnosis.

16.3.3 The Ill-formed Structures Repository

The second component to be considered was the rules of the controlled grammars; they mainly consist of things to be avoided (too long sentences, too complex compounds, too many passive constructions, ambiguous prepositional phrases, etc.). The phenomena were collected from an examination of the relevant literature (cf. Schmitt 1989).

The first task here is to reformulate the statements of the controlled grammars in terms of linguistic structures and features: Which structures should be flagged when a sentence should not be "too complex"? Which structures indicate an "ambiguous prepositional phrase attachment"? The result of this step was a list of structures, annotated with features, the occurrence of which indicated an ill-formed construction.

The next step was to find a representation for these structures. It had to be as declarative as possible, which led to two requirements:

- the structures should be stored in files, not in programs, not only in order to ease testing, but also to change applications (and languages) later on (e.g. from German Siemens Nixdorf Styleguides to English AECMA controlled languages);
- the structures should be declared in some simple language, describing precedence and dominance of nodes, presence and absence of features / feature combinations and values. Any linguist should be able to implement their own sets of controlled grammar phenomena and call them by just specifying their specific diagnostic file.

Both requirements were fulfilled in the final TWB demonstrator; the ill-formed structures are collected in a file which is interpreted at runtime; and the structures are described in a uniform and easy way (cf. Thurmair 1990).

16.3.4 The Matcher

The matcher is the central component of the verification software. It matches the structures of the ill-formed structure repository with the input sentence, applying the feature and tree structure tests to the input tree. This process has to be done for all subtrees of a given syntax tree recursively (as there may be diagnosis information on all levels of a tree). For every positive match, the matcher puts a feature onto the root node of the input tree, the value of which indicates the kind of ill-formedness, and gives a hint for the production of the diagnostic information.

As a software basis for the matcher, we were able to use a component of the METAL software which performs tree operations. The output of the matching process is the input analysis tree, modified by some features if ill-formed structures were found.

16.3.5 The Output Generator

The last component is the output generator. The diagnostic information must be presented in a way which is easily understandable and optimally usable for the users.

There are two kinds of information to be presented:

- **Sentence specific** information flags ill-formed structures in sentences. This information should be given together with the sentence it occurs in. This could be achieved either by splitting the input text into single sentences and flagging them if necessary, or by writing comments into the document itself (using an additional right column). The latter presentation is preferable but requires some layout information from the document (to find the respective text line) and is therefore restricted to a given editor;
- The other kind of information is **global** and refers to a text as a whole; examples are flags like

  - too many passives in a text

  - nominal style

  - overall readability

  This information could be presented in a header of the text as a whole, and could even be represented graphically (e.g. by bar charts).

The existing TWB prototype only supports sentence-based diagnosis and represents it as pairs of <sentence ; diagnosis>. This has to be improved; also, experiments related to a good readability score have to be performed in order to meet users' intuitions on this issue.

16.3.6 Test Experiments and Results

Several experiments have been carried out with the Controlled Grammar Verifier (cf. Thurmair 1992):

In order to test its functionality, a set of test sentences was written which was used for functional tests.

In addition, we analysed several "real life" documents, mainly user manuals in data processing. They consisted of about 220 sentences. The result was that 100 were flagged; this turned out to be too much; but 44 just flagged "abstract nouns" (from a guideline that asked authors to avoid abstract nouns). If this was eliminated, one out of four sentences was flagged which for the texts chosen was considered to be acceptable.

A closer look at three phenomena showed encouraging results. In the case of complex prenominal modifications, all cases (13 overall) had been identified and flagged correctly. In the case of unclear PP attachment, all cases (23 overall) had been found if the sentences could be parsed; ambiguities not identified (overall 11) were due to parse failures. In the case of wrong specifier formations, all cases (overall 8) except one had been found. These results show that on the basis of a good large coverage analysis, precise and helpful diagnosis is possible.

What turned out to be a problem is the treatment of parse failures (about 25% of the texts could not be parsed). In this case, the diagnosis can be erromeous; e.g. if the system flags an incomplete sentence structure which is due to the fact that the parser could not find all predicate parts). This requires improvements both in the parsing and analysis phase (the verifier must know if a sentence could not be parsed) and in the diagnosis phase (be more robust here).

16.3.7 Next Tasks

In order to make the Controlled Grammar Verifier really productive, the following tasks must be performed:

- **Port** the Controlled Grammar Guidelines to other applications. This should demonstrate if the modular architecture which is based on specification files really works. This task has begun with an external pilot partner.
- **Tune** the system to find out if what it flags is what human users would flag as well. For example: Are all constructions marked as "too complex" by the system also considered to be complex by human readers? This also relates to the number of flags to be allowed for the construction to be acceptable.
- **Improve the quality** of the output component. We must be able to refer to the original text in giving diagnostics. For example, if a sentence contains three large compounds, we must tell the users which of them the message "unclear compound structure" refers to. We also need good text related scores (e.g. for readability).
- Finally, we need a better **user interface** which allows for the selection of some parameters (do not always check everything) and other more sophisticated operations.

17. Automatic Syntax Checking

Peter Hellwig

17.1 Introduction

A correct translation includes the correct construction of phrases. Obviously, the knowledge involved in this task is very complex. A great deal of the efforts in learning a language must be devoted to syntactic properties like admissible complements of words, word order, inflection and agreement.The opportunities for making mistakes are as many as the number of appropriate syntactic constructions . Therefore a tool for assessing the syntactic correctness of a translation is a very desirable module of the Translator's Workbench. Such a module is under development at the Institute for Computational Linguistics of the University of Heidelberg.[1] The present work relies on basic research conducted in the framework of the PLAIN system (Programs for Language Analysis and INference) starting in the mid-1970s.[2] The linguistic theory underlying the application is Dependency Unification Grammar (DUG).[3]

There are three levels of syntactic support for text processing systems which are characterized by increasing complexity. The first level supplies mere recognition of ill-formed phrases. Any parser should master this level, since a parser must, by definition, accept well-formed phrases and reject ill-formed ones.

The second level of support consists in flagging the portions of the phrase which are incorrect. However, this goal is not easy to achieve. Even correct sentences contain a lot of local syntactic ambiguities and, hence, a lot of dead-ends, which are removed only when the final stage of a correct parse is reached. If the latter situation does not occur because the input is invalid, "normal" dead-ends of the analysis and the incorrect portions of the phrase which are responsible for the parsing failure are hard to distinguish.

The most comfortable level of support is the automatic creation of the correct phrase. While the first two tasks belong to language analysis, the correction of an ill-formed phrase is an instance of language synthesis. To our knowledge, linguistic theory has not expended much effort on clarifying the mechanisms of error correction and has not yet elaborated a general and uniform solution to this problem. In any case, it is obvious that syntax checking up to the third level ranks among the greatest challenges of computational linguistics.

Error correction is a problem which is in conflict with the set-theoretic foundation of the theory of formal languages which, in turn, is the basis of natural language processing. A language L is formally defined as the set of well-formed strings which are generated by a

---

1. The following personnel have contributed to the project: Bernhard Adam, Christoph Bläsi, Jutta Bopp, Vera Bub, Karl Bund, Ingrid Daar, Erika de Lima, Monika Finck, Marc-Andre Funk, Peter Hellwig, Valerie Herbst, Christina Kläne, Heinz-Detlev Koch, Harald Lüngen, Imme Rathert, Corinna Romke, Ingo Schütze, Henriette Visser, Wolfgang Wander, Christiane Weispfennig.

2. See Hellwig 1980.

3. See Hellwig 1986.

grammar G from an inventory V of words. A parser P is an algorithm which recognizes any string contained in L given a grammar G and assigns a syntactic structure S to it. There are various formalisms for writing a grammar, e.g. constituency grammars versus dependency grammars, rule-based grammars versus categorial grammars. Furthermore, there are various algorithms that assign a structure to a phrase, given a certain type of grammar, e.g. top-down versus bottom-up parsers, shift-reduce parsers, parsers with back-tracking mechanisms or with well-formed substring tables, derivation-based or network-based parsers, etc.[4] In any case, however, an ill-formed string is not part of L, it must not be generated by G and, hence, cannot be recognized by a parser P.

What are the possibilities for handling ill-formed input without undermining the formal notion of languages, grammars and parsing?[5] One suggestion is to resort to methods for the syntax checker independent of the classical theory of formal languages as, for example, the evaluation of transition probabilities between the parts of speech of adjacent words.[6] If the product of probabilities is below a certain threshold, the sentence is likely to be ill-formed and the words with the lowest transition probability between their categories might be the ones causing the error. If no parsing is involved, this method will probably yield a syntax checker of poor quality. The algorithm will, for example, fail to detect violations of complex agreement relationships common in inflectional languages. If a parser is at hand, statistical calculations might be beneficial in order to delineate the erroneous portion of a phrase when the parser fails and, hence, they might contribute to a syntax support of the second level.

Another reaction to ill-formed input is the relaxation of the syntactic rules of the grammar, often accompanied by an increasing reliance on semantic criteria. The system ignores the violation of syntactic rules as long as a plausible meaning can be reconstructed. This reaction is known as "robust parsing", and most of the literature on parsing ill-formed input is devoted to this topic. This approach makes sense in the framework of information retrieval, but it is questionable when the assessment of syntactic correctness is the goal. Theoretically, the relaxation of rules results in the replacement of the correct grammar G by a grammar G' which accepts the language L'. L' contains ill-formed strings in addition to the correct strings of L. Various devices like subsequent filters or fitting procedures have been invented to narrow L' post festum in order to diagnose the errors.[7]

Another solution often implemented in practical systems is based on the anticipation of errors. There is a grammar G which contains rules for the correct phrases of L and a so-called peripheral grammar G' which generates the anticipated ill-formed phrases L'. The parser applies the rules of G' as well as G and, hence, is able to parse the ill-formed phrases successfully. If a rule of G' has been applied in a successful parse, then a specific error message is issued and an associated correction device might be called. From the formal point of view, there are no objections to this approach. The rules of G' must be drawn up empirically, i.e. they must be based on a typology of errors which has to be elaborated for each input language.[8] This typology might be arranged according to the reasons which caused the errors, which might be a good basis for procedures to correct mistakes by "un-

4. See, for example, the 16 prototypical parsers in Hellwig 1989.
5. The following survey of the state of the art is based on work of Christoph Bläsi.
6. Compare Atwell 1987, Atwell 1988.
7. Compare Jensen et al. 1983, Kudo et al. 1988, Borissova 1988.

doing" them. At the first view, this explanatory approach to ill-formed phrases is psychologically appealing. Ill-formedness is rule-based, as Weischedel and Sondheimer point out.[9]

The disadvantage of error anticipation is the tremendous empirical work which is necessary for drawing up the peripheral grammar. The "rules" according to which the erroneous phrases are constructed are often introduced by interference from the rules of the native language of the translator. It is, of course, impossible to take into account all the languages of the world and their impact on making mistakes in the target language. Therefore, an anticipation-based syntax checker will never be exhaustive.

If we turn from the psychology of the translator to the psychology of the corrector, we notice that the latter is able to correct a phrase even if he has not been confronted with the same mistake before. He does not need to know why the translator made that mistake. The only knowledge the corrector needs is a knowledge about the correct phrases of the target language which are defined by the grammar G. As a consequence, it is reasonable to model an automatic syntax checker similar to a native speaker of the target language who is to proof-read and correct a translation.

We decided to adhere to the following guidelines for the implementation of our syntax checker: In the same way as the parser, the algorithm for error detection and correction must be uniform and language independent. It must not require any linguistic data in addition to the grammar that generates the correct syntactic constructions of the language in question. Drawing up the lingware necessary to parse correct sentences is already difficult and costly enough. The portation of the system to a new language should not be burdened with the task of anticipating the errors that can be made in that language. On the contrary, the exchange of one grammar for another should at the same time enable the parser to assign a structural representation to another input, as well as enabling the syntax checker to detect and correct mistakes made in the new language.

The possibility of correcting a distorted text results from the contextual redundancy of natural languages. The words in a phrase give rise to the expectation of other words with certain properties and vice versa. The basic mechanism of error correction applied in proofreading seems to be the reconciliation of such expectations with the actual context. As long as there are sufficiently precise expectations of what the complementary context should look like, the actual data is likely to be adjustable even if it is ill-formed. This leads to the conclusion that the key to error correction without peripheral grammar is the availability of extensive expectations created by the parser.

The Dependency Unification Grammar (DUG) used in the PLAIN system advocates a lexicalistic approach, i.e. the notion of syntactic structure is derived from the combination capability of words rather than from the constituency of larger units. The combination capability of words (i.e. their contextual expectation) is described by means of templates

8. An empirical study of approximately 1000 syntactic errors occurring in examination papers of German as a foreign language has been conducted by our group.

9. See Weischedel/Sondheimer 1983. Anticipation of errors is assumed, too, by Guenthner/Sedogbo 1986, Mellish 1989 and Schwind 1988.

that assign slots to the word in question. The parser tries to fill the slots with appropriate material. When an error occurs, there will be a gap between the portions of the text analysed so far, because the latter do not meet the expectations of one another. The syntax checker inspects the analysed portions around a gap for open slots that specify the correct context. At the same time, all forms of the inflectional paradigm of the adjacent portion are generated and the one that meets the expectations stated in the corresponding slot is chosen.

We will concentrate in the sequel on the following important features of the PLAIN parser and syntax checker:

- a word-oriented approach to syntax as opposed to a sentence-oriented approach;
- syntax description by equations and unification;
- parsing based on the slot and filler principle;
- parallelism as a guideline for the system's architecture;
- error detection and correction without any additional resources.

17.2 A Word-Oriented Approach to Syntax

Syntax has traditionally been conceived as the study of words and their combination capabilities. With the introduction of formal syntax (which is a prerequisite for machine processing), a shift occurred towards an abstract notion of sentence structure constituting the domain of syntax. Chomsky starts his influential book *Syntactic Structures* (1957) with the assumption: "From now on I will consider a language to be a set (finite or infinite) of sentences, each finite in length and constructed out of a finite set of elements."[10] The goal of a syntactic theory is now to define the set of sentences of a language and to study their structure.

For this purpose, a formal device is introduced that generates all the sentences of a language, starting with an abstract symbol S and arriving, after a series of rewriting operations, at a sequence of categories which are eventually substituted by concrete words. This device is called a generative grammar. The variation of sentences is dealt with on the abstract level of non-terminal symbols which are arranged in various ways by means of rewriting rules. Terminal symbols, i.e. words, are involved only after the abstract structure of any sentence is already generated.

The set of examples shown in Fig. 43 gives an impression of the variations which must be taken into account

It can be seen from the interlinear symbols that each sentence has a different structure and, hence, asks for a different rewriting of the start symbol S. The verbs must be categorized by different symbols (V1, V2, ... , V9) in order to account for their correct co-occurrence with the other categories in the (context free) rewriting rules. However, providing many different symbols for the same part of speech is awkward from the sentence-oriented point of view. The following rule, which contains just one symbol V for all verbs, is more revealing with respect to the abstract structure of the example sentences.

10. Chomsky 1969 (originally 1957), p. 13.

Arthur	left		
NP1	V1		
Arthur	attended	the meeting	
NP1	V2	NP2	
John	gave	a present	to Mary
NP1	V3	NP2	PP_to
John	gave	me	a present
NP1	V3	NP3	NP2
Sheila	reminds	me	of the meeting
NP1	V4	NP2	PP_of
I	differ	with you	about this matter
NP1	V5	PP_with	PP_aboutd
That you have a clean record			helps
CL_that			V6
That Arthur attended the meeting			amazes me
CL_that			V7 NP2
Sheila	agrees	that Arthur should leave	
NP1	V8	CL_that	
Arthur	agreed	to attend the meeting	
NP1	V8	INF	
Sheila	persuaded	him to attend the meeting	
NP1	V9	NP2 INF	
I	wonder	whether he left	
NP1	V10	CL_whether	

Fig. 43: Example sentences with non-terminal symbols

There must be a method to restrict the substitution of the symbol V in the above rule in order to avoid ill-formed sentences like "That Arthur attended the meeting left with you about this possibility." Chomsky introduces context-sensitive subcategorization rules for this purpose.[11] The subcategorization of the verbs in the lexicon might look as shown in Fig. 45.

The entries in Fig. 45 read as follows: Replace the symbol V in a sequence of symbols generated according to Fig. 44 if this sequence is equal to the sequence of symbols in the square brackets with V being substituted for the underscore.

11. Compare Chomsky 1965, pp. 90ff.

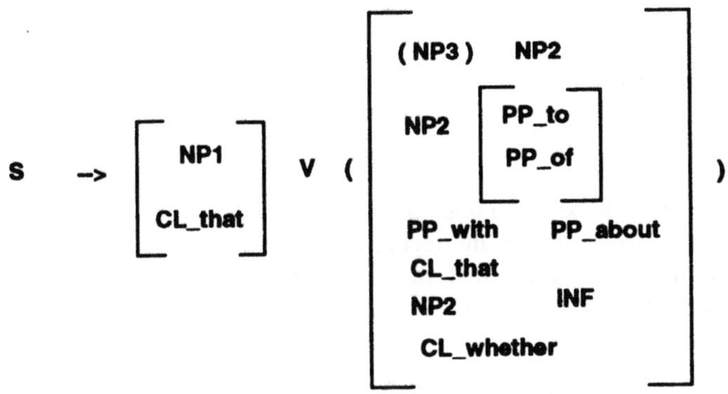

Fig. 44: Abstract sentence rule

The constructs in Fig. 45 are remarkable from several points of view. First of all, the data in square brackets is a precise representation of the contextual expectations which are associated with the respective words. Making them available is an important step towards the strategy for error correction which we have sketched above. As opposed to simple distributional categories, like V1, V2, ..., V9, the complex categorization in Fig. 45 is transparent.[12] Each complex category denotes explicitly the syntactic properties of the words in question. If a categorization according to Fig. 45 is available, there is little information which the rule in Fig.44 adds to it, except the fact that the presence of the elements mentioned in the subcategorization results in a sentence. If we neglect the position of V for the moment, we can replace the rule in Fig. 44 by the more abstract rule in Fig. 46.

leave	V	[NP1 _]
attend	V	[NP1 _ NP2]
give	V	[NP1 _ NP2 PP_to]
	V	[NP1 _ NP3 NP2]
remind	V	[NP1 _ NP2 PP_of]
differ	V	[NP1 _ PP_with PP_about]
help	V	[CL_that _]
amaze	V	[CL_that _ NP2]
agree	V	[NP1 _ CL_that]
	V	[NP1 _ INF]
persuade	V	[NP1 _ NP2 INF]
wonder	V	[NP1 _ CL_whether]

Fig. 45: Context-sensitive subcategorisation of verbs

12. This notion is introduced in Hausser 1985, p. 8.

S --> V [X] X

Fig. 46: An abstract sentence rule

The variable X in Fig. 46 is to be instantiated by the symbols in square brackets associated with the verbs in the lexicon. In fact, the recent development in phrase grammar theory tends to the use of increasingly abstract rules, shifting the burden of the description towards the lexicon. This means, however, that the general development is in favour of a word-oriented approach to syntax.

So far we have argued in the framework of constituency grammars. A much more natural framework for word-oriented decriptions of syntactic structures is dependency grammar, introduced in Tesniere 1959. The version of dependency grammar we use is augmented by various features.

Each node in a dependency tree is labelled by a set of categories. There are three main types of information in this set: a role, a lexeme and a morpho-syntactic category. The latter consists of a symbol for the part of speech and, possibly, a set of typed grammatical features. A simplified representation of the dependency structure of one of the example sentences is depicted in Fig. 47. Role, lexeme and part of speech are separated by a colon.

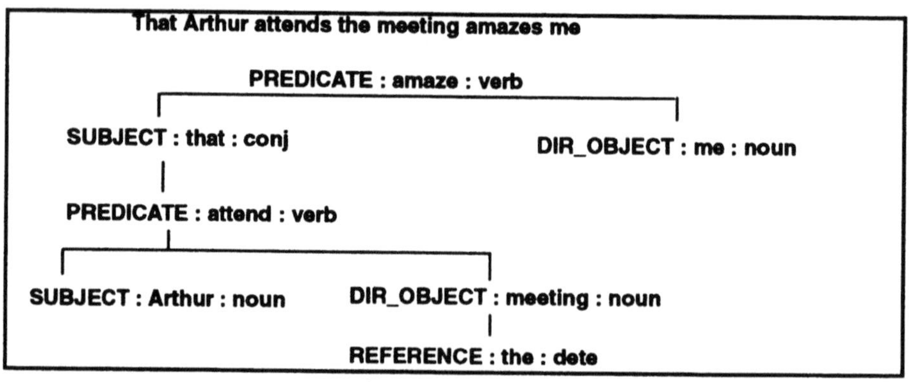

Fig. 47: A DUG representation of an example sentence

Note that dependency is not a relationship between individual words as the tree might suggest. Dependency grammar has been misinterpreted in this respect even by its advocates. In reality, the dependency relationship holds between individual words and their complements which might be quite complex. For example, "amaze" has two complements: SUBJECT and DIR_OBJECT. We might paraphrase the function of these two complements as "the amazing fact" (SUBJECT) and "the one being amazed" (DIR_OBJECT). Of course, the expressions denoting these functions can consist of several words. (This is the case for the SUBJECT complement of "amaze" as well as for the DIR_OBJECT complement of "attend".) Formally, dependency is a relationship between a dominating node and a dependent tree rather than a relationship between two nodes. The role label in a dominating node holds for the whole subtree and not just for the single node.

These stipulations of DUG reconcile the notions of dependency and constituency. Each subtree that constitutes a complement is a constituent. Internally, this constituent is structured according to dependency principles and, hence, is represented again by a dependency tree. With respect to the dominating word, the constituent functions as a whole. If we give names to the complements, we can characterize the constituents which co-occur with the words of our examples as follows.

leave	verb	(+subject)
attend	verb	(+subject, +direct_object)
give	verb	(+subject, +direct_object, +indirect_object)
remind	verb	(+subject, +direct_object, +prep_object_of)
differ	verb	(+subject, +prep_object_with, +prep_object_about)
help	verb	(+subject_clause)
amaze	verb	(+subject_clause, +direct_object)
agree	verb	(+subject, +object_clause)
persuade	verb	(+subject, +direct_object, +object_clause)
wonder	verb	(+subject, +whether_clause)
should	verb	(+infinitive)
meeting	noun	(+determination)
matter	noun	(+determination)
record	noun	(+determination)
of	prep	(+noun_phrase)
to	prep	(+noun_phrase)
with	prep	(+noun_phrase)
about	prep	(+noun_phrase)
that	conj	(+subclause)
whether	conj	(+subclause)
to	conj	(+infinitive)

Fig. 48: Assignment of complements to words in the lexicon

The similarity between the subcategorizations in Fig. 45 and the complement assignments in Fig.48 are obvious. Both specify contextual expectations.

The next step is to describe the building of structure and the morpho-syntactic properties. In most grammars, a set of rules serves this purpose. The DUG uses templates which mirror the dominating and the dependent nodes in the dependency tree directly. A template consists of a dominating node which carries the template's name and, possibly, a morpho-syntactic category which restricts the form of the governing word. The template's name can be the individual lexeme of a word. In this case, the template will apply to that word directly. The other templates apply to a word if they are assigned to it in the lexicon. Figure 48 is an example of such assignments.

A template consists, furthermore, of a so-called slot or, possibly, a disjunction of slots. A slot functions as a variable for a subtree which is to be subordinated to the governing node. The slot contains a precise description of (the dominating node of) the complement that is to fill the slot. Normally, a slot includes a role marker, a variable for the filler's (top-most) lexeme, and a more or less complex morpho-syntactic characterization. There might also be a selectional restriction associated with the lexeme variable. An important augmentation of DUG, as opposed to traditional dependency grammars, is the inclusion of positional categories in the node labels.

Dependency trees, including templates, are represented in the PLAIN system by bracketed expressions. We turn to this format in the subsequent illustrations. Some (simplified) templates necessary for the construction of the example sentences are presented in Fig. 49.

```
(* : +subject
        (SUBJECT: _ : noun position[1]))
(* : +direct_object
        (DIR_OBJECT: _ : noun position[3]))
(* : +indirect_object
        (,      (IND_OBJECT: _ : noun position[2])
                (IND_OBJECT: _ to : prep position[4])))
(* : +prep_object_of
        (PREP_OBJECT: _ of : prep position[4]))
(* : +prep_object_with
        (PREP_OBJECT: _ with : prep position[4]))
(* : +prep_object_about
        (PREP_OBJECT: _ about : prep position[5]))
(* : +subject_clause
        (SUBJECT: _ that : conj position[1]))
(* : +object_clause
        (,      (OBJECT_CLS: _ that : conj position[4])
                (OBJECT_CLS: _ : verb form[inf_to] position[4])))
(* : +determination
        (REFERENCE: _ : dete position[1]
(* : +noun_phrase
        (: _ : noun adjacent[to_the_right]))
(* : +subclause
        (PREDICATE: _ : verb adjacent[to_the_right]))
(ILLOCUTION : assertion
        (PREDICATE: _ : verb adjacent[to_the_left]))
```

Fig. 49: Templates of complements

("*" denotes a variable role. "_" is a variable to be substituted by a filler's lexeme. The last template in Fig. 49 is attributed to the individual lexeme "assertion" which is the internal representation of the period at the end of the sentence. The role (ILLOCUTION) of this lexeme is fixed.)

When a word in the input is processed, the templates are looked up which have been associated with the word in the lexicon. The slots in the templates are then ascribed to the word itself. For example, the word "amaze" is specified in Fig. 48 for +subject_clause and +direct_object. When the parser reaches the word in the input, the following structure will be the result of consulting the lexicon: Figure 50 illustrates the way in which the DUG centers the grammatical information around the individual words, thus giving a detailed account of the contextual expectations which arise with each word. In a rule based phrase structure grammar, this information is not as overtly available. As we have argued above, just these contextual clues are crucial for the corrector if something went wrong in a phrase and has to be fixed.

```
( * : amaze : verb
        (SUBJECT: _ that : conj position[1])
        (DIR_OBJECT: _ : noun position[3]))
```

Fig. 50: Slots for the complements of "amaze"

17.3 Syntax Description by Equation and Unification

Up to this point, we have simplified the descriptions for the sake of perspicuity. In reality, the morpho-syntactic properties of words and their relationships in a sentence might be very complex. For example, the personal and the reflexive pronoun as complements of the German verb "sich ärgern" (to feel angry) must agree in number and person with each other and the verb. The paradigm of correct phrases looks as shown in Fig. 51:

ich ärgere mich	I feel angry
du ärgerst dich	you feel angry
er ärgert sich	he feels angry
wir ärgern uns	we feel angry
ihr ärgert euch	you feel angry
sie ärgern sich	they feel angry

Fig. 51: Example of morpho-syntactic agreement

DUG represents morpho-syntactic properties by sets of typed features. Each feature, e.g. singular or plural, is classified according to its type, e.g. number. For instance, singular is represented as number[singular]. The expression in square brackets is called a "value". This representation is widely accepted now in modern grammar theories. As opposed to other grammars, DUG allows atomic values only (i.e. a value cannot be a typed feature again). However, a set of alternate values is admitted, e.g. person[1st,3rd].

The advantage of the explicit indication of types lies in the fact that agreement between features can now be formulated in terms of the feature type. Instead of stating that singular must go with singular and plural must go with plural, one can state that number must equal number. (Of course, this is what traditional linguists have always done.) The categories in syntactic descriptions function in the same way as constants and variables in an equation. The instantiations of variables must be in agreement with each other. This principle has already been applied in the abstract rule in Fig. 46. The calculation of consistent variable instantiations in a syntactic formula is called "unification". The term has been taken over from logic theorem proving. Grammars which employ similar techniques are known as "unification grammars".

DUG is based on the unification of partial dependency trees, especially on the unification of slots and fillers. This is the only device for building and recognizing phrases. There are no production rules which have to be applied in order to create structures. The unification of features is not a blind mechanism in DUG, but can be tuned to the specific situation. The requirement of agreement between features of a certain type is explicitly stated by means of the special values C (bottom-up agreement) and U (top-down agreement).

The agreement phenomena in Fig. 51 are accounted for by the following assignment of templates to the verb "ärgern":

```
ärgern                          verb (+subject, +reflexive)
(* : +subject
     (SUBJECT: _ : noun case[nomin] person[C] number[C] position[1])
(* : +reflexive
```

Fig. 52: Templates with agreement indication

Syntactic features are specified in slots, they are compared with those of a potential filler and they are propagated across the nodes of the dependency tree if the value "C" is specified. If a feature type is marked for agreement in two categories, then the intersection of values of both sets is formed. If this process results in an empty set for any type, then the unification has failed and the filler must not enter the slot.

Let us assume that the inflected word form "ärgern" (not to be confused with the lexeme "ärgern") is encountered in the input. The corresponding entry in the morphological lexicon and the templates in Fig. 49 would yield the description of this word and its contextual expectations shown in Fig. 53:

```
(* : ärgern : verb person[1st,3rd] number[plural]
     (SUBJECT: _ : noun case[nomin] person[C] number[C] position[1])
     (REFL: _ : reflpron case[acc] person[C] number[C] position[3]))
```

Fig. 53: Features of the inflected word "ärgern"

The personal pronouns which are potential fillers of the subject slot and the reflexive pronouns which are potential fillers of the REFL-slot must be specified in the morphological lexicon in a way similar to Fig. 54.

```
(* : ich : noun case[nomin] person[1st] number[singularl])
(* : wir : noun case[nomin] person[1st] number[plural])
(* : sie : noun case[nomin,acc] person[3rd] number[singular,plural])
(* : uns : reflpron case[acc] person[1st] number[plural])
(* : sich : reflpron case[acc] person[3rd] number[singular,plural])
```

Fig. 54: Lexical features of personal and reflexive pronouns

The following phrases built with "ärgern" and the material in Fig.54 would result from a successful unification of pronouns and slots:

wir ärgern uns	(unified by person[1st] number[plural])
sie ärgern sich	(unified by person[3rd] number[plural])

The unification would fail for the following input:

ich ärgern uns	(number fails)
ich ärgern sich	(number and person fail)
wir ärgern sich	(person fails)
sie ärgern uns	(person fails)

17.4 Parsing Based on the Slot and Filler Principle

Given the morphological and contextual information associated with each word, the basic parsing algorithm is extremely simple. The parser scans the input from left to right and stores each word together with its slots. In a bottom-up fashion, the parser then tries to fit adjacent words as well as larger units which resulted from former steps into the available slots, thus forming a dependency tree which covers both units. When the last word of a phrase is reached, there will be at least one dependency tree which includes nodes for all words of the phrase, except when the input is ill-formed.

Figure 55 sketches the parser's steps with an example. For each step, we list the segment of the input with its right and left margins (in terms of word positions), the structural representation which is either the result of the lexicon consultation or the fitting of a filler tree into a slot, and the templates which specify the remaining contextual expectations. The concrete contents of the templates can be found in Fig. 49.

17.5 Parallelism as a Guideline for the System's Architecture

The reality of parsing texts is, unfortunately, much harder than the above presentation might suggest. Even such a data-driven approach as the DUG-parser faces problems of combinatory explosion. There are hundreds of slots to be checked and thousands of features to be compared. Under these conditions, on-line parsing for the purpose of error correction might still be too costly under many circumstances. Therefore, it is important to keep pace with advances in computing.

One very promising development is the increasing availability of multi-processors for parallel computing. Transputer boards, which can already be integrated in a PC, offer a cheap solution to the hardware problem. So, parallelism might be a realistic option in order to surmount the complexity barrier of linguistic applications.

The availability of parallel processors, however, is not yet a warrant for efficient programs. What is needed are algorithms that optimally solve a problem in parallel steps. To develop such algorithms is, first of all, an intellectual challenge for each domain of application.

In the course of the re-implementation of the PLAIN system for the Translator's Workbench, we decided to revise the architecture, so that it would lend itself to future implementations on multi-processors. It turned out that our word-centered orientation is an advantageous starting point for the introduction of parallelism. If the contextual expectations of each word or segment are locally available, then each pair of a word and its potential complements can be processed at the same time without interference.

1 *That* 1
(* : that)
+subclause

2 *Arthur* 2
(* : Arthur)

3 *attends* 3
(* : attend)
+subject, +direct_object

2 *Arthur attends* 3
(*: attend (SUBJECT : Arthur))
+direct_object

4 *the* 4
(* : the)

5 *meeting* 5
(* : meeting)
+determination

4 *the meeting* 5
(* : meeting (REFERENCE : the))

2 *Arthur attends the meeting* 5
(*: attend (SUBJECT : Arthur) (DIR_OBJECT : meeting (REFERENCE : the)))

1 *that Arthur attends the meeting* 5
(*: that (PREDICATE : attend (SUBJECT : Arthur) (DIR_OBJECT : meeting (REFERENCE : the))))

6 *amazes* 6
(* : amaze)
+subject_clause, +direct_object

1 *That Arthur attends the meeting amazes* 6
(* : amaze (SUBJECT : that (PREDICATE : attend (SUBJECT : Arthur) (DIR_OBJECT : meeting (REFERENCE : the)))))
+direct_object

7 *me* 7
(* : me)

1 *That Arthur attends the meeting amazes me* 7
(* : amaze (SUBJECT : that (PREDICATE : attend (SUBJECT : Arthur) (DIR_OBJECT : meeting (REFERENCE : the)))) (DIR_OBJECT : me))

8 . 8
(ILLOCUTION : assertion)

1 *That Arthur attends the meeting amazes me .* 8
((ILLOCUTION : assertion (PREDICATE : amaze (SUBJECT : that (PREDICATE : attend (SUBJECT : Arthur) (DIR_OBJECT : meeting (REFERENCE : the)))) (DIR_OBJECT : me)))

Fig. 55: Trace of the parser's steps

The basic object of the PLAIN+ parser is the "bulletin". A bulletin provides all the information about a segment of the input, its coverage, its morpho-syntactic features, its dependency representations, its associated templates which indicate the combinatorial potentials. Bulletins can be accessed via a "bulletin board". The bulletin board reports which bulletins are already existant with respect to the input segments.

The overall control of the parser is achieved by means of an agenda. The agenda is a list of processes and arguments. As soon as there is free computing power, a process is taken from the agenda and is executed. Each execution consists of a sequence of actions, possibly producing new data (e.g. new bulletins). All processes on the agenda can be executed in parallel. The main processes are:

- the scanner, which reads the next word from the input and extracts the morpho-syntactic information for this word from the lexicon;
- the predictor, which collects all of the combinatorial information for the word from the lexicon;
- the selector, which chooses the pairs of bulletins that should be compared for compatibility;
- the completor, which tries to combine segments on the basis of the information in their bulletins in order to construct a coherent dependency tree;
- the assess-result process, which checks the presence of a successful parse.

Except for the initial process (i.e. the scanner for the first word), processes and their arguments are put on the agenda by other processes. The scanner puts a scanner process for the next word on the agenda. Furthermore, it puts one predictor process for each reading of the actual word on the agenda. If the scanner encounters a sentence boundary, then it puts the assess-result process on the agenda.

The predictor constructs a bulletin for the reading in question and supplies, most importantly, the templates which specify the combination capabilities of the word. There might be alternate combination frames. For each frame, the predictor puts an instance of the selector process on the agenda.

The selector looks up all bulletins which are to be compared with the actual one. The selector consults the bulletin board for this purpose. The selector puts a completor process on the agenda for each pair of bulletins it has chosen. If the heap of appropriate bulletins is exhausted, the selector process might have to wait until more bulletins have been produced by other processes.

The completor tries to fit one of the two structures described in the bulletins into a slot of the other one, and vice versa. In each of the successful cases (there might me more than one possibility), the completor draws up a new bulletin. This bulletin provides the data about the resulting structure and is put on the agenda as the argument of a selector process. This technique will cause a recursive application of the completor to larger and larger units. The parser will stop when a sentence boundary has been encountered and the agenda is empty.

17.6 Error Detection and Correction Without any Additional Resources

We have pointed out that the only resource for correcting ill-formed phrases should be the grammar which defines the well-formed phrases. The crucial point of our solution is the word-oriented formulation of our grammar. All the possible syntactic relationships and features of the grammar are attached to the individual words by means of the templates. What other grammars put into abstract rules, is turned into contextual expectations of individual words and stated in the form of slots. Such expectations are always available, although the context might not meet them, because the phrase is ill-formed.

Given these prerequisites, the correction of a syntactic error is a comparatively simple task. What we have to do is to inspect the available but unsatisfied slots, inspect the context and reconcile the two. Technically, the latter is done in two steps. First we vary the context, and then we check whether any of the new contexts fits the given slots.

The following additional processes are involved in the task of error detection and correction:

- the revisor, which calculates the paths of segments covering the phrase, chooses the shortest path (the one with the fewest segments) and proposes one segment after the other for correction;
- the generator, which creates the alternative forms of the syntactic paradigm of which the given segment is an instance.

The assess-result process was the last one on the aganda during the phase of ordinary parsing. It yields the correct parse if there is one. Otherwise, it puts the revisor process on the agenda. The revisor compiles a path and restricts the bulletin- board to the bulletins of that path. For each promising segment in the row (i.e. for each one that either contains an expectation or is likely to be adjustable to the expectation of another segment), the revisor puts an instance of the generator process on the agenda. At the end of the path, the revisor also puts the assess-result process on the agenda.

The generator creates all the forms of the paradigm of which the given segment is an instance. This task is achieved by a special mechanism which is inherent to our morpho-syntactic lexicon. The mechanism allows all inflectional word forms and their categories to be generated for a given word. If the segment to be varied is a complex unit, all the words in it are varied, too, according to the internal agreement requirements of the complex unit. The generator also creates items according to the selectional restrictions in the slots if there is no corresponding item in the input. The generator draws up a bulletin for each new segment and puts it on the agenda as an argument of the standard selector process.

The selector looks up all bulletins in the restricted bulletin board which are to be compared with the bulletin for the generated segment. The rest is done just as in the case of ordinary parsing. The selector puts a completor process on the agenda for each pair of bulletins it has chosen. The completor process works in the usual way trying to fit the (revised) fillers into the available slots. Parsing will continue until the assess-result process is the only one left on the agenda.

The assess-result process proposes the successful parses as candidates for the correction. If no such result has been achieved, then the revisor process is put on the agenda again in order to check on another path.

We conclude with an example. Let us assume that the input is "Sheila agree Arthur leave".

```
1 Sheila 1
(* : Sheila : noun person[3rd] number[singular]

2 agree 2
(* : agree : verb person[1st,2nd] number[singular]
                (SUBJECT: _ : noun person[C] number[C] position[1])
                (OBJECT_CL: _ that : conj position[3]))

2 agree 2
(* : agree : verb person[1st,2nd,3rd] number[plural]
                (SUBJECT: _ : noun person[C] number[C] position[1])
                (OBJECT_CL: _ that : conj position[3]))

3 Arthur 3
(* : Arthur : noun person[3rd] number[singular]

4 leave 4
(* : leave : verb person[1st,2nd] number[singular]
                (SUBJECT: _ : noun person[C] number[C] position[1]))

4 leave 4
(* : leave : verb person[1st,2nd,3rd] number[plural]
```

Fig. 56: Parsing failure for "Sheila agree Arthur leave"

The initial parsing attempt will fail completely. The situation at the end of this phase is shown in Fig. 56. There is just one path covering the input which consists of as many segments as there are words. The revisor initiates the generator, which creates the complementary word forms of the respective paradigms shown in Fig. 57:

```
2 agrees 2
(* : agree : verb person[3rd] number[singular]
                (SUBJECT: _ : noun person[C] number[C] position[1])
                (OBJECT_CL: _ that : conj position[3]))


4 leaves 4
(* : leave : verb person[3rd] number[singular]
                (SUBJECT: _ : noun person[C] number[C] position[1]))
```

Fig. 57: New items generated

Now parsing is resumed. It yields the result shown in Fig. 58.

```
1 Sheila agrees 2
(* : agree : verb person[3rd] number[singular]
             (SUBJECT: Sheila : noun person[C] number[C] position[1])
             (OBJECT_CL: _ that : conj position[3]))
3 Arthur leaves 4
(* : leave : verb person[3rd] number[singular]
```

Fig. 58: Parsing the revised phrase

There is still no complete parse. Therefore, the revisor is activated again. There is a new path consisting of two segments (as displayed in Fig. 58). However, the generator cannot create any new word forms. In this situation the slots of the segments are inspected. The generator encounters the selectional lexeme "that" and creates the corresponding word. The parser now tries again and comes up with the result shown in Fig. 59.

```
2' that 2'
(* : that : conj
             (PREDICATE: _ : verb adjacent[to_the_right])

2' that Arthur leaves 4
(* : that
             (PREDICATE : leave : verb person[3rd] number[singular] adjacent[to_the_right]
             (SUBJECT: Arthur : noun person[C] number[C] position[1]))

1 Sheila agrees that Arthur leaves 4
(* : agree : verb person[3rd] number[singular]
             (SUBJECT: Sheila : noun person[C] number[C] position[1])
             (OBJECT_CL: that : conj position[3]
             (PREDICATE : leave : verb person[3rd] number[singular] adjacent[to_the_right]
             (SUBJECT: Arthur : noun person[C] number[C] position[1]))
```

Fig. 59: Corrected Output

18. Greek Language Tools

Stratis Karamanlakis, Alexios Zavras

18.1 Introduction

The modern Greek language is the result of a continuous evolutionary process that spans over 3000 years. This long evolutionary process resulted in a language that is both rich and loosely-defined.

The Greek language is characterized by the unavailability of a concrete and unambiguous definition, and by its complicated grammatical and orthographic rules. This complexity has hindered the development of electronic processing tools for the language. Furthermore, the relatively small market size made investments in language tools not an obvious proposition.

The TWB provided the opportunity by which a number of internal developments by L-CUBE were assembled to a coherent set of language tools. A lexicon of 40000 lemmas has been developed, a spelling checking / thesaurus / hyphenation engine has been built and has been ported to UNIX, Apple, and DOS environments. Finally tight bindings have been implemented with Quark XPress in the Apple environment and FrameMaker under UNIX.

18.2 Background

The Greek language has to be understood as a continuum of types and rules whose origin lies in ancient Greek, coexisting with more recent ones, and where the proper spelling of a word or its types is quite often up to interpretation. Looking back only two hundred years, there are at least two major definitions of the "Greek language" that have been proposed and widely used. The first one contains vocabulary and rules closer to the ancient Greek (which in itself is a uniquely defined entity), while the second is closer to the everyday spoken Greek. A variant of the latter has been adopted by the Greek Government as the official form of the language since the early 1980s. This form of the language has been chosen to be supported by the Greek Language Tools. The decision has been based on consultations with potential users of the tools, and also from the fact that inclusion of words or types belonging to other forms of the language was problematic at least for PCs, since available character sets have no provision for the plethora of accents that will be required.

Another issue for the development of language tools for the Greek language is the character encoding for the Greek characters. There exists an International Standard (which is also a standard of the Hellenic Organization for Standardization, ELOT), which specifies the representation of Greek characters. This standard is ISO 8859-7 (also known as standard ELOT-928), and it specifies that each Greek character should be encoded in an 8-bit byte. The standard is actually an extension of the usual ASCII representation, with the Greek characters occupying the positions 128 to 254 (decimal).

Unfortunately, in the DOS world a different encoding than the one specified by the standard is used almost exclusively, and in the Apple Macintosh world yet another one is used. Although there are tendencies for convergence to the standard, it is clear that a product currently being developed and aiming at supporting all major platforms has to address the peculiarities of each and every one of them. In the X -Window environment on UNIX platforms, Greek characters usage is not yet widespread and in the course of the development special Greek fonts were produced, with the encoding specified in the ISO 8859-7 standard.

In the Greek Language Tools, an internal encoding scheme that was capable of representing all characters of the Greek language was defined. This way all internal processing and data are platform-independent, and translation to the character encoding of the host machine is implemented only for human interface reasons.

18.2.1 The Greek Language Model

Greek is a heavily inflective language. Although ancient forms of the language were far more complex, modern Greek is still inflective enough to make lexicon building a very time-demanding operation. The Greek inflective words have two parts: the stem of the word, which is joined with a series of suffixes, thus forming complete words. Although this scheme describes most European languages, the number of suffixes that may be combined with one stem is much higher in Greek. Furthermore, when a suffix is juxtaposed to a stem, the accent of the stem may be shifted by one or two syllables. These shifts is a very common phenomenon in Greek and there exist inflectional models that differ only in the way the accent changes positions. Finally, there is no rigorous and, more important, unambiguous way to describe how words are formed by stems and suffixes, along with the accent shifts induced. However, a tool targeted to the document processing market should accommodate for all, if possible, opinions on the language and let the user enforce the style of his own choice.

An efficient scheme describing the entries of a spelling dictionary is obviously of critical importance. The denser such a scheme is, the less storage it occupies, the more words can be kept in memory during checking, and the faster the correction is. The possible suffixes have been grouped into inflectional paradigms that describe how a word is formed by these suffixes, and what accentuation shifts may occur. Many lemmas do not abide fully to the grammatical and spelling rules, and hence exceptions arise. The defined model takes special care in order to minimize the exceptions that have to accompany the lemmas concerned, thus saving space and processing time.

An extension of the approach taken for the suffix decomposition is not straight forward for the prefixes of Greek words. The way prefixes are handled by the contemporary Greek language, has dramatically changed in the past few years. Since a spelling checking system must be open to current and future changes in the language, relying heavily in prefix removal was not considered appropriate.

18.2.2 The Spelling Checking Problem

The spelling correction process can be decomposed to the following two basic stages:

1. detection, where an input word is classified as either correctly or incorrectly spelled
2. correction, where the software must determine the correctly-spelled word, that was most llikely originally meant.

If a word is seen as a point in a multidimensional space of letter sequences, then the quest for a correct word that is similar to an erroneous one, can be divided in three phases:

1. a neighbourhood of the input word is defined so as to avoid searching the whole pattern space and instead limit the search where it is more probable to succeed,
2. this neighbourhood is traversed in a way that the most promising parts are checked first, and
3. words found are compared with the given one and certain similarity criteria are checked.

Knowledge of the way spelling errors were introduced in a document helps in order to define this neighbourhood and the traversal criteria. Errors fall basically in three categories: author ignorance of correct spelling, typographical errors when text is typed, and acquisition of data by the computer system. All of these errors can be modelled by four basic operations, namely insertion, deletion, substitution, and transposition. These operations are useful in order to establish a way to measure the difference between two words.

Depending on the operational environment (OS, memory size, etc.), a number of design choices can be made for the efficient implementation of a spelling checker. These design choices for the overall implementation are discussed in the sequel.

18.3 Greek Language Tools

The functionality of the developed Greek language tools is in the following areas:

- Spelling correction
- Thesaurus
- Hyphenation
- Lexica Tools

The architecture of these tools and the various modules that comprise them are described below.

18.3.1 The Detector Engine

The Greek Spelling Checker is comprised by two functionally independent modules, the detector module and the corrector module. They both operate on a spelling dictionary of Greek words, that contains approximately 40000 lemmas.

The detector is the module that accepts as input a word, and tries to match it with the dictionary entries. If the word is found in the dictionary it is considered correct, otherwise it is considered erroneous.

In a simplified description, the detector tries to decompose morphologically the input word. The ending part of the word is checked against the set of valid suffixes, and for each matching suffix, the detector searches the dictionary for the corresponding stem. When a stem is found, the validity of the stem-suffix combination must be verified with respect to suffix set, accent position etc.

Since the detector is the module that necessarily handles the whole input document (and not only the misspelled words as the corrector does), its efficiency is critical for the whole system. The following two-level search strategy was implemented, which highly speeds the detector operation: When a word is given it is first checked against a table of most frequently used words and only if this look-up fails the word is morphologically decomposed and searched for in the main dictionary. Since a few hundreds of words account for the great percentage of words utilized in any document, there is high probability that this search will succeed, thus avoiding a series of accesses to the main dictionary.

The organization of the table of most commonly used words is based on the trie data structure. The trie has the advantage that it compares a character at a time instead of whole strings, and the number of comparisons needed equals the string length. This structure is also used to organize the suffixes thus speeding up the morphological decomposition phase described above.

18.3.2 The Corrector Engine

The corrector is the module that accepts as input an erroneous word (a word not found in the dictionary during the detection phase), and tries to find a word (or words) similar to the given one.

As mentioned before, the corrector considers as candidates for replacement of an erroneous word, only these dictionary entries that fall inside this word's neighbourhood. In order to define such a neighbourhood, the erroneous word goes through a series of transformations producing a list of strings. These strings define neighbourhood in the dictionary. For each entry in the area its distance from the erroneous word is calculated. If it is below a suitable threshold, the entry is appended to a list of replacements of the erroneous word, which will be proposed to the user.

The distance between words has a rather ambiguous content, which among others strongly depends on the flavour of similarity of the individual user. This similarity can be described in terms of the Damerau-Levenstein distance function. This approach considers as distance between two words the sum of the costs of the primitive editing operations (insertion, deletion, substitution, transposition) that were defined above.

The Damerau-Levenstein criterion does not compare other aspects of candidate words, such as phonetic resemblance, accented syllables etc., that seem to contribute to the feeling of similarity. The approach chosen is based on Damerau-Levenstein with properly adjusted costs for the editing operations. In addition, the words are compared in a form in which there is no distinction between similarly uttered vowels.

The distance threshold against which candidate words are compared also requires subtle treatment. If it is too high, the user will be flooded with suggestions, while if too low, there will be many situations where the corrector will fail to suggest anything at all, simply because the correct suggestion is outside the threshold. The threshold is therefore dynamically adjusted to the results of the dictionary search.

18.3.3 Lexicon Organization and Memory management

The two modules interact with the file system via a disk paging mechanism. Due to memory constraints that can exist in bindings for certain platforms, only a fixed number of pages reside in main memory, at every given moment. Therefore, when this number of pages is already in memory, no more requests can be satisfied unless some pages are released. The page replacement policy selected is the LFU (Least Frequently Used).

Both modules have access to the same lexicon structures in order to increase space exploitation, and to centralize data management. It must be noted that general purpose data organization schemes did not seem fit for the requirements of these two modules. Among the most important of these requirements, are

1. direct access when a suspect word is at hand (detection)
2. efficient scanning of some neighbourhood of a target word when searching for similar words (correction)
3. efficient storage of structures that have a totally variant number of fields.

To cover these requirements, a specialized hashing function was devised, based on the soundex code, a method originally used to overcome the erroneous spelling of words that were phonetically dictated. The function is essentially a mapping of the input alphabet to an alphabet of much fewer symbols, and generates a hash code that can be up to six bytes long. Furthermore, this mapping hides characteristics of the source word, that are particularly error-prone, such as double letters and phonetically equivalent letters or dipthongs.

Its most important property is that the neighbourhood of the hash code obtained for a target word corresponds to hash codes of words in the neighbourhood of the original target. This means that instead of modifying the target word, one can modify its hash code and use the transformed codes to search the lexicon. Two advantages become apparent:

1. Since the definition domain of a hash code is much narrower than that of a regular word, the number of resulting codes is significantly smaller than that of the words produced under the same transformations, resulting in a significantly lower number of disk requests.
2. Since the disk image of the dictionary is organized by the hash codes of its entries, then hash codes that neighbour according to the transformations of the correction phase also neighbour physically, on disk. Page swapping is therefore reduced, with obvious gains in the correction speed.

The two modules share also a memory management mechanism. The need for such a mechanism becomes apparent if one considers the number of operations involved in checking a word for correct spelling, and trying to suggest a similar one. The general purpose memory allocation routines introduce several problems: calls to allocate and release memory to the operating system result in a considerable overhead that can not be ignored. Furthermore, since general purpose routines ignore the nature of the data involved, they can not apply any specific optimization algorithms in the way data are allocated or released, and thus can not avoid the memory fragmentation that further undermines the optimal operation of the system.

The memory management system implemented has two main components:

1. A dictionary memory buffer, where the dictionary entries are loaded. It offers allocation and release of blocks of arbitrary size and reorganization of the allocated blocks when fragmentation (inevitably) becomes disturbing.
2. An object cache. Various data objects are frequently allocated and released. The cache can hold released objects, up to a limit, and hence allocation requests are satisfied without using conventional allocation routines, unless the cache is empty.

18.3.4 Hyphenation and Thesaurus

The objective of the Hyphenation and Thesaurus development, was a portable engine that can work in conjunction with the developed spelling checking tools.

Hyphenation is essential in document processing, mainly because without it no proper text formatting can take place. Hyphenation in Greek must cope with inconsistencies of the current grammatical rules. Additionally, these rules, that some times took the phonetic approach to hyphenation to extremes, are very seldom followed in every day writing.

The design took into account the various opinions about how Greek words have to be hyphenated, by implementing in the same module all known ones, and leaving this way to the user the freedom to choose one of the possible variants. The same was done for more than one language variant, since their usage is still widespread.

The Greek Thesaurus gets its information from a lexical database that currently contains only a few hundred words. The database contains lemmas and the relations between them. Each lemma in the database has a unique identifier associated with it. Each entry contains the lemma concerned and the identifiers of lemmas that are related with it.

Given an input word, the thesaurus invokes the spelling detector. The detector must verify that the word is correctly spelled, because otherwise there is no point in continuing to work with it and the user should instead try to correct it. If the word is accepted, the detector returns the lemma of the input word. The thesaurus then consults the database for any entries concerning this lemma. If an entry is found, the lemmas whose identifiers are contained in it are retrieved and presented to the user.

18.4 Lexicon Development

The development of a lexicon is a costly and time-consuming process, requiring the coordination of individuals from different fields. Moreover, minor omissions in the initial phases may result in considerable overhead for corrections later, due to the volumes of data. The most important issues that should be noted are:

1. First, a large part of lexicon development involves manual (as opposed to automated) work. The grammatical information pertinent to a lemma can only be provided by a group of linguists.
2. Second, the accuracy and consistency of a lexicon is of crucial importance for the success of any language tool that is based upon it. Selection of lemmas, entry in the lexicon and validation of the lexicon should be carried out with extreme care in order to cover as many as possible of the errors that unavoidably occur.

3. Third, a lexicon records some aspect of the language or languages it covers. Since the language evolves, a lexicon should be capable of following this evolution. Thus the development of lexicon is a continuous process.

In order to construct the lexicon of the Greek Spelling Checker, the following steps were undertaken:

1. Selection of lemmas. In order to rapidly develop a prototype of the lexicon and clarify some of the issues involved, a corpus of 4000 lemmas was selected by experienced linguists. The criterion for selection was their frequency of usage, which due to lack of statistical data, had to be judged by the linguists involved. After this step, a commercial dictionary was selected and approximately 40000 lemmas were entered into the lexicon.
2. Grammatical information entry. For each lemma entered in the lexicon, a linguist provided the grammatical information related to it. This information includes inflectional models, accentuation shifts and formation and recording of derived types, that are often omitted as obvious from human lexica. The interface through which this information is provided must account for user-friendliness and consistency. A special software, with the appropriate interface, has been developed for this phase.
3. Lexicon validation. The lemmas entered into the lexicon have been exported along with the complete information related to them. This information was extensively checked. This process, necessarily carried out by the linguists involved, posed considerable logistic problems.
4. Spelling Checker and Thesaurus lexicon. A tool for document processing has specific requirements in performance, resources, etc., that make the general purpose grammatical lexicon not suitable for it. Instead, data structures more appropriate to the specific exploitation of the lexicon must be designed, and the lexicon data must be projected on these formats. A suite of transformation tools was developed for that purpose. On the other hand a database meant to be the source of the various lexica has been developed.

18.5 Statistical Information

Statistical information about the language concerned is essential for document processing tools. Knowledge of frequencies of words, digrams or n-grams in general, suffixes etc., can significantly improve the performance of these tools, when incorporated in the data structures and algorithms involved.

Focusing into the spelling checker requirements, statistical information is necessary for the construction of the dictionary of common words, the arrangement of data on the main dictionary so that rarely used words do not hinder the retrieval of more common ones etc. Another point where statistical information is needed, is when the suggestions of the corrector should be presented to the user. As aforementioned, if the criterion for ordering these words is solely their Damerau-Levenstein distance, the result might be counterintuitive for the user. Therefore, the ordering criterion should be extended to include knowledge of the word frequency.

In order to extract the statistical information, large amounts of text files have been acquired from a number of sources. It has to be recognized that the logistic effort required has been originally underestimated. The data came in any kind of file format, character encoding and media, and conversion and translation effort, most of it necessarily with human attendance, was almost always required. In acquiring the necessary texts, issues of copyright and confidentiality proved to be a serious problem. Especially acquiring business related documents was an extremely lengthy process.

The acquired text, after passing through the filtering and conversion process in order to be converted to a common format, were fed to a modified UNIX version of the spelling detector, that was communicating with the lexicon module. The lemmas or types found in the lexicon were passed to the statistics gathering modules.

The parameters of major relevance to the spelling checker were the frequencies of lemmata and words, the frequencies of individual letters, digrams and trigrams, and the frequencies of suffixes and suffixes sets. The main results are summarized in the following:

The overall rejection ratio (percentage of words not found in the lexicon) was around 9%. After subtracting geographical terms and various linguistic extremes the rejection ratio was about 3% and more than half of it represented words that had to be included in the lexicon. About thirty percent represented diminutive types of noun or adjectives. The most common of these terms are incorporated in the lexicon, but a linguistic analysis of the phenomenon is in progress to evaluate the feasibility of facing the problem on a semi-algorithmic basis without undue increase of the lexicon size.

Concerning the common words dictionary, it was found that 40 lemmas have a cumulative probability of more than 28%. The table of common words used by the spelling checker has been modified on the basis of the findings.

18.6 Exploitation

The Greek Spelling Checker operates on all major computing platforms, namely Apple Macintoshes, DOS machines (IBM PCs and compatibles) and UNIX workstations. These bindings and the exploitation plans are summarized in the sections that follow.

18.6.1 Macintosh

The Macintosh is perhaps the most popular platform in Electronic Publishing. Among the most important software packages in this area is Quark XPress, a page layout program that is extensively used for professional production of a variety of publications, ranging from small leaflets to daily newspapers. An important feature of Quark XPress is its open architecture. Based on the concept of code resources that are native to MacOS, XPress allows integration with modules that communicate through a high-level functional interface. This modules are called Quark Xtensions.

The Greek Spelling Checker was integrated with Quark XPress through this mechanism. It appears to the user as a menu item, along with the menu items of corresponding tools for English. When activated, it checks the document for errors, notifying the user for suspect words, and suggests the candidates for correction when prompted by the user. It must be noted that all these actions take place in seamless cooperation with the host application. The interface to the user is consistent with the Apple Human Interface Guidelines, whereas the suggestions of the spelling checker always retain the attributes of the original text.

18.6.2 DOS

In the DOS arena, a diversity of document processing tools and even differences in platform make it difficult to integrate with any particular product. For example, although the Microsoft Windows is a successful environment, it is only partially established in Greece, mainly due to its considerable resource requirements. On the other hand, existing word processing or page layout products are rather "closed" as far as integration with other software is concerned.

These are the reasons why currently the Greek Spelling Checker exists for DOS only as a stand-alone program, supporting text files. However, the company is working for a product aiming at the Windows platform.

18.6.3 UNIX

The document processing tools that were previously described benefit greatly from their port to a UNIX platform.

The major improvement comes from the different architecture used for the tools: since UNIX is a multiprocessing operating system, there was no need for the totality of the document processing tools to be a single program (process). Therefore, they were transformed into a client-server architecture, where the servers run continuously in the background and service requests from the clients. This client-server architecture is implemented using the Remote Procedure Call (RPC) protocol, resulting in a completely distributed system.

There are distinct servers for each of the services the tools provide, i.e., detection, correction, hyphenation and thesaurus. However, it is perfectly legal to have a multitude of servers of the same kind running, each one servicing a specific kind of request. For example, one can envision an environment where there is a dedicated spelling correction server for words relevant to medical sciences, one for words used in legal documents, etc. These servers are functionally equivalent; they just use specialized dictionaries. With this architecture, when a client issues a request, any server that knows how to handle it answers, thus achieving minimum delay, since a client never waits for a busy server to be free, while there is another server sitting idle.

Access to these servers is provided by either character-based clients, much in the manner of the original UNIX spell program, and a graphical interface, based on the X Window System.

The X interface to the tools was tailored to communicate with FrameMaker, by Frame Corporation, which is one of the best word processing and page layout software available for UNIX workstations. The user uses FrameMaker to write his document, and the Greek Spelling Checker tools to work on it. The words produced by the Greek Language Tools can be automatically incorporated in the FrameMaker document.

The intercommunication between FrameMaker and the Greek Spelling Checker X11 Front End is automatic, and based on well-defined interface mechanisms, namely the X-Selection Buffer and RPC commands, that are supported among different versions of both the X11 system and FrameMaker.

Since there is no widely available font, for displaying Greek text in the X Window System environment, Greek fonts according to the ISO 8859-7 encoding were developed. Furthermore, in order to be able to input Greek characters, a toggling mechanism between English and Greek keyboard states was implemented, based on the translation mechanism of the X Toolkit, which is an integral part of the X Window System. The complete implementation of the Greek keyboard driver is accomplished solely through resources, without any modification of the X Window System code.

18.6.4 Summary

The development work had the commercial exploitation built-in. The code for the various modules has been designed to be portable to the extreme, physical memory requirements are small for all implementations, and storage requirements for the lexicon are very modest (just over one megabyte). Also the lexica work went to great lengths to ensure that the linguistic decisions made will be acceptable by the largest possible customer base. The seamless binding to popular word processors and page layout products was also a target from the beginning of the development.

Two such bindings exist currently, with XPress for the Macintosh world, and with FrameMaker for the UNIX platforms. The first one is basically a production grade implementation, while for the second one some product development work is still carried out. These two implementations will be commercially available in June 1992 and September 1992 respectively, as shrink-wrapped packages.

The engines of the various tools will also be integrated in turnkey systems that the company is installing for the Editing/Publishing Sector. Such an integration has been carried out for a daily newspaper editorial system, and another one is currently under progress for a subtitling facility for a major Greek Video Studio.

Future plans include the lexicon improvement in coverage (70000 words), a WordPerfect binding, and the supply of the same facilities in an integrated English-Greek environment.

V. Towards Operationality -

A European Translator's Workbench

19. Integrating Translation Resources and Tools

Beate von Kleist-Retzow, Marianne Kugler, Gabriele Stallwitz, Klemens Waldhör, TA Triumph-Adler AG

Two prototypes were developed in the course of the Translator's Workbench project: the fully integrated UNIX workbench[1] and a more reduced DOS version running under MS Windows. For each of these versions some guidelines had to be followed by the partners willing to integrate their software. The interface and integration activities are described in the following chapter.

19.1 Translation Assistant Editor - Multilingual Text Processing with Personal Computers

19.1.1 How Can Translators Get Help by a Text Processing System?

Machine translation has been intensively worked on during the last decades, but hardly any acceptable translation system is available for personal computers yet: Although there is already some software on the market, the qualitiy of these translations is not acceptable. Another handicap is that most of these systems even use their own text format, which forces the users to convert their text into the translating system's special format, start the translation, and then re-convert and load it into the text format of their own word processing system.

This is quite an effort, obviously (PC-Welt 11/91). Our approach ships around this cliff by simply connecting a professional text editor and TAE tools in a way the user does not need to convert texts - which normally even causes loss of format information - and even does not need to interrupt his or her text processing session. A user simply edits the source text, checks it for misspellings with the help of the Proofreader, opens a target text window, positions both windows on the screen by using a TAE function, and starts translating. As soon as the user finds a word he or she does not know exactly how to translate, he or she selects it and sends it to a dictionary application that comes up with translation suggestions and additional information. The user can browse through the dictionary index for getting further information or just for looking up other entries. Furthermore, a Translation Memory tool provides the possibility of storing and retrieving frequently used phrases of special purpose languages and their translations. This is useful, for example, for translators who do a lot of similar translations, like computer manuals, patent texts and so on.

19.1.2 Drilling Hooks into WinWord

So far for the underlying idea - but how can it be realized? For being able to use windows applications within Winword, a special interface is necessary. This interface must be capable of establishing Dynamic Data Exchange (DDE) links to applications that act as DDE servers, while WinWord acts as DDE client. Further, there must be a possibility of adapting the standard WinWord surface to the task of a Translator's Workbench. Both problems can be solved by WinWord's macro language, WordBASIC, a BASIC dialect that provides

1. We would like to thank Thomas Glombik, SNI, for his work on the FrameMaker integration.

both features necessary for designing individual user interfaces and special functions for communicating with other Windows applications. By starting WinWord, the TAE interface is built up by a special macro which comes up with a dialog box asking the users whether to use the TAE extensions or not. Additionally, users can choose the languages they wants to work with and arrange windows as they please.

19.1.3 The Translator's Workbench User Interface

What a translator really needs while editing and translating texts is a chance to compare source and target texts directly. He or she also needs a help for stepping through one text pagewise and quickly finding the corresponding text part within the other text: All this is done by a Parallel Scrolling function. Furthermore, there must be a possibility of arranging texts on the screen either horizontally or vertically, and to change the arrangement whenever it is necessary. The WinWord based TAE provides both functions - and thus it provides an editing support for translators. Figure 60 shows the TAE surface with source and target language texts arranged vertically. The main menu displayed on the menu bar has already been extended by starting WinWord with the TAE option: Within the Window menu you find the additional functions recently discussed. The Utilities menu is extended by the TAE features Proofreading, Translation Memory and HFR Dictionary which are to be discussed within the next sections.

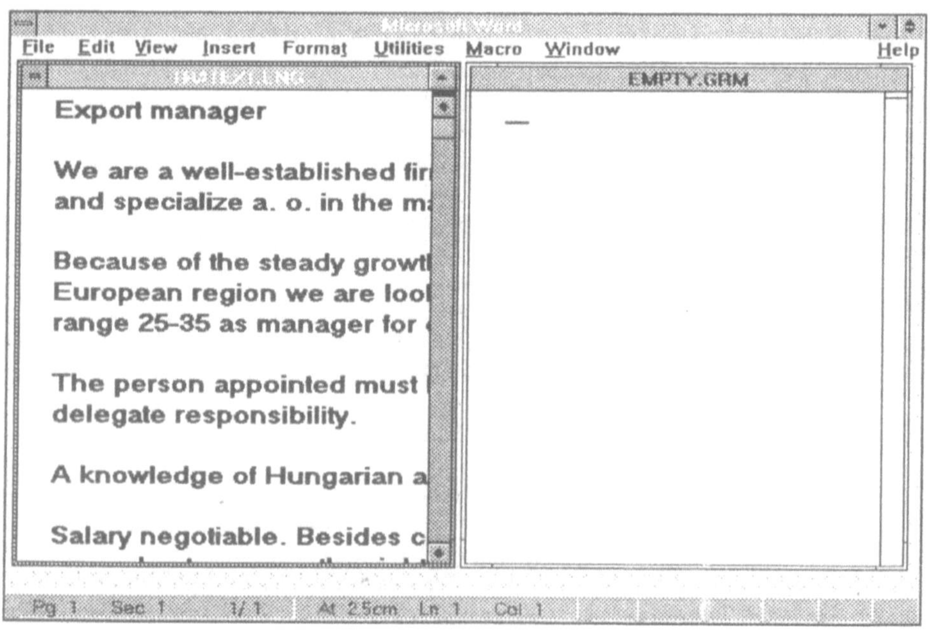

Fig. 60: The WinWord TAE interface

19.1.4 It's Not Magic - It's Just Proofreading!

WinWord already comprises a spellchecking tool. Why does the TAE extension have its own Proofreading tool? This question can be answered very easily: In a first step, the TAE Proofreading tools finds typing errors and misspelling within words, like any other spellchecking programs. But what is new is that in a second step even those errors can be corrected that can only be recognized by scrutinizing not single, isolated words but multi-words and words in context. This extended spelling software has been developped at the TA Triumph-Adler Laboratories and has been built into several MS-DOS and UNIX applications already. For TAE purposes, the program has been modified slightly and designed as a Windows DDE server application. WinWord can call this application via a WordBASIC macro that initiates and controls the DDE communication channel. It also ensures that the right parameters are handed over to the server application. For that reason, a dialog box (Fig. 61) checks the parameters for the Proofreading run.

Besides the language you want to check, you can also choose one out of three modes. Default is Checking Run, which selects your text starting with the cursor position and sends it to the Proofreading application. If Dictionary Lookup is selected, the paragraph of text recently typed in will be selected and checked. This mode is very helpful if the user feels unsure about the spelling of the phrase just typed in. In both cases, the WordBASIC macro sends the selected text to the Proofreading application. Whenever the Proofreading application finds a mistake - either a simple misspelling or a higher-order, cognitive error - the system comes up with a dialog box that helps the user correcting the error by.

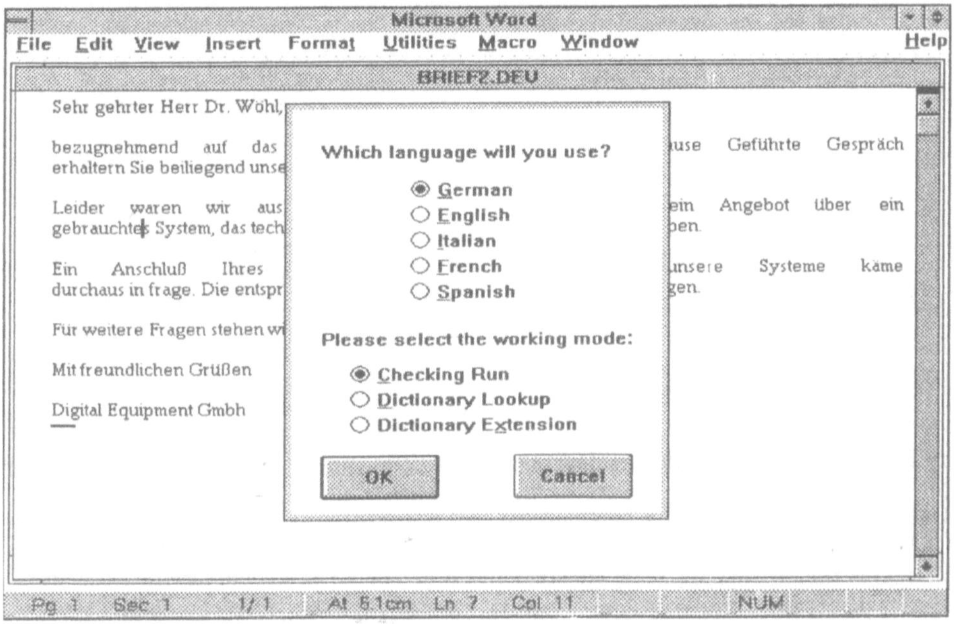

Fig. 61: After calling the TAE proofreading tool, the user is asked to check some parameters

displaying an explanation or rule that is presented together with a correction proposal - see Fig. 61 for example. The Proofreading application provides an explanation or rule for each error

The Dictionary Extension mode allows adding multi-words or words in context to the dictionary. As the user has to type in information concerning the word in focus, the left and right context and what possible misspellings could look like, this option should be used by experienced users only. But if users want to add isolated words like e.g. idioms, names, and trade marks, they can do it while running the Proofreading tool in one of the checking modes: Whenever the first step of the Proofreading program comes up with a name the system does not know yet, the Add... button can be pressed and the word (or whatever word the user types in) can be added the the user dictionary. The message box displayed in Fig. 62 enables the user to accept the suggested correction, ignore it and continue checking, or to cancel the checking run .

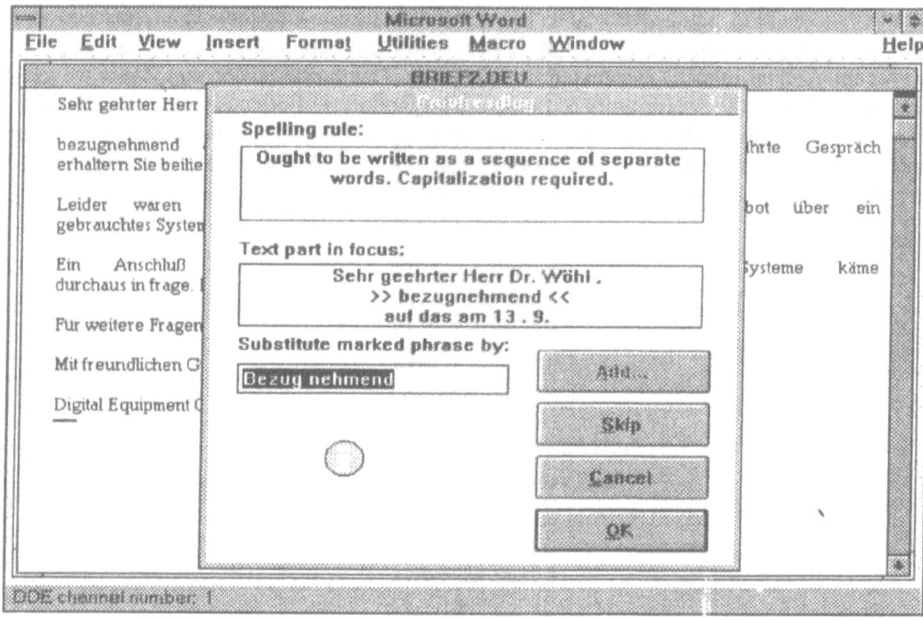

Fig. 62: The proofreading application provides an explanation or rule for each error

19.1.5 Problems, Bugs and Beetles...

Unfortunately, implementing complex applications always causes some problem - the TAE Proofreading tool is no exception in this case. Although a rather reliable prototype version is already running, there are still some problems to be solved. One of those problems is the fact that WinWord does not provide any possibility to hide or protect the WordBASIC macros constituting the TAE surface. This means, every user can read and even change or destroy the macros. This lack might be removed with WinWord version 2.0 - the future will give us the answer. A rather annoying fact is that WordBASIC has no function that returns selected text plus format information. That means that it is impossible to conserve format information that has been inserted in the text before the checking run. At the moment we are trying to find a good solution for this problem.

19.1.6 No More Printed Dictionaries Are Necessary - Everything Is Online

As described above, DDE communication is a good way of connecting WinWord to other applications. Various external programs and functions can be built into WinWord this way. A very powerful connection is the one from the TAE editor to the HFR Dictionary application, because the user can look up words of special purpose languages during the editing. resp. translating session. Translations found within the dictionary can be copied to and inserted into the text directly by the help of the *Transfer* button. As a detailed description has already been given in the section on Lexica, no more details on the HFR Dictionary application will be mentioned here. To get an overview of its functionality, see Fig. 63:.

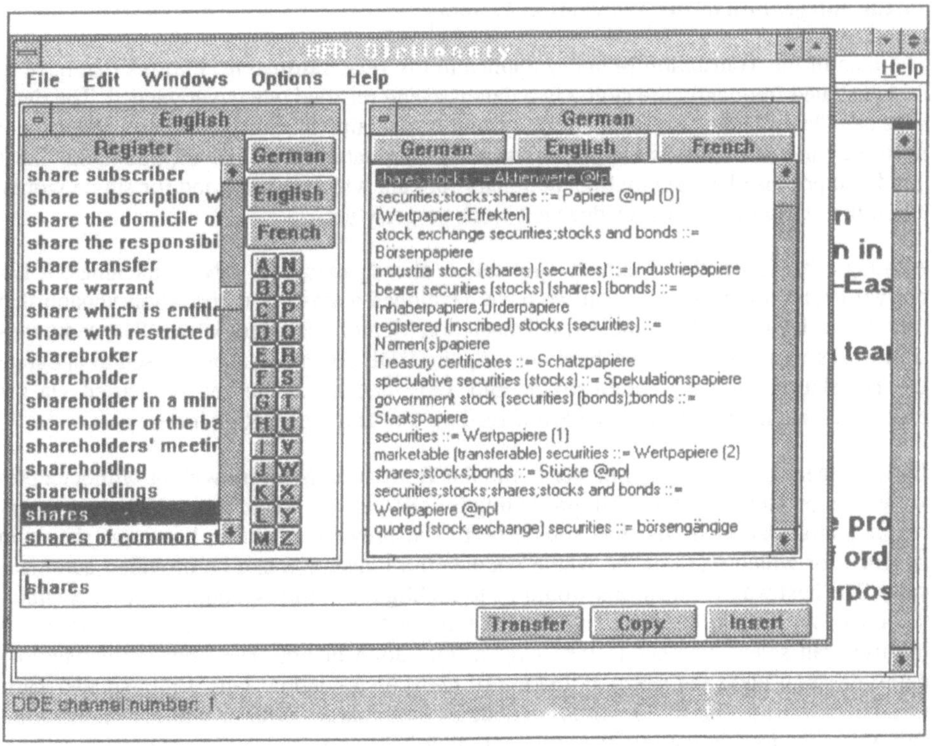

Fig. 63: User interface of the HFR dictionary

On the left hand side, there is an index bar where the user can browse through the dictionary. As soon as an entry is selected, its translation and some further lexical information are displayed in the translation window on the right hand side. For looking up quickly, there is also an edit line where the user can type in the word under consideration. Besides the *Transfer* button there are two other function buttons which allow to copy text to (*Copy*) and insert text from (*Insert*) the Clipboard. The menu bar of the HFR Dictionary follows the SAA standard.

19.1.7 Performance Problems

Although the FRF Dictionary is a successful feature already, and the stand-alone version even has product status already, there are still some performance problems to be solved with the TAE integration. The main problem is that WinWord does not get the input focus automatically after the Transfer button has been used: Instead, the TAE title bar blinks, and the users normally look puzzled until they find out that they simply have to click into the editing window where the transferred text should be inserted to. Another annoying detail is that changing the size of the HFR Dictionary window takes very long, because it consists of very many child windows, and each of them must be resized separately. Solutions for both problems still have to be found.

19.1.8 Integration of the Translation Memory

The idea of the Translation Memory application is very transparent: Phrases that have to be transllated frequently are stored in a database and recalled whenever needed. The database can "learn" new phrases, and the system is also able to translate phrases that do not have the same structure as the phrases stored in the database. All in all, this looks like a good compromise between online dictionary lookup, which is just good for single words, and full text translation, which does not work properly yet.

Although the Translation Memory application already exists for UNIX machines, it has not yet been ported to DOS. But we have developed a small demonstration version that can give a clue how a TAE integrated Translation Memory could look like. This demo version works on a very small database only. Again, DDE communication is used to integrate the Translation Memory demonstrator into TAE, and the demo can be started via the extended main menu, just like the Proof-reading tool and the HFR Dictionary.

Initially, there is a choice of whether to run the Translation Memory with or without a preview prompt. Running it without prompting is called an automatic run, which does a very rough pretranslation of the full source text. The preview function, however, shows in advance for which parts of the whole document a translation can be provided automatically. The best way to show this would be to highlight the corresponding text parts simultaneously. At present, however, we list the phrases to be translated in a box, from which the user can select whether to take over a translation or not. The Translation Memory demo program takes the selected text out of the source window, cuts it into smaller parts (sentences, phrases up to 25 words), translates these parts - with or without interaction - and writes the translation into the target window. Text parts which did not receive a translation can be marked with an asterisk.

For the first "real-life" version, several improvements of the functionality of the user interface have to be made. Porting of the system to the DOS environment, a well-designed user interface, good solutions for training and extending the database interactively remain the tasks for the near future.

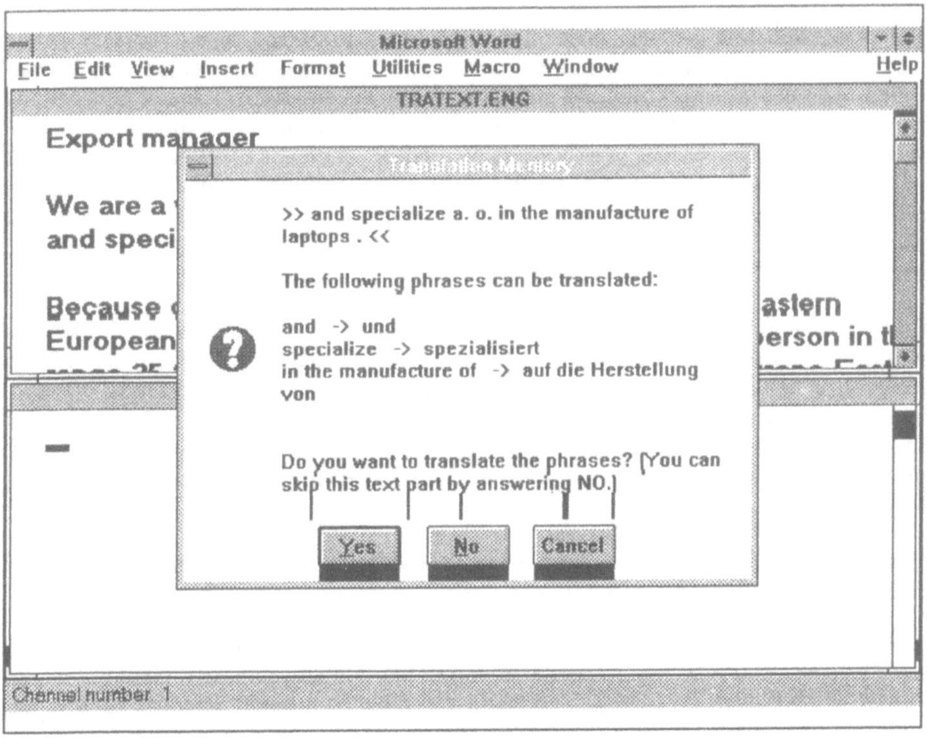

Fig. 64: The translation memory demonsatrtor comes up with translation suggestions

19.2 The UNIX Integration Procedure

Whereas the PC prototype integrates only a limited number of tools, the UNIX prototype has been designed to fully integrate the TWB modules. A message system was designed to cater for the different needs of the individual tools.

Figure 60 gives an architectural overview over the TWB UNIX components. It consists of a central management unit (TWB_MANAGER) and a set of modules (applications). The TWB_MANAGER is responsible for the activation and correct termination of modules. It communicates with the modules using messages which describe the tasks for each module (e.g. passing parameters). On the other hand messages are used by the modules to inform the TWB_MANAGER about the progress and results of their activities. Modules are not allowed to communicate directly. Communication management (distributing messages) is handled by the TWB_MANAGER.

The main goal of the architecture and message passing system is to decouple the individual applications (modules) from most of the initialization work normally needed and to provide a uniform communication architecture. This enables the addition of new modules without influencing other modules.

19.2.1 Basic Message Handling

The communication mechanism for the TWB UNIX prototype uses a message passing mechanism which enables the communication between the central 'organising module', called the TWB manager, and the individual tools. No direct module communication is allowed, every message has to be passed on to the TWB manager (for control and redistribution). A message consists of a message-id, a sender (a unique identification), a receiver (a unique identification), a command specification and parameters for the command. For each module the possible commands and the parameters are specified. A description is provided of how a typical module should interact with the TWB manager. Possible error messages describe the action which have to be taken in case of different errors.

Communication between modules and the TWB-manager is achieved using messages. A message describes a task to be done by the receiver for a sender or an information for the receiver, eg that a message has been received. Messages can only be exchanged between a module and other modules using a communication path established by the TWB-manager. No direct module communication is allowed. If a model specifies a module as the receiver of a message which does not exist an error is signalled (this is checked by the TWB_-MANAGER).

Within the message system two basic message types are distinguished based on a classification of the <command> argument:

common messages: Such a message is known and can be interpreted by all modules and the TWB_MANAGER. They contain messages like initialization, terminating a module and so on. Common messages should not be redefined by different modules because they are executed in a special way.

private messages: These messages and their interpretation are not known to every other module, but are restricted in most cases to the TWB_MANAGER and the appropriate module (e.g. messages concerning the data transfer between the spelling checkers and the TWB_MANAGER). This includes also messages which are sent from one module to another module (via the TWB_MANAGER).

Additionally messages may be divided into task messages and answer messages. Task messages contain a task or informations for other modules or the TWB_MANAGER. Answer messegas represent the answer of one module for another module with regard to a task message.

Sending and Receiving Messages

Modules and the TWB_MANAGER may send as well as receive messages. Two possibilities for sending a message exist:

A module sends a message to the TWB_MANAGER directly. The TWB_MANAGER will execute the command (= task) specified in the command slot (<command>)[2].

2. Please see the annex to this section for a definition of the message formats.

A module sends a message to another module. The message will not be received DIRECTLY by the receiver module but will first be checked by the TWB_MANAGER. TWB_MANAGER checks the content of the command and if it finds a command which can be interpreted by the TWB_MANAGER it will execute it regardless of the receiver. It follows that commands which can be interpreted by the TWB_MANAGER cannot be used by other modules! When the TWB_MANAGER finds a command it cannot interpret it will pass the message to the receiver of the message. In this case it is the responsibility of the receiver to check if an allowed command has been specified by the sender. If not it must send an error message to the sender. The following pictures illustrates this message passing. Modules can only communicate with each other via the TWB_MANAGER, thus allowing the manager to switch off a module when timeout problems occur.

19.2.2 Module Execution

A module is executed by doing some initializing work, carrying out some operations within the module and finishing the module. The following phases can be distinguished.

Init phase

Execution phase

Termination phase.

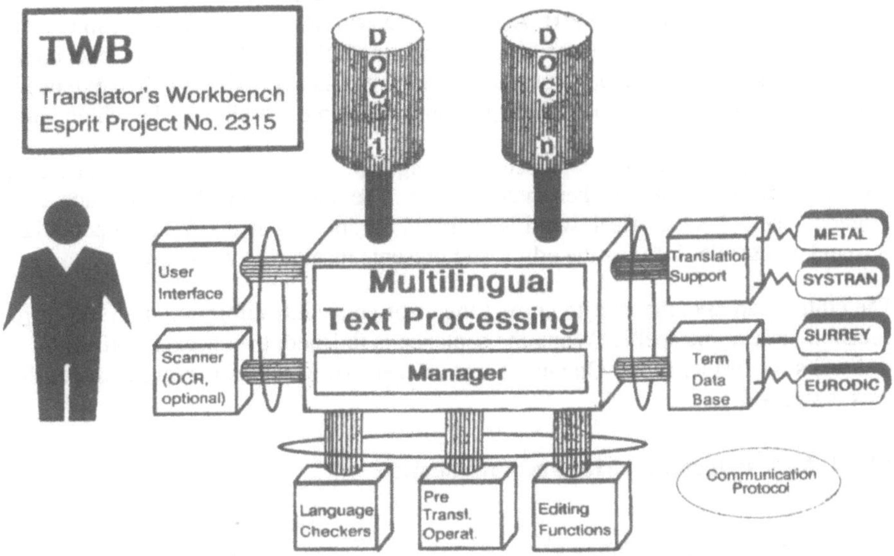

Fig. 65: TWB integration architecture

Within the init-phase the following procedure applies: First, the TWB_MANAGER starts (executes) the appropriate module. Then TWB_MANAGER sensd a test command

(TWB_ACK) to the module using message passing. The module returns a message which indicates wether the initialization has been done correctly (TWB_ACK_OK). After receiving this message the TWB_MANAGER passes initial parameters to the module using the TWB_INIT_MODULE command. The init-phase is supported by a special init-call in C (see technical annex).

In the next phase (execution phase) a set of messages is passed between the TWB_MANAGER and the module doing some module specific work.

Two possibilties for terminating a module exist. In the first case the module signals that its task has been finished sending a TWB_FINISH_MODULE message to the TWB_MANAGER. In the other case the TWB_MANAGER signals the module to terminate. This is done by sending a TWB_END_MODULE message to the module. In both cases the module itself is not allowed to terminate without contact to the TWB_MANAGER. The module has to terminate when it receives a TWB_END_MODULE message. Before it terminates it has to send TWB_MODULE_EXIT message to the TWB_MANAGER indicating that termination is correct.

19.2.3 Language Checker Message Specification

As an illustration of the mechanism described above, the communication between editor and language checker is presented exemplarily.

The checker can be called from any position in the edited file. First of all, communication is established (TWB_ACK, TWB_ACK_OK). Depending on the user selection the checking mode is any combination of checks mentioned above. The order of execution (not noticed by the user) is always: first standard spell checker (Proximity), then extended spell checker, both working on words; then grammar checking, working on the whole sentence.

The initializing information is passed, e.g. language of the text, user dictionaries, type of checking selected. The checker then receives a sentence from the editor and calls the extended spell checker. Each word is analysed for spelling errors. When a potential error is found, the speller informs the editor and presents its alternative spelling.

The editor then asks the user to correct the error and sends information on the correction decision back to the speller. When the sentence is finished, the checker notifies the editor and waits for further input. On end of text or user exit or internal error messages the process is stopped.

19.2.4 Annex: Technical Message Specification

A message is defined as follows[3]:

<message >:= <msg-id> <sep> <sender> <sep> <receiver>

---

3. The following syntax description is used throughout this specification:

syntax symbol semantics

< ... >non terminal symbol | alternative { ... } repetition; (0 .. n) { ... }+ repetition (1 .. n) [...] optional
underlining default uppercase indicates constants

<sep> <command> <sep> <parameters> <end>
<sep> := "::"
<end> := "\n\0"
<msg-id> := four digit number
<sender> := <module-id>
<receiver> := <module-id>
<module-id> := two digit number
<command > := two digit number

Meaning of the various components:

<sep> message seperator the string "::"
<msg-id> message identification (a four digit number)
<sender> sender of the message (a two digit number)
<receiver> receiver of the message (a two digit number)
<command> command to be executed by the module
<parameters> parameters for the command

The names of the modules are represented as constants in C and are available through a header file (see technical annex).

Module Names

TWB_MANAGER TWB manager
TWB_CHECKER various spelling checkers
TWB_PRE_TRANSLATION pretranslation module
TWB_TERM_DATA_BASE term data base module
TWB_TRANSLATION translation module
TWB_EDITO editor module
TWB_ALL dummy module, specified when any of the above module should be used as <sender>

20. Software Testing and User Reaction

Monika Höge, Andrea Hohmann, Khai Le-Hong

As pointed out in Chap. 4, user participation is the only means to guarantee that the software developed in the course of a software project reaches a certain quality standard. However, the common understanding is that "... a software product, as object of evaluation, does not lend itself (in the current state of the art of software engineering) to any empirical-analytical investigation like the usual products of handicraft and industry" (Christ et al. 1984/ii). Thus the first step in developing a user-oriented evaluation approach for TWB was to define the term "quality" as precisely as possible.

20.1 Software Quality - The User Point of View

The notion of evaluation implies a judgement, a comparison between a certain target quality standard and the actual software quality. Ideally, the three parties involved in the development of a software system - management, developers, users - should at an early stage come to terms with regard to two crucial questions:

- what should be the target quality of the envisaged software product
- how can it be tested.

There have been numerous attempts to define quality in terms of quality factors and corresponding quality criteria. The most sophisticated decompositions of software quality date back to McCall in 1977 and Boehm in 1978. However, none of the existing quality models provides any clue with regard to the question, how the different criteria can be measured or even tested. Moreover, existing decompositions of software quality are based on the assumption that a software product is an entity on its own and thus a particular software quality factor applies to the whole software product equally. Strictly speaking, however, the final performance of a software product depends on the quality of the user-interface, the quality of the functions offered, and, finally, in some cases (e.g. term banks) on the quality of the informational content offered.

For TWB a three level approach was developed, in which measurable quantities were defined for different user-oriented quality factors. Depending on the level (functional, interface and content) on which the quality criteria are applied, different measurable quantities had to be found (see Fig. 66).

This list of quality factors, the corresponding criteria, and the measured quantities function as a basic guideline for the specification of acceptance tests. In order to get detailed information on the current software quality, these criteria had to be operationalized and applied in user tests (for details see final report "Evaluation of the Translator´s Workbench - Operationalization and Test Results").

The testing framework of TWB covered the basic inspection of the TWB software, three scenario tests, where a number of translators had to work with the modules available in a near-to-real-life situation, and longterm testing where the functionality of the system was checked by a team member - not necessarily a translator - over a longer period of time.

<table>
<tr><th rowspan="2">QUALITY FACTOR</th><th rowspan="2">CRITERIA</th><th colspan="3">MEASURED QUANTITY</th></tr>
<tr><th>functional level</th><th>interface level</th><th>content level</th></tr>
<tr><td>reliability</td><td>task adequacy</td><td>checklist items</td><td>WYSIWYG</td><td>ratio of searched/found terms
actual/detected errors
searched/found information cat.
suitability of presented information for specific purpose</td></tr>
<tr><td></td><td>correctness</td><td colspan="2">number of failures
mean time to failure
time when failure occurs
number of cumulative failures
failure type</td><td>correct/incorrect data output</td></tr>
<tr><td></td><td>error tolerance</td><td colspan="2">undo facility
escape function
error messages</td><td></td></tr>
<tr><td>usability</td><td>ease of learning</td><td colspan="2">time needed for training program
frequency of help/documentation use
time spent using help/documentation
time needed to achieve a performance criterion
number of error messages</td><td></td></tr>
<tr><td></td><td>ease of use</td><td>time needed for task</td><td>actual/minimal number of keystrokes</td><td></td></tr>
<tr><td></td><td></td><td colspan="2">actual/maximal number of function usage
availability of help facility/documentation
success/failure of completing a given task</td><td></td></tr>
<tr><td></td><td>task relevance</td><td colspan="2">number of available functions not used
frequency of use of available functions</td><td></td></tr>
<tr><td></td><td>comprehensibility</td><td>understandability of
help facility
documentation
system messages</td><td>clarity of layout
mnemonic labels</td><td>comprehensibility of output texts (definitions etc.)</td></tr>
<tr><td></td><td>consistency</td><td colspan="2">similarity in performance</td><td></td></tr>
<tr><td></td><td></td><td></td><td>consistent layout</td><td></td></tr>
<tr><td>efficiency</td><td>execution efficiency</td><td>response time for queries
response time for batch programs
storage space needed</td><td>time needed with button/ menu version</td><td></td></tr>
<tr><td></td><td>performance efficiency</td><td colspan="3">amount of text translated in a given time compared to conventional methods
success/failure of completing a given task in a fixed amount of time</td></tr>
</table>

Fig. 66: Quality factors, criteria and measured quantities

20.1.1 Operationalisation of the TWB Quality Approach

The first step to defining the overall quality of a software module is to lay down the technical scope of the software in a software inspection phase. For this purpose, the MB testing team developed a question catalogue for translation software, where the evaluator has to answer different questions determining to which extent the different software quality factors relevant for TWB were considered.

When performing scenario tests with users, the evaluators fill in an observer's checklist, where all relevant data such as system failures, user errors, user remarks etc. can be put down in a systematic way. The data of the different observer's checklists are interpreted and discussed with the users in a post-testing interview. The results of the test (including interview) are put down in an on-line test sheet, again distinguishing between the functional, interface and content level.

Different on-line test sheets were developed for longterm tests. The evaluator checks all available software in terms of functionality, interface and content, puts down the problems identified and, if possible, also gives proposals for modification. Whenever system failures occur, he fills in a failure sheet, describes the failure situation, tries to detect failure cumulations etc.

No matter whether scenario or longterm test, the test results are presented and discussed with the developers. The remarks given by developers in terms of suitability and feasibility are put down on the result sheets, which form the guideline for further improvements and developments. Priorities and deadlines for modifications are put down jointly by user representatives and developers. Any further software test starts with a comparison between the developers earlier commitments and the actual state of the software.

After performing the different tests by the aid of the test sheets developed in the course of TWB, the data has to be interpreted, i.e. the software has to be evaluated in terms of the different software quality factors (for details see Höge/Hohmann 1992).

20.2 Results of Tests and Evaluation

The main focus of testing was put on the UNIX version of TWB. The test results were achieved with both longterm and scenario tests.

20.2.1 The UNIX Version of TWB

The UNIX version of TWB covers the professional editor FrameMaker, term bank, language checking (German: Extended Speller, grammar and style checker, Spanish: spell checker, grammar checking (METAL parser), translation memory (including phrase training business language (de, en, es)), converters between text processors and, as stand alone tools, MATE, Greek spell checking).

There are a number of preconditions for successful testing and evaluation, which could not be met with regard to all tools of TWB. The following figures give an outline of the achievements and deficiencies of the tools for which the technical environment was provided, which could be installed at the testing site, which were in a testable state and last but not least for which sufficient user guidance was available.

20.2.2 TWB on the PC Platform

There are two different ongoing developments of TWB on the PC platform:

1. based on the professional editor WinWord, TA integrated the German and English extended spell checking, a legal/finance/commerce dictionary (German, English, French) and a version of the Translation Memory.

Integrated TWB/UNIX		
TOOL	ACHIEVEMENTS	DEFICIENCIES
EDITOR - Framemaker	- State-of-the-Art Publishing System - efficient spell checking in a number of languages	- complex functionality - inflexible interface language (lacking spanish interface) - cumbersome access to different charactersets - difficult to define individual keyboards
Toolbox	- all tools at one sight - all tools can be called separately	- lack of hourglass symbol for initiated processes
Profile	- adjustable to individual needs	- not all tools adjust their interface accordingly
Termbank	- framework for most useful information categories available - exemplary content for the domain catalytic converter - additional exemplary information categories •encyclopaedic units •transfer comments - retrieval interface including •user interfaces in English, Spanish, German •retrieval specification •list search •encyclopaedia browser	- data structure cannot be modified by user directly - lack of graphics - not all information categories were filled with data - only few entry remarks and transfer comments available - inflexible search modes (no constrained search) - lack of smart print facility
Translation Memory	- retrieval of previous translations - translation proposal for similar sentences	- only rough translation - needs vast storage capacity

Fig. 67: Achievments and deficiencies of integrated TWB/UNIX

2. based on the UNIX version of MATE, the TELISMAN tool, an additional tool initiated by MB is being implemented by the University of Surrey. It covers a terminology elaboration tool, a parallel corpus management tool, and a termbank, which can be accessed from WinWord and thus be used by the translator *during* the translation process.

Stand-Alone TWB/UNIX		
TOOL	ACHIEVEMENTS	DEFICIENCIES
Translation Memory	- training facility - improving quality after training	- very complex user interface - no modification facility for background databases - training is time-consuming
Cardbox	- allows definition of different card types - supports the linking of information - supports retrieval of linked information	- only one cardbox can be viewed at a time - the different modes of card retrieval, modification and creation are not clearly distinguished
MATE	- provides smart terminology elaboration environment, including •corpus manager •term browser •term refiner •term publisher - provides sophisticated tools for term elicitation (KonText)	- can only handle full ASCII text files at the moment

Fig. 68: Achievments and deficiencies of stand-alone TWB-UNIX

Since the developments on the PC platform have started only in the second phase of the TWB project, it was hardly possible to assess the final software quality by means of scenario tests and extensive longterm testing.

In Fig. 69 the findings gained during the longterm test of the demo version of TWB/PC developed by TA are described briefly (for details see Höge et al., 1992). The TELISMAN tool development is well under way and the versions which were demonstrated at MB were promising. Due to its basic similarity with MATE/UNIX, the findings gained during the longterm test of MATE/UNIX could be applied directly to the development of the TELISMAN tool (for details see Höge et al. 1992). Extensive testing will be performed as soon as the basic functions have been implemented on the PC platform.

20.3 Concluding Remarks

The developments made in the course of the TWB project are all on the right way to support the translators in their daily work. However, there are still a number or technical and organisational problems which have to be considered in further projects. Most of the aspects which were put forward by the testing team were taken up in the specification of TWB II, the follow-up project of TWB on the PC platform.

PC Version TA		
TOOL	ACHIEVEMENTS	DEFICIENCIES
extended Speller	- integrated into WinWord - integrates lexicon on typical errors which cannot be handled by ordinary spelling checkers such as • irregular plurals • capitalization • punctuation etc. - includes grammatical rules - gives correction rules (for German)	- integration into normal WinWord spell checker not yet complete - not all correction rules implemented - overgeneration of corrections for German compounds - program not yet fully stable
legal/ finance/commerce dictionary	- integrated into WinWord - retrieves selected words - shows alphabetic environment, if word is not in lexicon - allows alphabetic scrolling in	

Fig. 69: Achievments and deficiencies of PC version TA

21. Products

Gerhard Heyer, Gregor Thurmair

21.1 Tangible Products: SNI

The products planned by Siemens Nixdorf referring to results of TWB or developed in the same area as TWB are the following:

- The **converter** between ODIF and MDIF, developed as part of the remote access to METAL, has been improved and customised; it will be released as a Add-on product for METAL before 6/92.
- The **lexicon lookup** interface between the editor and the Term Bank has been stabilised and connected with the Term Bank of Siemens Nixdorf (called "Term-PC"). It is in internal use in Siemens Nixdorf's translation and documentation department, and it is planned to release it as a product in 12/92 (a similar product under DOS and Windows is already on the market).
- The **Controlled Grammar Verifier** is in internal and external pilot applications (also in the documentation department). As explained above, it needs some refinement and tuning; a beta release is planned to be available in 12/92.
- Talks have been started to attach some of the **MATE functions** to the "Term-Tools" terminology products marketed by Siemens Nixdorf; in particular the corpus based tools are of interest if they can be connected to the Term-PC.
- A facility to offer **remote translation services**, integrating parts of the work done for the remote METAL access, has been set up in Munich; its first version was completed in 9/91. It is run and maintained by the Siemens Nixdorf translation department.

21.2 Products Planned by TA

Several products are developed at present, some are being presented to the public on the CeBIT Fair in Hanover, March 1992.

- The extended spell checker for German (**ORTHODIC**) will be available as a stand-alone Windows application in mid '92, it has already been shown in its version integrated into the screen typewriting system BSS 300
- The HFR dictionary of commerce, finance, and law (**HFRDIC**) is being presented at the CeBIT '92, implemented as a stand-alone MS Windows application; a version integrated into Word for Windows is expected later this year.
- A basic dictionary of German/English (**TRANSDIC**), implemented on TA's typewriter Gabi PFS is being shown at the CeBIT '92 and is released as a product shortly after the fair.
- Work on the **ATN noun phrase parser** is expected to lead to a grammar checking product within the next year.
- Together with the IAO, TA plans to turn the **Translation Memory** into a product, in its MS Windows version

References

Ahmad, K., Fulford, H., Holmes-Higgin, P., Langdon, A., Rogers, M., (1989): A 'knowledge-based' record format for terminological data, Guildford: University of Surrey.

Ahmad, K., Fulford, H., Holmes-Higgin, P., Rogers, M., Thomas, P., (1990): The Translators Workbench Project. In: C. Picken, ed., Translating and the Computer II, London: ASLIB.

Ahmad, K., Fulford, H., Griffin, S., Holmes-Higgin, P., (1991), Text-based knowledge acquisition: a language for special purposes perspective. In: I.M. Graham, and R.W. Milne, eds., Research and Development in Expert Systems VIII, Cambridge: Cambridge University Press.

Ahmad, K., Fulford, H., Rogers, M., (forthcoming): The elaboration of special language terms: the role of contextual examples, representative samples and normative requirements. Proc. EURALEX, Tampere, Finland, August 4-9, 1992.

Ahmad, K., Holmes-Higgin, P., Langdon, A., (1990): A computer-based environment for eliciting, representing and disseminating terminology. Report of ESPRIT Project 2315, Translators Workbench, Guildford: University of Surrey.

Ahmad, K., Rogers, M., (in preparation): Knowledge Processing - An AI Perspective. Guildford: University of Surrey.

Albl, M., Kohn, K.; Pooth, S., Zabel, R. (1990): Specification of terminological knowledge for translation purposes. Report of ESPRIT Project 2315, Translator's Workbench. University of Heidelberg

Albl, M., Kohn, K., Mikasa,., Patt, C., Zabel, R. (1991). Conceptual design of termbanks for translation purposes. Report of ESPRIT Project 2315, Translator's Workbench. University of Heidelberg.

Alcina Fr., Juan, Blecua Jos Manuel (1991): Gramática Española. Barcelona. Ariel.

Alford, M., (1971): Computer Assistance in Learning to Read Foreign Languages: An Account of the Work of the Scientific Language Project, Cambridge: Literary and Linguistic Computing Centre.

Alonso, J. (1990): Transfer Interstructure, designing and 'interlingua' for transfer-based MT Systems. Proc. 3rd Intern. Conf. on Theoretical and Methodological Issues in MT, Austin, TX.

Appelt, W. (1992): Document architecture in open systems: The ODA standard. Berlin: Springer-Verlag.

Atwell, E.S. (1987): How to detect grammatical errors in a text without parsing it. In: Proceedings of the 3rd Conference of the European Chapter of the Association for Computational Linguistics. Copenhagen, pp. 38ff.

Atwell, E.S. (1988): Grammatical analysis of english by statistical pattern recognition. In: Proceedings of the 4th International Conference on Pattern Recognition. Cambridge, UK, 1988, pp. 626ff.

Bahl, L.R., Jelinek, F., Mercer, R.L. (1983): A maximum likelihood approach to continuous speech recognition. IEEE Transactions on Pattern Analysis and Machine Intelligence, PAMI Vol.5, No. 2, pp. 179-190.

Boehm, B.W. et al. (1978): Characteristics of Software Quality. TRW Series on Software Technology, Vol. 1, Amsterdam.

Boguraev, B., Briscoe, T., (eds.), (1989): Computational Lexicography for Natural Language Processing, Longman: London.

Borissova, E. (1988): Two component teaching systems that understands and corrects mistakes. In: Proc. 12th International Conference on Computational Linguistics (COLING 1988). Budapest 1988. Vol. I., pp. 68ff.

Brown, P., Cocke, della Pietra, S., della Pietra, V., Jelinek, F., Mercer, F., Roossin, P., (1988): A statistical approach to language translation. Proc. 12th International Conference on Computational Linguistics (COLING) 1988, Budapest, pp. 71-76.

Brown, P., et al. (1990): A Statistical Approach to Machine Translation. Computational Linguistics, Vol. 16, No. 2, pp. 79-85.

Bush, V., (1945): As we may think. Atlantic Monthly, 176, No. 1, 101-108, July 1945.

Caeyers, H., Adriaens, G. (1990): Efficient parsing using preferences. Proc. 3rd Intern. Conf. on Theoretical and Methodological Issues in MT, Austin, TX.

Calzolari, N. (1989): The development of large mono- and bilingual lexical data bases, contribution to the IBM Europe Institute Computer based Translation of Natural Language: Garmisch-Partenkirchen.

Carbonell, J. (1986): Requirements for Robust Natural Language Interfaces: The Language CraftTM and XCALIBUR experiences, Proc. 11th International Conference on Computational Linguistics (COLING) 1986, Bonn.

CCITT (1988): CITT Study Group VII, Message Handling System: X.400 Series of Recommendations.

CCITT (1988), Recommendation T.502: A Document Application Profile PM1 for the interchange of Processable Form Documents.

CEC (1991): ECHO User Manual.

CEN/CENELEC ENV 41 510 (1989): ODA Document Application Profile Q112 - Processable and Formatted Documents - Extended Mixed Mode.

CEN/CENELEC ENV 41 509 (1989): ODA Document Application Profile Q111 - Processable and Formatted Documents - Basic Character Content.

Chen, P. (1975): The Entity-Relationship Mode: toward a unified view of data. ACM Transactions on Database Systems, Vol.1, No.1, 9-36.

Chomsky, N. (1956): Three models for the description of language. IRE Transactions on Information Theory, IT-2, pp113-124.

Chomsky, N. (1957): Syntactic Structures. The Hague, Mouton

Chomsky, N. (1965): Aspects of the Theory of Syntax. Cambridge, M.: The MIT Press.

Christ et al. (1984): Software Quality Measurement and Evaluation. Final Report Volume II Project MO: Measuring Quality of Software Products and Software Production Aids, GMD, Sankt Augustin, FRG and NCC, Manchester, UK.

Conklin, J. (1987): Hypertext: An introduction and survey. IEEE Computer September 1987, 17-41.

Damerau, F.J. (1964): A technique for computer detection and correction of spelling errors, Communications of ACM, pp. 171-176, March 1964.

Delgado, J., et al. (1988): A user interface for distributed applications. In: ESPRIT'88, North-Holland.

Delgado, J., Perramon, X. (1990): ODA converters and document application profiles. In: Message Handling Systems and Application Layer Communication Protocols, North-Holland.

EWOS (1990): ODA Document Application Profile Q113 - Processable and Formatted Documents - Enhanced Mixed Mode.

Fulford, H., Höge, M., Ahmad, K. (1990): User Requirements Study. Report of ESPRIT Project 2315, Translator's Workbench.. Mercedes Benz AG Stuttgart.

Fulford, H., Rogers, M., (1990): Draft Guidelines for the Selection of Contextual Examples, Guildford: University of Surrey.

Geer, D., Mayer, R. (1990): Specification of the user interface layout. Report of ESPRIT Project 2315, Translator's Workbench. Fraunhofer Society IAO Stuttgart.

Gomez J., Meya, M. (to appear): Spanish Language Checking in the Translator Workbench ESPRIT Project. To appear in Computational Linguistics.

Gross, M. (1986): Lexicon - Grammar. In: Proc. 11th International Conference on Computational Linguistics (COLING) 1986, Bonn

Guenthner, F., Sedogbo, C. (1986): Some remarks on the treatment of errors in natural language processing systems". Forschungsstelle für natürlich-sprachliche Systeme. University of Tübingen.

Hall, P.A.V., Dowling, G.R. (1980): Approximate string matching, Computer Surveys, pp. 381-401, December 1980.

Hausser, R. (1985): NEWCAT: Parsing natural language using left-associative grammar. Lecture Notes in Computer Science 231. Berlin, Springer-Verlag.

Heid, U. (1991): Study Eurotra-7: An early outline of the results and conclusions of the Study, Stuttgart

Heidorn, G.E., et al. (1982): The EPISTLE text-critiquing system. In: IBM System Journal, Vol. 21, Nr. 3. 1982, 305-326.

Hellwig, P. (1980): PLAIN - A program system for dependency analysis and for simulating natural language inference". In: L. Bolc (ed.): Representation and Processing of Natural Language. Munich: Hanser & Macmillan, pp. 271ff.

Hellwig, P. (1986): Dependency Unification Grammar. In: Proc. 11th International Conference on Computational Linguistics (COLING 1986). Bonn, pp. 195ff.

Hellwig, P., Bub, V., Romke, C. (1990): Theoretical basis for efficient grammar checkers. Part II: Automatic error detection and correction. Appendix: Empiricial feasibility study. Report of ESPRIT Project 2315, Translator's Workbench. University of Heidelberg.

Hellwig, P. (1988): Chart parsing according to the slot and filler principle. In: Proceedings of the 12th International Conference on Computational Linguistics (COLING 1988). Budapest: Vol. I., pp. 242ff.

Hellwig, P. (1989): "Parsing natürlicher Sprachen: Grundlagen - Realisierungen". In: I.S. Batori, W. Lenders, W. Putschke (eds.): Computational Linguistics. An International Handbook on Computer Oriented Language Research and Applications. Handbücher zur Sprach- und Kommunikationswissenschaft vol. 4, pp. 348ff. Berlin: De Gruyter 1989

Heyer, G. (1990): Probleme und Aufgaben einer angewandten Computerlinguistik. In: KI 1/90

Herbst R., Readett, A.G. (1985): Dictionary of Commercial, Financial and Legal Terms: Englisch - German - French, Volume I, Translegal, Thun, Switzerland, 1985

Herbst R., Readett, A.G. (1989): Wörterbuch der Handels-, Finanz- und Rechtsspache: Deutsch - Englisch - Französisch, Band II, Translegal, Thun, Switzerland, 1989

Herbst R., Readett, A.G. (1987): Dictionnaire des termes Commerciaux, Financiers et Juridiques, Francais - Anglais - Allemand, Volume III, Translegal, Thun, Switzerland, 1987

Höge, M., Wiedenmann, O., Kroupa, E. (1991): Evaluation of the TWB. Report of ESPRIT Project 2315, Translator's Workbench. Mercedes Benz AG.

Höge, M., Hohmann, A, Mayer, R., Smude, P. (1992): Evaluation of the Translator's Workbench - Operationalization and Test Results. Report of ESPRIT Project 2315, Translator's Workbench. Mercedes Benz AG, Stuttgart.

Holmes-Higgin, P., (1992), The machine assisted terminology elicitation environment, AI International Newsletter, Issue 3, pp. 9-11.

Holmes-Higgin, P., Griffin, S., (1991): MATE User Guide, Guildford: University of Surrey.

ISO 7498 (1984): Information processing systems. Open systems interconnection. Basic reference model.

ISO 8613 (1989): Information Processing - Text and Office Systems - Office Document Architecture (ODA) and Interchange Format, Parts 1-8.

ISO 8824/8825 (1988): Abstract Syntax Notation 1, ASN.1.

ISO 8879 (1986): Information Processing - Text and Office Systems - Standard Generalized Markup Language, SGML.

ISO 10021 (1988): Message Oriented Text Interchange System, Parts 1-7.

ISO DISP 10610 (1991): FOD-11, Profile for the Interchange of Basic Function Character Content Documents.

ISO DISP 11181 (1991): FOD-26, Profile for the Interchange of Enhanced Function Mixed Content Documents.

ISO DISP 11182 (1991): FOD-36, Profile for the Interchange of Extended Function Mixed Content Documents.

Jensen, K., Heidorn, G.E., Miller, L.A., Ravin, Y. (1983): Parse fitting and prose fixing: getting a hold on ill-formedness. In: Computational Linguistics 9/3-4, pp 147ff.

Keck, B. (1989): Theoretical study of a statistical approach to translation. Report of ESPRIT Project 2315, Translator's Workbench. Fraunhofer Society IAO Stuttgart.

Keck, B. (1991): Translation Memory: A translation aid system based on statistical methods. Report of ESPRIT Project 2315, Translator's Workbench. Fraunhofer Society IAO Stuttgart.

Kittredge, R., and Lehrberger, J. (eds), 1982: Sublanguage: Studies of Language in Restricted Semantic Domains. Berlin: DeGruyter.

Knops, U., Thurmair, G. (1993): Design of a multifunctional lexicon. In: H.B. Sonneveld, K.G.Loening, eds., Terminology: Applications in interdisciplinary communication. Amsterdam: J. Benjamins B.V.

Knuth, D.E. (1973): The Art of Computer Programming, Volume 3: Sorting and Searching, Addison-Wesley.

Kohn, K. (1990a). Translation as conflict. In P. H. Nelde (ed.). Confli(c)t. Proceedings of the International Symposium 'Contact+Confli(c)t', Brussels, 2-4 June 1988. Association Belge de Linguistique Applique: ABLA Papers 14, 105-113.

Kohn, K. (1990b). Terminological knowledge for translation purposes. In R. Arntz, G. Thome (Hrsg.). Übersetzungswissenschaft. Ergebnisse und Perspektiven. Festschrift für Wolfram Wilss zum 65. Geburtstag. Tübingen: Narr, 199-206.

Krause, J. (1988): Sprachanalytische Komponenten in der Textverarbeitung. Silbentrennung, Rechtschreibhilfen und Stilprüfer vor dem Hintergrund einer kongnitiven Modellierung des Schreibprozesses. In: J. Röhrich (ed.): Handbuch der Textverarbeitung.

Kudo, I., Koshino, H., Chung, M., Moromoto, T. (1988): Schema method: a framework for correcting grammatically ill-formed input. In: Proc. 12th International Conference on Computational Linguistics (COLING 1988). Budapest, pp. 341ff.

Longhurst, J., Mayer, R., Smude, P. (1991): Cardbox. Report of ESPRIT Project 2315, Translator's Workbench. Fraunhofer Society IAO Stuttgart.

Longman Dictionary of Contemporary English (1987): Essex: Longman.

Lothholz, Kl. (1986): Einige Überlegungen zur Übersetzungsbezogenen Terminologiearbeit, TEXTconTEXT 3, 193-210.

Marchionini, G.; Shneiderman, B. (1988): Finding Facts vs. Browsing Knowledge in Hypertext Systems. IEEE Computer 21(1), 70-80.

Mayer, R. (1990): Benutzerschnittstelle für eine Terminologiedatenbank. In: Endres-Niggemeier, B. et al. (Hrsg.): Interaktion und Kommunikation mit dem Computer. Proc. GLDV-Jahrestagung. Informatik Fachberichte 238. Berlin: Springer-Verlag.

Mayer, R. (1990): Investigation of Retrieval Strategies. Report of ESPRIT Project 2315, Translator's Workbench. Fraunhofer Society IAO Stuttgart.

McCall, J.A., Richards, P.K., Walters, G.F. (1977): Factors in Software Quality. Vol 1: Concepts and Definitions of Software Quality. Springfield.

Mellish, C. (1989): "Some chart-based techniques for parsing ill-formed input". In: Proc. 27th Annual Meeting of the Association for Computational Linguistics (ACL), Vancouver, pp. 341ff.

Meya, M., Rodellar, X (1992): Evaluation of the Spanish Spell Checker. Report of ESPRIT Project 2315, Translator's Workbench. CDS Barcelona.

Microsoft Corp. (1992): New directions for Microsoft. Do all roads lead to Redmond? In: Language Industry Monitor No.7, January - February 1992.

Okuda, T., Tanaka, E., Kasai, T. (1976): A Method for the Correction of Garbled Words Based on the Levenstein Metric, IEEE Transactions on Computers, pp. 172-178, February 1976.

Patterson W., Urrutibeheity, H. (1975): The lexical structure of Spanish. The Hague: Mouton.

Partee, B. H., et al. (1990): Mathematical Methods in Linguistics. Dordrecht 1990.

Peterson, J.L. (1980): Computer Programs for Detecting and Correcting Spelling Errors, Communications of ACM, pp. 676-687, December 1980.

Picht, H., Draskau, J., (1985): Terminology: An Introduction, Guildford: University of Surrey.

PODA (1988): (ESPRIT Project 1024), Stored ODA (SODA) Interface.

Rimon, M., Herz, J. (1991): The Recognition Capacity of Local Syntactic Constraints. EACL, pp. 155-160.

Romano J. (1984): Un sistema automático de Síntesis de habla mediante semisílabas. in: Boletín 2 Procesamiento del Lenguaje Natural. San Sebastian.

Saras, J.A., et al. (1988): CACTUS: Opening X.400 to the low cost PC world, in: Proc. ESPRIT'88, North-Holland.

Schmitt, H., (1989): Writing Understandable Technical Texts. Report of ESPRIT Project 2315, Translator's Workbench. Siemens Nixdorf, Munich.

Schnelle, H. (1991): Beurteilung von Sprachtechnologie und Sprachindustrie, Colloquium Sprachtechnologie und Praxis der maschinellen Sprachverarbeitung, Reimers-Stiftung: Bad Homburg.

Schwanke, M. (1991): Maschinelle Übersetzung, ein Überblick über Theorie und Praxis. Berlin: Springer-Verlag.

Schwind, C. (1988): Sensitive parsing: error analysis and explanation in an intelligent language tutoring system. In: Proc. 12th International Conference on Computational Linguistics (COLING 1988). Budapest, pp. 341ff.

Sinclair, J., ed., (1988): Collins Cobuild English Language Dictionary, London and Glasgow.

Taul, M., Alonso, J.A. (1990): Specification of String Syntax for Spanish. Report of ESPRIT Project 2315, Translator's Workbench. CDS Barcelona.

Thurmair, G. (1990a): "Parsing for grammar and style checking". Proc. 13th International Conference on Computational Linguistics (COLING) 1990, Helsinki.

Thurmair, G. (1990b): Complex lexical transfer in METAL. Proc. 3rd Intern. Conf. on Theoretical and Methodological Issues in MT, Austin, TX.

Thurmair, G. (1990c): METAL, Computer integrated translation. In: J. McNaught, ed.: Proc. SALT Workshop 1990, Manchester.

Thurmair, G., (1990d): Style checking in TWB. Report of the ESPRIT Project 2315, Translator's Workbench. Siemens Nixdorf Munich.

Thurmair, G., (1990e): Parsing for grammar and style checking. Proc. 13th International Conference on Computational Linguistics (COLING) Helsinki.

Thurmair, G., (1992): Verification of controlled grammars. Proc. Workshop Bad Homburg. To appear

Turba, T.N. (1981): Checking for spelling and typographical errors in computer-based text, SIGPLAN Notices, pp. 298-312, June 1981.

Ullman, J.R. (1977): A binary n-gram technique for automating correction of substitution, deletion, insertion and reversal errors in words, The Computer Journal, pp. 141-147.

Weaver, W. (1955):Translation. In: W.N. Locke and A.D. Booth (eds).: Machine translation of languages. Cambridge, MA: MIT Press.

Weischedel, R.M., Sondheimer, N.K. (1983): Meta-rules as a basis for processing ill-formed input". In: Computational Linguistics 9/3-4 (1983), pp 161ff.

Williams, Gr. (1987): HyperCard. BYTE 12, 109-117, 1987.

Winkelmann, G. (1990): Semiautomatic Interactive Multilingual Style Analysis. Proc 13th International Conference on Computational Linguistics (COLING) 1990, Helsinki.

Voliotis, A., Zavras, A. (1990): Extending 4.3BSD to support greek characters, Proceedings of the European Unix Users Group Conference in Nice, France, Fall 1990.

Yang, H., (1986): A new technique for identifying scientific/technical terms and describing science texts. Literary and Linguistic Computing 1 (2), pp. 93 - 103.

Zimmermann, H. (1987): Textverarbeitung im Rahmen moderner Bürokommunikationstechniken. PIK 10, München, pp. 38-45.

Index of Authors

Springer-Verlag and the Environment

We at Springer-Verlag firmly believe that an international science publisher has a special obligation to the environment, and our corporate policies consistently reflect this conviction.

We also expect our business partners – paper mills, printers, packaging manufacturers, etc. – to commit themselves to using environmentally friendly materials and production processes.

The paper in this book is made from low- or no-chlorine pulp and is acid free, in conformance with international standards for paper permanency.

MIX
Papier aus verantwortungsvollen Quellen
Paper from responsible sources
FSC® C105338

If you have any concerns about our products,
you can contact us on
ProductSafety@springernature.com

In case Publisher is established outside the EU,
the EU authorized representative is:
Springer Nature Customer Service Center GmbH
Europaplatz 3, 69115 Heidelberg, Germany

Printed by Libri Plureos GmbH
in Hamburg, Germany